Intersections Between Feminist a

Intersections Between Feminist and Queer Theory

Edited by

Diane Richardson

Janice McLaughlin

and

Mark E. Casey
University of Newcastle, UK

First published in hardback 2006
This paperback edition published 2012 by
PALGRAVE MACMILLAN

Palgrave Macmillan in the UK is an imprint of Macmillan Publishers Limited, registered in England, company number 785998, of Houndmills, Basingstoke, Hampshire RG21 6XS.

Palgrave Macmillan in the US is a division of St Martin's Press LLC, 175 Fifth Avenue, New York, NY 10010.

Palgrave Macmillan is the global academic imprint of the above companies and has companies and representatives throughout the world.

Palgrave® and Macmillan® are registered trademarks in the United States, the United Kingdom, Europe and other countries

ISBN-13: 978–1–4039–4531–0 hardback
ISBN-13: 978–0–2302–9635–0 paperback

This book is printed on paper suitable for recycling and made from fully managed and sustained forest sources. Logging, pulping and manufacturing processes are expected to conform to the environmental regulations of the country of origin.

A catalogue record for this book is available from the British Library.

Library of Congress Cataloging-in-Publication Data

Intersections between feminist and queer theory / edited by Diane Richardson, Janice McLaughlin, and Mark E. Casey.
    p. cm.
Includes bibliographical references and index.
ISBN 1–4039–4531–4
    1. Homosexuality – Philosophy. 2. Feminist theory. I. Richardson, Diane, 1953– II. McLaughlin, Janice, 1968– III. Casey, Mark E.

HQ76.25.1585 2006
306.76'601—dc22   2006040123

10 9 8 7 6 5 4 3 2 1
21 20 19 18 17 16 15 14 13 12

Printed and bound in Great Britain by
CPI Antony Rowe, Chippenham and Eastbourne

Contents

Preface to the Paperback

Janice McLaughlin, Diane Richardson and Mark Casey

When we published this book in 2006 part of the rationale was to show how the feminist social sciences had (eventually) responded to ideas associated with queer studies from within a range of disciplines, but particularly the arts and humanities. We catalogued how that response had been to both draw in ideas around cultural representations into considerations of equality and recognition and also to bring back to people's notice the ways in which feminist social sciences have had and do have an interest in cultural exploration and its links to everyday identity negotiations and formations. Through the book we highlighted the rich range of on-going work which is crossing the boundaries of both feminist studies and sexuality studies and also social sciences and arts and humanities. We would suggest that the work represented here continues to provide exemplars of the ideas being developed across these boundaries. We would also suggest they continue to be highly relevant to understanding contemporary social, political, cultural and economic intersections that revolve around sexuality and gender.

Where are we now?

We assert that the theoretical tools and creativity produced by working across sexuality/queer studies and feminist studies remains the best way to explore contemporary realities and identities at the intersection of gender and sexuality (indeed a number of new texts have appeared which also make that argument (Giffney and O'Rourke 2009; Browne and Nash 2010)). There is much changing at that intersection and its relationship to other sources of social, cultural, political and economic categorisation and identity formation. Below, very briefly, we highlight just a few of these changes, while acknowledging there is a more globally varied complex picture than we can produce an account of here.

Since the book was first published marriage and family has become an increasingly dominant preoccupation in sexualities politics, particularly in the global north. Interestingly, much of the campaigning and celebrations of victories won have appeared remarkably divorced from and/or unaware of the legacy of feminist work critiquing both institutions as important vehicles for the subjugation of women. As a result of such campaigns several countries have now gone down the route of providing some form of legal recognition for same sex couples. Such legal opportunities – even when full marital status is not provided – have proved to be very popular. This is probably of little surprise given the demand for legal recognition that predated the changes in law and the presumed (but some would argue not equally available) legal, particularly financial, protections which come with it. Alongside marriage, a greater range of countries now provide same-sex couples with adoption and fostering rights (see Casey, 2011).

At a cultural and political level, there is evidence of greater, more frequent and more varied representations of sexualities and sexual lives. It has almost become common place and no longer newsworthy for politicians to come out or acknowledge their sexuality (for example, in 2009 in Iceland Johanna Sigurdardottir became the first openly gay prime minister of any country). Even a limited number of conservative politicians have sought to court the 'gay vote'. There is now hardly a TV drama or comedy programme without lesbian and gay characters (even the occasional bisexual and transgender person too), including characters whose role is broader than being the straight girl's 'gbf' [gay best friend], or to be killed half way through. In the arena of professional team sports a small number of competitive sports men (in women's sport it has been the opposite presumption of lesbian sexuality which has been the problem) have come out.

After a period, when at least in the global north, feminism had appeared to have become a dirty word, there is evidence that a new generation of women, seeking to bring different perspectives and demands to feminist politics, is emerging. The social and material position of women in the global south has meant that feminism never really did go away, particularly within development agendas, but in the north a period of quiet or at least disinterest appears to be coming to an end. One of the interesting aspects of this is that much of the new campaigns and demands of contemporary feminists are focused on issues of sexualities rights – whether this be the right to travel the streets or be at home without the threat of sexual violence, or the right to be sexual, in attitude and desire, without the consequence being seen either as a 'slut' or someone who 'asked for it'. As the world has continued to witness the commercialisation of the female body and female (hetero)sexuality, tied to claims that 'equality' has been achieved, the recent and rapid spread of 'in your face' feminist politics is refreshing and aligned to tactics associated with queer activism/politics. As with other areas of contemporary political activism the global dimension of new tactics of feminist direct action and political networking is helping the range of people and issues that can be highlighted and challenged.

Theorists within and across queer and feminist interests have continued to explore the conceptual significance of these areas of change. Two
new terms have entered the debates which are worth highlighting.
While neither is strongly present in the book, they reflect the concerns
we have sought to include. The first is the growing concern with the
intersection of sexual identities with other multiple identities (such as
class, ethnicity, gender, disability) (see Casey, 2009; Taylor et al., 2010).
One benefit of this work is that it has allowed for an increasing presence
for feminist work that has been undertaken away from the global north
(Stella, 2010).This new focus on intersectionality (distinct from the
intersection we sought to explore) has been positioned by some as a
product of the need to move past limitations within feminist thought
that have prioritised specific identities e.g. gender, age, ethnicity over
others, e.g. sexuality (see, McDermott, 2010). However, intersectionality
can also be connected to the focus given in feminist work to wider
engagement with the material realities of women (and men) in diverse
social, material and geographic locations. This reading of intersectionality is more in keeping with our perspective.

The second term is associated with Duggan (2002) who explores the
existence of a 'new *homonormativity*' which '.... does not contest dominant
heteronormative assumptions and institutions but upholds and sustains
them, while promising the possibility of a demobilized gay constituency
and a privatised, depoliticized gay culture anchored in domesticity and
consumption' (2002:50, our emphasis). The debates around the current
preoccupation highlighted above with marriage within sexualities politics
make much use of this term. While a valuable term for evaluating 'where
we are now' it is nonetheless one open to critical analysis (Brown, 2009).
For example, it would seem important to distinguish a lack of political critique of institutions such as marriage from positively desiring and enact-
ing forms of 'homonormative' practices (Richardson and Monro 2012).
This seems an important distinction to make, in particular in relation to
on-going debates over the effects of normalisation and the relative extent
of the diffusion of neoliberal governance into LGBT lives. Such 'choices'
may be ones made necessary, rather than wanted, by the economic and
social conditions of contemporary intimate life.

Framing contemporary sexualities politics

How are we to theorise and understand the contemporary position of
sexualities politics and rights? In particular, what do they suggest are the
current possibilities and limitations for sexualised and gendered

citizens? We would argue that there is good reason to be concerned about how current trends will affect the lives of LGBT citizens and the consequent need to theorise new contexts. There is a continued need for vigilance on how gender and sexualities continue to be important sources of individual and collective regulation as well as personal identity and desire (Phelan, 2001, Cooper 2004, Weeks 2008).

An important strand in theoretical evaluation of the contemporary prioritisation of marriage and family asks whether what we are seeing is the convergence of contemporary lesbian and gay politics with neoliberal state practices (Cooper 2002; Richardson 2005; Smith 2005). Namely, are LGBT subjects being asked to become self-regulating homosexual citizens who are located in long-term, monogamous, relationships modelled on (hetero) normative marriage and family values (Richardson, 2004; Hull 2006; Rimmerman and Wilcox 2007; Weeks 2008; Badgett 2010)? If so, this means that citizenship is contingent on conforming to a 'responsibilised' model of sexual citizenship, which (re)asserts the idea of sexuality as a private concern and at the same time constitutes a normative public who get to define what are acceptable forms of living (Warner, 1999; Phelan, 2001; Duggan, 2002; Richardson, 2004). What this implies is that current forms of citizenship relate to claims of universal belonging and, connected with this, the belief that it is not the individual's belonging to a group that confirms 'worth' in terms of recognition as equal citizens, but the worth of every individual as an individual (Phillips, 2006). This new era of equalities initiatives extending citizenship rights to LGBT individuals may establish 'formal equality' in society, but it also narrows the sphere of concern to individual prejudice and discrimination or, alternatively (and worse), 'tolerance' and 'acceptance', rather than institutionally embedded patterns of inequality (Leckey and Brooks 2010). This amounts to a depoliticisation of difference. The cost is that these approaches deny important material and social realities – particularly those related to capital, race, gender and sexuality – that remain significant in the production of systematic and long term inequalities and marginalisation (Brown 2008).

The apparent predominant demand of this individual citizen is to be recognised as an ordinary citizen – 'just like you' (Richardson, 2004, 2005; Taylor, 2011). It is hard to ignore, in the continued demand for and enactment of 'gay marriage', an evocation to be treated like everyone else. Weeks (2008) sees the appeal of ordinariness as a desire for validation and a commitment to shared norms and values, what he describes as the 'ordinary virtues of care, love, mutual responsibility'. However, the desire to be seen as 'ordinary' can also be understood in terms of a claim for individuality. Historically, lesbians and gay men were typically understood through their sexuality: to be 'homosexual' was to be nothing but 'a homosexual.' Ordinariness in this sense can be seen as a desire for 'difference' to be incidental, one aspect of a person's life and identity, allowing lesbians and gay men an individualised personhood (Coleman-Fountain 2011).

It is also possible to read such claims to ordinariness as containing the potential for a different kind of radical everyday politics, which arguments about regulation and assimilation may miss. Jackson (2008) has argued that there is a need to theorise mundane everyday sexual lives in order to counter balance academic fascination with the 'extraordinary'. Is there something subtly radical in living out an openly gay, lesbian, bisexual or transgendered life as an everyday possibility that can be done in any location – rather than the particular cosmopolitan spaces where liberation politics existed in the past? The imaginaries of marriage, parenthood, monogamy, cohabitation and the protections provided from pensions, life insurance, inheritance, and welfare benefits, do not speak to a politics of flamboyance, theatricality or fluidity. Instead they speak to a quest for permanence and domesticity. It is important to understand the contexts which make that appealing and at times a radical move. In an era of neoliberalism is it possible that to be seen as responsible, healthy, self sufficient and productive *and* be visibly in a same sex relationship or define oneself as bisexual or transgendered, just might be a version of radical politics that is both possible now and also more expansive than previous versions of sexual radical politics?

Continued relevance of the accounts contained here

The questions the changes in law, cultural representations, political rights and social responsibilities generate includes whether they negate the need for sexuality studies and feminist studies – never mind their intersection. Such moves towards ordinariness and sameness imply that for some at least, sexuality and gender, may be thought of as trivial or incidental to the lives they lead, the politics (if any) they articulate and the battles they face over maintaining their individual familial and intimate relations. We would like to argue that questions of sexuality and gender remain imperative in understanding such lives, politics and battles and that the contributions contained within the book offer approaches to doing so. Below we highlight what types of accounts are still necessary and how the different authors in the book continue to provide that.

One of the key themes of the book is the need to provide approaches that enable a thorough synthesis of material and cultural dynamics affecting people's lives and the contexts around them. It is clear that a key influence on the demand for civil partnerships and marriage are the presumed material benefits and protections which come with them. We can also see the ways in which new economies are emerging around them with companies offering 'unique services' to the 'gay marriage market', including divorce lawyers offering services for both those preparing to enter civil partnerships or marriage and those preparing to leave. However, it seems churlish to ignore that such ceremonies are rich in their cultural significance, offering new possibilities for not just how to mark an intimate commitment through public continued, but also how to form and explore kinship ties, which just might – via the alternative imaginaries they provide culturally – push at the boundaries of what are seen as 'normal' families and 'good' citizens. Meeks and Stein in their chapter offer their argument for such a possibility emerging in the US contexts over the moves towards legalising (and resisting) gay marriage. In the very different context of labour rights disputes in the factories on the border of Mexico and the United States Hennessy in her chapter offers up a still highly relevant account of how even in economic and material disputes which seem far removed from questions of gender and sexuality, both are visibly present via the cultural articulation of who can demand rights and what is included within those rights claims.

Some of the contributions in the book also offer reasons for at least some caution over the politics of sameness and ordinariness. The state and cultural modes of recognition may be offering up ways in which people can be both good citizens and also open as gay, lesbian, bisexual or transgendered. However, if being recognised as ordinary requires an allegiance to normative assumptions about sexuality and gender, and the desirability and necessity of marital-style sexual coupledom, then are a new set of hierarchies being produced: new versions of the good homosexual and dangerous queer (Smith, 1994)? The problem identified here is that a particular version of what it is to be lesbian or gay (as well as heterosexual) is privileged in demands for 'equality', with the potential for creating 'new social, economic and moral divisions between lesbians and gay men, between heterosexuals and across the heterosexual/homosexual divide' (Richardson 2004: 405). There is a need to continue, as Richardson argues for in the book, to interrogate the intersection of gender and sexuality and the 'patterned fluidities' (Richardson 2007) that exist at different levels of analysis between different categories of gender and sexuality, as well as within the practices and institutions of citizenship (Richardson and Monro 2012).

The main theme of the book – the cultural, social and political difficulties involved in separating out gender from sexuality – is as true now as it was when we first published. From the gendered iconography of marriages and civil partnerships, to the different social responses to gay and lesbian parents which reflect back to gender, to the continued gender dynamics of violence towards gay and lesbian people – whether that be homophobic attacks on gay men in the UK or sexual assaults on lesbians in South Africa. Both Jackson and McLaughlin explore the importance of feminist work which capture the significance of social interaction and material specificity in the production of gendered and sexual identities. Such work helps understand the contexts that are informing some contemporary explicit or implicit rejections of the politics of feminism and queer and also their continued articulation in local and global protest movements.

Finally the kinds of accounts present in the book also remind us of the limitations of how far change has come. For every out gay or lesbian actor, politician or sports person there remain very many more publicly quiet about their sexuality for fear – not just of their careers, but in many places their lives. The introduction of hate crime legislation in the UK has brought new appreciation of the continued presence of such violence and intimidation in people's lives. The US has seen high profile murders and suicides of young lesbian and gay people, which highlight the very real limitations to recognition. Sexuality continues to be a source of bullying in school and at work. While state recognition of gay and lesbian rights is often seen as proof of a country's entry into the network of 'advanced civilised states', this does not equate to a reduction in day to day discrimination and violence and state sanction of such acts in those same countries. The accounts in this book place possible advances in gender and sexual politics within their historical place. Garbor stresses the need to remain conscious of the politics that produced some of the rights advances seen around gender and sexuality in order to remain aware of the fragility of where we have got to. Likewise Halberstam stresses the need to be aware of political history, while also stressing the importance of not being prisoners to that history in order that we may create new strategies of identity politics and invention. Wilson provides a bridge across these two accounts by seeking both recognition of the importance of past politics, while also calling for new inventive ways to do a politics which speaks to now.

The collection as a whole demonstrates the continued need for articulating and recognising feminist and queer theorising and politics.

References

Badgett, M.V. L. (2010) *When Gay People Get Married: What Happens When Societies Legalize Same-Sex Marriage*. New York: New York University Press.

Brown, G. (2009) 'Thinking Beyond Homonormativity: Performative Explorations of Diverse Gay Economies', *Environment and Planning A.*, 41: 1496–1510.

Browne, K. and Nash, C. J. (2010) (eds) *Queer Methods and Methodologies: Intersecting Queer Theories and Social Science Research*. Farnham: Ashgate.

Brown, W. (2008) *Regulating Aversion. Tolerance in the Age of Identity and Empire*. Princeton, NJ: Princeton University Press (paperback edition).

Casey, M (2009) 'Tourist Gay(ze) or Transnational Sex: Australian Gay Men's Holiday Desires', Leisure Studies 2009, **28**(2), 157–173.

Casey, M. (2011) 'Sexual Identity Politics: Activism from Gay to Queer and Beyond' in A. Elliott (ed.) *Routledge Handbook of Identity Studies*. London: Routledge.

Coleman-Fountain, E. (2011) *Making Sexual Selves: A Qualitative Study of Lesbian and Gay Youth*. Unpublished PhD thesis, Newcastle upon Tyne: Newcastle University.

Cooper, D. (2002) 'Imagining the Place of the State: Where Governance and Social Power Meet', in D. Richardson and S. Seidman (eds) *Handbook of Lesbian and Gay Studies*. London: Sage.

Cooper, D. (2004) *Challenging Diversity: Rethinking Equality and the Value of Difference*. Cambridge: Cambridge University Press.

Duggan, L. (2002)' The New Homonormativity: The Sexual Politics of Neoliberalism', in R. Castronova and D.D. Nelson (eds) *Materializing Democracy: Toward a Revitalized Cultural Politics*. Durham, NC: Duke University Press.

Giffney, N. and O'Rourke, M. (2009) (eds) *The Ashgate Research Companion to Queer Theory*. Farnham: Ashgate.

Hull, K.E. (2006) *Same-Sex Marriage: The Cultural Politics of Love and Law*. Cambridge: Cambridge University Press.

Jackson, S. (2008) 'Ordinary Sex', *Sexualities*, 11(2–3): 33–37.

Leckey, R. and Brooks, K. (2010) (eds) *Queer Theory: Law, Culture, Empire*. London: Routledge.

McDermott, L. (2010) 'Multiplex Methodologies: Researching Young Peoples Well Being at the Intersections of Class, Sexuality, Gender and Age', in Taylor, Y., Hines, S. and Casey, M. (eds) (2010) *Theorizing Intersectionality and Sexuality*. Basingstoke: Palgrave Macmillan.

Phelan, S. (2001) *Sexual Strangers: Gays, Lesbians, and Dilemmas of Citizenship*. Philadelphia, PA: Temple University Press.

Phillips, A. (2006) *Which Equalities Matter?* Cambridge: Polity Press.

Richardson, D. (2004) 'Locating Sexualities: From Here to Normality', *Sexualities*, 7(4): 391–411.

Richardson, D. (2005) 'Desiring Sameness? The Rise of a Neoliberal Politics of Normalisation', *Antipode*, 37(3): 515–53.

Richardson, D. (2007) 'Patterned Fluidities: (Re) Imagining the Relationship Between Gender and Sexuality', *Sociology*, 41 (3): 457–74.

Richardson, D. and Monro, S. (2012) *Sexuality, Equality and Diversity*. Basingstoke: Palgrave Macmillan.

Rimmerman, C. A. and Wilcox, C. (2007) *The Politics of Same-Sex Marriage*. Chicago: University of Chicago Press.

Smith, A-M. (1994) *New Right Discourse on Race and Sexuality: Britain, 1968-90*. Cambridge: Cambridge University Press.

Smith, M. (2005) 'Resisting and Reinforcing Neoliberalism: Lesbian and Gay Organizing at the Federal and Local Levels in Canada,' *Policy and Politics*, 33(1): 75–93.

Stella, F. (2010)' The Language of Intersectionality: Researching 'Lesbian' Identity in Russia', in Taylor, Y., Hines, S. and Casey, M. (eds) (2010) *Theorizing Intersectionality and Sexuality*. Basingstoke: Palgrave Macmillan.

Taylor, Y. (2011) 'Lesbian and Gay Parents' Sexual Citizenship: Recognition, Belonging and (Re) classification', in J. McLaughlin, P. Phillimore and D. Richardson (eds) *Contesting Recognition: Culture, Identity and Citizenship*. Basingstoke: Palgrave Macmillan.

Taylor, Y., Hines, S. and Casey, M. (eds) (2010) *Theorizing Intersectionality and Sexuality*. Basingstoke: Palgrave Macmillan.

Warner, M. (1999) *The Trouble with Normal: Sex, Politics and the Ethics of Queer Life*. New York: Free Press.

Weeks, J. (2008) *The World We Have Won*. London: Routledge.

Acknowledgements

The chapters presented here continue to take forward debates on sexuality, gender, feminisms and queer theory in new and exciting directions. We have enjoyed working with the chapter authors, each of whom is making a vital contribution to the debates in question. Sadly, since the first edition of this book Chet Meeks, who co-authored an excellent chapter to this book, died in 2008. We would like to remember him here and acknowledge the contribution his work has made to debates in the fields of sociology and sexuality studies.

Newcastle University
September 2011

Notes on Contributors

Mark Casey is a Lecturer in Sociology at Newcastle University, UK. His interest in sexuality is reflected in his current British Academy research grant examining sexuality, identity and space in the North East of England. He has written upon gay male identity and mental health (Casey, M. 2009, Addressing Key Theoretical Approaches to Gay Male Sexual Identity, in *Critical Public Health*, 19(3–4): 293–306). He has undertaken research and published on gay male travel in Australia and is currently undertaking research funded by the School of Geography, Politics and Sociology in the island of Mallorca examining the impacts of the current economic downturn on British residents based there. He teaches across the three stages of the Sociology degree at Newcastle including the modules 'The Sociology of Tourism' and 'Regulating Sexuality'.

Linda Garber is Associate Professor of Women's and Gender Studies at Santa Clara University, US. She is author of *Identity Poetics: Race, Class and the Lesbian-Feminist Roots of Queer Theory* (Colombia University Press, 2001) and *Lesbian Sources: A Bibliography of Periodical Articles, the Tower: Lesbians/Teaching/Queer Subjects* (Routledge, 1994).

Judith Halberstam is Professor of English and Gender Studies at University of Southern California, US. She is the author of several books including *Female Masculinity* (Duke University Press, 1998) and *The Drag King Book with Del LaGrace Volcano* (Serpent's Tail, 1999) and *In a Queer Time and Place* (New York University Press, 2005). Her new book, *The Queer Art of Failure* is forthcoming from Duke University Press in 2011 and she is finishing another book, *Gaga Feminism* for The Feminist Press to be released in Spring 2012.

Rosemary Hennessy is Professor of English and Director of the Center for the Study of Women, Gender, and Sexuality at Rice University in Houston, Texas. She has published widely in contemporary culture theory, feminist, and sexuality studies, including the co-edited collection *NAFTA From Below: Maquiladora Workers, Campasinos, and Indigenous Communities Speak Out on the Impact of Free Trade in Mexico* (Coalition for Justice in the Maquiladoras 2007); *Profit and Pleasure: Sexual Identity in Late Capitalism* (Routledge, 2000); *Materialist Feminism: Class, Difference and Women's Lives* (Routledge, 1997); and *Materialist Feminism and the*

Politics of Discourse (Routledge, 1993). Her book, *Fires on the Border: The Passionate Politics of Organizing on the Mexican-US Frontera and Elsewhere* is forthcoming.

Stevi Jackson is Professor of Women's Studies and Director of the Centre for Women's Studies at the University of York, UK. Her main research interests are feminist theory and sexuality, with a particular emphasis on heterosexuality. She is the author of *Childhood and Sexuality* (Blackwell, 1982), *Christine Delphy* (Sage 1996) *Heterosexuality in Question* (Sage 1999), co-author, with Sue Scott, of *Theorizing Sexuality* (Open University Press, 2010) and, with Momin Rahman, of *Gender and Sexuality: Sociological Approaches* (Polity, 2010). She has co-edited a number of collections, most recently *East Asian Sexualities: Intimacy, Modernity and New Sexual Cultures* (Zed Books 2008), with Liu Jieyu and Woo Juhyun. Recent journal articles include: 'Self, Time and Narrative: re-thinking the contribution of G.H. Mead' *Life Writing*. 7 (2): 123–136 2010 and 'Rehabilitating Interactionism for a Feminist Sociology of Sexuality', *Sociology*, 44 (5):811–826 2010 (with Sue Scott). She is currently working on a comparative study of modernity, generational change and intimacy in Hong Kong and the UK with Sik Ying Ho.

Chet Meeks was an Assistant Professor of Sociology at Georgia State University, USA where he taught social theory and sexuality. He edited *Introducing the New Sexuality Studies* with Steven Seidman and Nancy Fischer (Routledge, 2006).

Janice McLaughlin is a Reader in the School of Geography, Politics and Sociology, and Executive Director of the Policy, Ethics and Life Sciences Research Centre (PEALS), Newcastle University, UK. Her research is focused on two interrelated areas. One is the examination of contemporary social theory, which is explored in her 2006 book *Feminist Social and Political Theory* and in the 2011 edited collection *Contesting Recognition: Culture, Identity and Citizenship* (co-edited with Diane Richardson and Peter Phillimore), both with Palgrave Macmillan. The other research focus is the examination of the construction of knowledge, meanings and values within healthcare, relating this in particular to professional boundaries, technologies and disability. This work is being taken forward via a number of Economic Social Research Council funded research projects and is explored in her book *Families Raising Disabled Children,* co-authored with Dan Goodley, Emma Clavering and Pamela Fisher and published in 2008 by Palgrave Macmillan.

Diane Richardson is Professor of Sociology at Newcastle University, UK. She has written extensively about gender and sexuality including *Rethinking Sexuality, the Handbook of Lesbian and Gay Studies,* co-edited with Steven Seidman (Sage, 2002), and with Vicki Robinson, *Introducing Gender and Women's Studies* (Palgrave Macmillan, 2007), now in its third edition. Her most recent books are *Contesting Recognition: Culture, Identity and Citizenship* co-edited with Janice McLaughlin and Peter Phillimore (Palgrave Macmillan, 2011), and *Sexuality, Equality and Diversity,* co-authored with Surya Monro (Palgrave Macmillan, 2012). Diane is currently working on an Economic Social Research Council funded project entitled Post- *Trafficking Livelihoods in Nepal: Women, Sexuality and Citizenship.*

Arlene Stein is Professor of Sociology at Rutgers University, US. She is the author of three books and the editor of two collections of essays. Among them is *The Stranger Next Door: The Story of a Small Community's Battle Over Sex, Faith, and Civil Rights,* (Beacon Press, 2003) which won the American Anthropological Association's Ruth Benedict Award in 2001. She received the Simon and Gagnon Award in 2006 for career contributions to the study of sexualities, given by the American Sociological Association.

Angelia Wilson is a Senior Lecturer at the University of Manchester, UK, she works at the intersection between feminist political theory, religion and politics, and policies regulating sexuality. Her publications include *Below the Belt, Activating Theory and A Simple Matter of Justice?* (Cassell, 2000). Her most recent book considers the role of welfare ideology in making Europe more 'lesbian and gay friendly'. Currently, as a Leverhulme Research Fellow, she is researching the construction of social values as a political strategy of the US Christian right.

Introduction
At the Intersections of Feminist and Queer Debates

Janice McLaughlin, Mark E. Casey and Diane Richardson

Gender and sexuality, complex categories within social theory, were ignored for much of the nineteenth and the first part of the twentieth century, and it was left to psychology and sexology to lay down the first arguments about the interrelationship and their influence on human character and social relations. Feminist writers were among the first to challenge such frameworks for understanding gender and sexuality. While much of this work is associated with the second wave of feminism, in particular the work of Marxist, radical and lesbian feminism, it also goes further back into the work of first-wave feminism and its important precursors such as Mary Wollstonecraft's *Vindication of the Rights of Women* in 1792. Once social theory opened up the private realm to investigation and certain givens of what generated gender and sexuality were dispelled, debates about how we conceptualise both gender and sexuality steadily grew. In the majority of feminist work exploring their influence on social relations and identity, it has been assumed that gender and sexuality have to be examined together, with gender taking precedence over sexuality. This notion remained relatively unchallenged (and led some lesbian writers and feminists to associate with lesbian feminism rather than lesbian and gay liberation in the late 1970s) until the advent of queer ideas on the theoretical scene. Key writers such as Eve Sedgwick (1990) and Gayle Rubin (1993), influenced by Michel Foucault amongst others, called for a radical separation of gender and sexuality, in order for the internal dynamics within the production of homosexuality and heterosexuality to be understood.

Queer theories, along with other postmodern and post-structuralist ideas, represent what Jane Flax once called a 'loss of innocence' (Flax, 1992) in how social theory is conceptualised and linked to real world debates. Feminism, in the light of the development of new ideas about identity, culture and politics, has found itself going through a period of de-stabilisation – a process that some feminists have asserted is a good thing (Ahmed *et al.*, 2000). Feminist theorising has become a more difficult activity in the light of the ideas that have emerged within queer, postmodern and post-structuralist debates. However at the same time, while many contemporary feminists are keen to explore the 'new' world of contingency, ambiguity and transgression opened up in queer ideas and tactics, they also still worry about what is left behind in the presumption that some of the 'certainties' of previous feminist theorising are wrong. In the light of the wide-scale debunking of feminist ideas that predate the emergence of Foucault and his important re-interpreters, in particular Judith Butler (1992), Diana Fuss (1989), Rubin and Sedgwick, feminists both from the past and present have sought to remind current debates about two things: first, the actual arguments made by feminists in the 1970s, and second, the continued importance of issues not best understood by the celebration of contingency, ambiguity and transgression, things like global capitalism, religious fundamentalism and the absence of genuine citizenship rights for many across the globe (Okin, 1994; Nussbaum, 1999a). It is not that feminists are unwilling to engage with questions of difference, particularly given the important contribution feminists have made to bring questions of difference to the theoretical table. Instead they warn that it is dangerous for feminist theorising and activism if postmodernism is given a monopoly 'on theorising diversity and complexity' (Jackson, 2001: 285). Theorists trying to work through acknowledgement of difference and of wider commonalities are therefore pulled between a wish to fully recognise the complexity of the local and still incorporate the presence of global contexts and structures, which for some writers and political activists are even more pressing and deadly than ever in a globalised and transnational world.

Due to the different positions that are associated with feminist and queer ideas much has been written about how feminist and queer writers think differently about how to theorise and how to engage with issues around gender and sexuality (Merck *et al.*, 1998). The tension between global and local theorising remains an important context within which these debates take place. As has been highlighted one of the first issues on which queer and feminist writers fell out was over the conceptualisation of gender and sexuality and their relationship to each other. For the majority of feminist writers to separate the two and to refute the primacy of gender is to fail to capture the structural presence of gender as a social division that shapes women and men's lives and ultimately shapes sexuality. For queer writers this fails to capture the significance of sexuality, in particular homosexuality as 'a whole cluster of the most crucial sites for the contestation of meaning in twentieth-century Western culture' (Sedgwick, 1990: 72). From this initial disagreement amongst some feminist and queer writers has developed a presumption that queer and feminist writings are theoretically incompatible in their modes of reference, their priorities and their calls for action. Key areas are seen as symbolic of the apparent dispute between the two areas. Contrasts and antagonisms are set up between queer interest in studies of discursive construction and linguistic exchange, and feminist interest in structural analysis of concepts such as patriarchy and capitalism. Queer writers explore the deconstruction and fluidity of transient identities and feminists explore the materiality of the body and the things done to women's bodies such as rape and violence. The politics of queer are said to centre on local activities of performative transgression, within which cultural realms tend to dominate, while for feminists the point of political engagement continues to aim for resonance with global struggle and the intent to participate in the state, political and economic arenas.

The starting point for this book is that while feminists and queer writers have participated in shaping the terms of the supposed dispute between their bodies of work, the dispute itself is inappropriate and unhealthy. This is for a number of reasons. First, it does little to reflect the wide variety of work going on within feminist and queer (and indeed feminist queer) writings. It is frustrating when feminist writers such as Nancy Fraser (1997), Jane Flax (1993) and Audre Lorde (1984) have been so central to the development of ideas around the multiplicity of identity, the significance of discursive constructions and the need for politics at different levels of engagement that feminism becomes so easily tagged as a theoretical framework that has been resistant to the politics of difference. Equally, queer writers are seldom as lacking in 'real world' interest as some of their critics present, for example, that queer debates have their roots in AIDS/HIV activism in the US is seldom acknowledged in accusations of political apathy and disinterest. Second, there are worlds of theorising and political activity that, while working with feminist and/or queer ideas, do not fit nicely into the categories of feminist versus queer. Disputes can be vital to the ongoing development and responsiveness of theoretical ideas; however, over time disputes can take on a life of their own, where the point becomes one of disagreement rather than looking to new ways of engaging with the issues said to be at stake. The issues themselves become rhetorical devices on which to throw mud at the other. Outside of the insularity of the disagreement and those who maintain it, are varied and rich explorations of matters that are vital to both local and global politics, cultural expression and material life. Some of this work is discussed in the chapters and includes citizenship debates, transnational feminism, postcolonialism, cyber politics and new reproductive technologies debates.

From different perspectives (academic, cultural and disciplinary), this book seeks to examine ways in which, and indeed whether it is possible, to bring together arguments that have emerged from within different areas of feminist and queer enquiry. Pursuing ways in which this can happen is important because it allows, through the intersections, ideas, debates and praxis, writers and activists to move beyond the dichotomies forced by the oppositional framework. In doing so new voices and ideas concerned with gender and sexuality can take greater prominence, with less time taken by debating or having to assert whether they are feminist or queer. Each of the contributors takes a different view on what forms such intersections should take and indeed whether they should occur. Moving beyond is a common metaphor in the chapters, what is happening through the collection is an attempt to move beyond some of the categories and the assumptions maintained within the rubric of feminist versus queer theorising. What most authors (to different levels) seek to do is move beyond/past the issue of which is better or what came first: gender or sexuality/material structures or identity. Instead, the writers here are working with an understanding that such categories or forms of living are interrelated and at specific points for particular political and social reasons one may be more important in framing life and demanding political action than the other.

The contributions fall broadly into two forms of engagement with the issue of intersection. The first five examine, in different ways, the theoretical debates about the apparent fault line between feminist and queer writings. Diane Richardson stresses the need to move beyond the logic maintained in the debate that assumes that since queer comes after feminism it supersedes it. Instead the need is to engage with more nuanced accounts that allow feminist arguments a genuine space within queer ideas and vice versa, through this ideas and strategies can develop which are useful in important areas such as, for example, citizenship debates. Stevi Jackson explores the relationship between gender and sexuality in order to maintain that there is a clear and politically significant distinction between gender and sexuality, which feminist writers continue to acknowledge far better than queer writers. Janice McLaughlin explores the terms of the dispute between feminist and queer arguments in order to assert that it is the structure of theoretical and academic

debate that maintains the dispute rather than the arguments themselves. Linda Garber explores her own torn position between lesbian
feminism and queer debates in order to discuss the implications of the
apparent divide. Like others, she sees falseness in the divide created by a
lack of proper engagement with the texts of lesbian feminism in particular. Judith Halberstam calls for forgetfulness, rather than better memory,
as a starting point for feminist, queer and transgender debates to come
together and generate new ideas. Through an examination of both popular film and counter narratives from natural sciences, she advocates the
potential for forgetfulness to release theorising from the disciplinary
influence of previous positions and theoretical claims.

The final three chapters analyse different aspects of contemporary
gendered and sexualised lives and within their analysis draw on both
feminist and queer tools of enquiry, in the process reflecting on what
such a drawing together allows for in their analysis. Rosemary Hennessy
takes the theoretical debates into the politics of transnational capitalism
in the US/Mexico border, exploring how the activities of capitalism and
labour relations become entangled with gendered and sexual identities
in forms that enhance the exploitation, marginalisation and political
challenge of people working at US factories in the Mexican border. Chet
Meeks and Arlene Stein explore the contemporary debates around same
sex marriage in the United States in order to challenge both feminist and
queer writings that see such moves to legalise and institutionalise same
sex marriage as inevitably bad. Instead they view such legal moves as
having the potential, in new contexts of intimate and familial relations,
to reshape notions of marriage and citizenship in ways that offer libera-
tory potential. Finally, Angelia Wilson explores the limitations in both
feminist and lesbian and gay studies accounts of their own developments. Like Halberstam, she identifies a generational dispute where new
writings are seen to move too far beyond the important claims and arguments put forward by previous writers. Wilson rejects the need for allegiance and deference and instead calls for new ways to bring together
concerns of justice and inequality with the queer tools of deconstruction and contingency.

The contributions brought together here therefore raise both
common themes to consider and questions to take forward. The rest of
this chapter will examine these themes and questions.

Queer or feminist?

As editors one of the main reasons for wanting to do this project was
that, despite the existence of numerous books on feminist theory and,

increasingly, on queer, we were mindful of the fact that, at present, there are few texts that bring the two together in a manner that explores the interconnections, as well as the contestations, between them (those that have to varying degrees include Jagose, 1996; Seidman, 1997; Merck *et al.*, 1998; Richardson, 2000; Jeffreys, 2002; McLaughlin, 2003). We consider the need for a text that does this all the more important given that queer theory is often written about as though it has no history or antecedents. Equally, we need to consider queer theory's potential to challenge ways of thinking about sexuality and gender, and the possible new directions that may emerge out of and at the interface of queer/feminist theory. A central theme of the book, therefore, is an examination of the interconnections between queer theory and feminism. What kinds of theoretical connections and alliances are being made? What are the particular issues focused on? These and related questions are explored in some detail by Richardson and in the following chapter by Jackson, and are returned to by others in subsequent chapters. Central to these debates is how we theorise the interrelationship between gender and sexuality and, as Jackson argues in her chapter, the significance of defining gender as a social division over sexuality as a set of social relations or cultural norms that can become fixed through institutional processes.

Also discussed in the book is the variety of ways in which the relationship between feminist and queer theory has been represented, from assertions that the two are in opposition to one another and that queer is damaging to the interests of feminism, to the extent that some regard queer theory as 'anti-feminist', through to examinations of the extent to which queer claims may be considered to be similar to feminist claims, especially in the context of feminism sometimes being constructed as an 'orginating source' from which queer theory emerged. In her discussion of these issues Richardson asks whether feminist and queer theory should be considered to be two fields of study. She suggests that 'any theoretical "division" between the two is a rather tenuous one, a division constituted – at least in part – out of the material interests of those who invoke such theory borders and the political and historical contexts associated with the emergence of such interests' (29). There are overlaps here with Garber's chapter, in which she examines the link between queer theory and earlier lesbian/feminist work in her account of the evolution of queer studies. Like Richardson, Garber seems to be suggesting that queer theory's emergence invoked a theory border with feminism, but that the context may be now changing in ways that have important implications for how both feminist and queer ideas can be received and understood in relation to one another. In discussing her experiences in using various feminist texts in teaching lesbian/gay studies, Garber identifies possible signs that 'lesbian-feminist ideas can once again be considered at face value, that the early need for queer theory to establish itself against its lesbian feminist forerunners has past' (88).

In the desire to appear distinct from feminism, one of the concerns expressed by some feminists has been that queer theory risks paying insufficient attention to gender in its analyses of sexuality and that, as a consequence, this will/may lead to the construction of a universal male subject at the heart of its theorising. This has been an important source of tension between some queer and feminist accounts and has led to the claim that queer theory is damaging to the interests of feminism, and to the study of both sexuality and gender. At the same time, as this collection testifies, there are feminist/queer writers who consider feminist and queer accounts to be mutually productive. Halberstam's contribution acknowledges how in many instances feminism and queer theory have been constructed as 'at odds with one another', in particular over the meaning of gender variance and transgenderism. Yet in her discussion of the contestation over female masculinities within feminism, both in the past and more recently, Halberstam seeks to avoid such divisions. Indeed, she states that her chapter is 'less of an attempt to summarize the impact of transgenderism on feminism and vice versa and more of a search for new ways of articulating some of the mutual projects of a politicized transgenderism and a gender-queer feminism' (102).

As a number of the contributors point out, there are important differences in the political strategies and goals for social transformation advanced both across and within feminist and queer accounts. At the same time, it is clear that there are important theoretical intersections and these are also drawn out in the book. Both feminist and queer accounts regard sexuality not as a 'private matter' of individual 'choice' or 'fate' that is somehow divorced from wider social and material contexts, but as a 'public matter'. As a number of the chapters in this volume demonstrate, there is much overlap with queer theory in feminist accounts that are critical of the privileging of heterosexuality. Indeed, as both Jackson and Richardson point out both feminist and queer accounts have contributed to a renewed interest in and the development of theories of heterosexuality over the last decade and a half. More specifically, they have highlighted how heterosexuality is interpreted as stable, necessary, universal, natural and normal in ways that, it is argued, structure and organise understandings of ourselves and the social worlds we inhabit. In challenging this, queer theorists are in

agreement with those feminists who see the need for radical social transformation, rather than social change through the normalising politics
that are currently advanced by many activists involved in sexual and
gender politics. These issues are addressed by a number of writers in this
collection, including Meeks and Stein who, in their chapter outlining
queer and feminist critiques of the institution of marriage, claim that
oppositions to the politics of normalisation 'are grounded in a tradition
of feminist and queer politics that views marriage as central to patriarchal, heterosexist, and class forms of domination' (137). Although they
see such critiques as 'indispensable', they also believe that such critiques
must respond to and confront what they describe as the 'post-queer'
realities of contemporary lesbian and gay lives.

The distance between the global and the local

One of the main benefits postmodern and queer theories have brought
to social theory is recognition of the validity of exploring everyday,
localised patterns of identity construction and power relations
(although Jackson is correct to argue elsewhere (1999a) that social interactionism got there first through the work of writers such as Erving
Goffman (1969, originally published 1959) and Mary McIntosh (1968)).
Embedded in what Michèle Barrett once famously called the 'cultural
turn' (1992) is increased space for exploring how sexual and gendered
identities are the product of local situations and contexts within which
such identities have meaning and value. Within such accounts concepts
such as capitalism or patriarchy have seemed clumsy and out of place.
Through examining the variability of sexual and gendered identities,
greater significance has been given to other aspects of identity such as
race and ethnicity, disability and cultural location. The means through
which identity is generated has also broadened to prioritise cultural
realms of production giving greater acknowledgement of the role of
clothing, music and popular cultures as sites of contested identity
production. While seeing richness to the localised discussions and
arguments that have followed writers both outside and inside of queer
studies have begun to question what is left to the side in these forms of
engagement. This questioning is taken forward by a number of writers
here who argue that queer studies needs to intersect with other theoretical
frameworks in order to achieve a viable global agenda.

What several contributors here seek is an engagement with the material realities of the everyday lives of women, lesbians, gay men and other
queer individuals within their respective localised settings, under the

shadow of the globalisation of the world's economy, workforce and political movements. In contrast, the playfulness and uncertainty of queer and its critique and lack of an engagement with the value that identity positions may have in challenging globalised forces of oppression and exploitation is met with concern. The globalisation of second wave feminist movements and 'women's rights' post 1970, symbolised in the United Nations Decade of Women (1976–85) and the adoption by 110 member nations of the Convention on the Elimination of All Forms of Discrimination Against Women (CEDAW), has not resulted some 20 years on, in the granting of basic rights or improving the material realities of the majority of the world's women. As McLaughlin (2003: 4) argues, many of the basic rights accorded to women in the West are still actively denied to women in countries where religious fundamentalism and nationalism are on the increase and where globalised patterns of trade and manufacturing are creating new patterns of exploitation. Hennessy in this volume echoes these concerns, through her ethnographic study of female and gay male workers in the maquiladoras of Northern Mexico. In challenging what she terms queer studies' 'pitting of the local against the global', Hennessy asks, 'but surely we should think twice before closing off the possibility of understanding the relation of a subculture's particularities to the dominant social relations of which it is part or against which it manoeuvres?'(118). The complex intersections that exist between local realities and global networks and the material consequences for the maquiladora workers reflect capitalism's transnational reach and its local impacts. Such large scale global restructuring is incorporating women everywhere into a (low paid) system regulated by market norms of the western (masculinist) world, particularly the World Bank and the International Monetary Fund, as well as individual multinational corporations (see Ollenburger and Moore, 1998: 88).

In addressing the intersections between the local and global, Garber in particular raises concern with the types of analysis and argument developing within 'global queer studies' due to their inappropriateness for those not living within rich western worlds or working within liberal western academia. Garber raises a number of concerns, first that the new global queer work may, through the dominance of discussion of male homosexuality, be replaying earlier sexist exclusions that occurred within lesbian and gay studies in the 1980s. Second, for Garber, the ability to name oneself and claim an identity position is denied through queer's concern with fluidity, transgression and fun. Through queer's call to reject identity politics, women, lesbians and gay men are denied the possibility of developing identity positions from which to name and challenge their oppression. As Garber argues in citing Ruth Vanita, 'it is usually those that have obtained most of their basic civil rights and liberties in first world environments who object to the use of these terms (*gay* and *lesbian*) in third world contexts' (81 original emphasis). McLaughlin echoes this point when she argues that denying the validity of claims based on the assertion of an identity in queer's search for fluidity takes 'the ground from which women can challenge the sources of oppression and exploitation' (63) at a time when the material contexts of many women and sexual others grow more difficult through political uncertainty, increased global terrorism, growing exploitation by powerful transnational corporations and environmental/'man' made disasters. For feminists wishing to maintain a global focus, queer's playfulness and uncertainty is problematic for addressing material and social inequalities, where uncertainty cannot always be experienced as a liberating experience.

For McLaughlin a global focus is occurring within transnational feminism, which engages with both cultural/linguistic and economic/material contexts:

> Transnational feminism examines the contemporary interactions between global economies, nationalism and national movements and gendered and sexualised identities and inequalities. Cultural values are understood as the product of particular economic, political and social contexts. (75)

Through drawing on the work of Gloria Anzaldúa and Irene Gedalof, McLaughlin suggests that much of this work 'connects the pain of identity construction and destruction to the economic and political contexts in which it takes place' (76), which she suggests is missing in much work associated with queer theory.

Hennessy identifies a shift within queer studies to include global material concerns within accounts of the construction of gender and sexuality. Such work could be the basis within which 'the politically urgent discourses of materialist feminism and queer studies converge' (119). For Hennessy:

> This materialist direction in queer studies situates analyses of specific sexual formations in relation to globalization's exploitative relations and imperial histories as they are shaped by race and ethnicity and the changing relations of labour throughout the modern period. (119)

Hennessy's reading of gender and sexuality as a 'second skin' situates the value given to identities in particular localities within a social ontology, placing the lived cultural values of identity in relation to the surplus value of capital. And it is within this that the insights offered by feminism and queer studies can intersect.

Bringing material and cultural analysis together

The wish to bring global and local dynamics together and the role a fusion of queer and feminist ideas can play within this, revolves around a desire to see material and cultural issues examined together. As identified earlier, the dispute between feminist and queer writers has solidified the notion that feminists prioritise the material over the cultural, while queer writers do the reverse. For contributors here there are both criticisms of writers who fall into the tendency of analysing one over the other and praise for attempts to genuinely bring their consideration together.

As several of the chapters point out, one of the criticisms that has often been made of queer theory by feminist and other writers is that in its focus on cultural practices it has not paid sufficient attention to issues of structure and materiality. This is a tendency that some queer writers such as, for example, Seidman see as needing to change. His interpretation of queer leads him to 'criticize queer theory to the extent that its social perspectives slide into textual or discursive idealism and have not seriously considered the ethical-political implications of making difference so fundamental to theory and politics' (Seidman, 1997: 16). Echoing such concerns, both Richardson and Jackson note that even Butler, whose work has been influenced by that of materialist feminists, appears to have little interest in discussing material inequalities between women and men or considering that heterosexuality might be related to male dominance. This is something Wilson and McLaughlin also draw attention to in their analysis of the critique made of Butler's work by Nussbaum who, as well as others, claims that the individualised approach and lack of a clear narrative for socio-economic change associated with Butler's queer approach serves to deconstruct 'the political' with calamitous effects for the economically, socially and politically excluded/marginalised.

Materialist critiques of queer theory are also intertwined with its criticism of 'identity politics'. At the heart of these discussions is the question of the political utility of gender and sexual categories such as lesbian/gay, woman/man, and their enabling and disciplinary effects.

Put simply, do we need such categories in order to articulate and contest material inequalities? One might also point to a lack of attention to materiality in queer theory in a different sense, in arguing that the focus on cultural norms often fails to address questions of how these norms are constituted and why they prevail. The claim that what is missing in much of the work associated with queer theory is an analysis of economic and political contexts in which cultural practices occur is taken up in the chapters by McLaughlin, Wilson and Hennessy. In her chapter Wilson discusses generational change in sexual politics, as does Garber, drawing out how a 'new generation of transgression' associated with queer has led away from 'a politics of social transformation' that she argues has had important implications for articulating material concerns such as poverty, racism and violence.

For Jackson the over prioritisation of cultural concerns within queer studies can be traced to a shift in the conceptualisation of 'the social' away from social structural definitions towards definitions of the social in terms of 'fluidity and mobility'.

> In *teasing* apart these intersections (between gender, sexuality and heterosexuality) I have drawn on some ideas from queer theory and insofar as I wish to challenge the connections that bind gender and sexuality into the 'heterosexual matrix' (Butler, 1990) my project converges with theirs. However, I have also argued the need to pay attention to aspects of the social that generally fall outside the scope of queer – particularly social structures and everyday social practices. (56)

One of the consequences of this she argues is that there has been an associated shift in definitions of gender, away from gender as social division towards an understanding of gender as cultural distinction. Because of this Jackson sees queer theory's analyses of the intersections between gender, sexuality and heterosexuality as delimited in a number of important respects. For instance, in identifying the need for a more sociologically grounded understanding of the self Jackson asserts that the 'impact of social structures in shaping our gendered and sexual beings is frequently ignored' (51). In addition, she also suggests that a more sociological understanding of the ways in which sexuality intersects with non-sexual social relations, will afford a fuller understanding of sexuality. It is here, that as Richardson suggests, there is the potential for a powerful intersection between feminist and queer ideas.

The lack of consideration given to material concerns identified in queer work leads several contributors to identify this as an important area within which intersections with feminism can (and indeed should) occur. However, for McLaughlin and others in the book: 'A simple return to past feminist agendas and concerns is not possible or advisable because old certainties are not appropriate to uncertain times' (73). Queer arguments are bringing to the fore new ways to engage with the challenges to social justice and citizenship embedded in unequal material conditions. For Wilson 'queer theory's deconstruction of modernity's definitions of justice, equality, freedom, identity and sexuality' (173) is potentially expansive of political dialogue. McLaughlin and Hennessy, albeit in different ways, develop this argument further through a discussion of the productive tension that exists between queer and feminism. In part, this 'tension' may be seen as arising out of the ways in which 'the cultural' and 'the social' have often been constructed in these arguments as binaries, which has hampered theoretical development. Acknowledging this, McLaughlin advances the view that

> Queer arguments cannot obtain greater relevance and political significance without a genuine engagement with material issues, while feminists concerned with matters that count, need to acknowledge the greater complexity involved in talking of such matters due to queer arguments about the presence of discursive and linguistic processes within material relations. (66)

Meeks and Stein offer one form of bringing queer and feminist ideas into new connection through their challenge to both their critiques of same-sex marriage because while 'queer and feminist critiques of the institution of marriage are indispensable, these critiques must also confront the "post-queer" reality of contemporary lesbian and gay life' (154). In analysing the possible political and social significance of same-sex marriage Meeks and Stein take arguments and approaches from both queer and feminist writings (and others, for example Giddens's work on the 'pure relationship' (1992), the use of which some may consider contestable due to the lack of empirical grounding to the arguments he makes) without being wedded to the conclusions such writers have made. This allows them to propose that same-sex marriage offers an opportunity to reframe what marriage is and for the politics of marriage to move 'beyond the liberation-versus assimilation deadlock, framing the debate in ways that speak to the changed realities of lesbian and gay lives today' (155). Similarly, Hennessy makes a convincing argument in her chapter for ways to reframe the material/ cultural binaries that often arise in debates across feminist and queer accounts in her discussion of the need for materialist feminism and queer studies to converge. Hennessy, through her innovative drawing together of arguments from within queer discussions of transgenderism and Marxist arguments about the structure of labour relations and capitalist manipulation of surplus value, paints a picture of possible intersections, contemporarily useful and non-deferential to theoretical legacies. Through this work she sees the following political possibilities:

> the most incisive politics of feminism and queer studies converge here: in addressing the social relations through which the material and cultural value of human being is filtered. Here both feminism and queer politics aim to transform the deprivation of *what is* into *what can be*. (133 original emphasis)

Generational legacy

Within the feminist contributions to the book there is repeated unease about the lack of apparent appreciation and knowledge of feminist writings within queer texts; a concern that has been raised before by writers such as Jeffreys (2003). While occasional feminists are mentioned in queer works, sometimes admirably more often to evoke distain, there is little genuine engagement with the legacy of feminist work. In response some feminists here and elsewhere challenge contemporary theorists to be more appreciative of previous work and to acknowledge more carefully within their critique of such work the contexts and aims that provided the foundations to the arguments they wish to now reject.

Various contributors here echo the concern of other feminists who fear that feminist politics and arguments have become lost, in Barrett's 'cultural turn' (1992) and which led Diana Coole to warn that 'the political momentum of feminism is being quietly deconstructed away as writers become increasingly reluctant to use terms like 'women (or worse, Woman)' (1994: 7). Feminists have investments in and knowledge of, a variety of arguments and political strategies that emerged out of hard fought battles in the 1970s and 1980s. There is wariness with apparently being required to step away from the arguments and demands of this period for the contingency and locality of contemporary accounts of gender and sexuality. Jackson argues against such a shift in her chapter, particularly because she wishes to assert that gender and sexuality are different and gender more significant: 'without gender categories we could not categorize sexual desires and identities along the axis of same-gender or other-gender relationships, as heterosexual, bisexual or homosexual/lesbian' (40). For her there is a laziness about queer accounts from writers such as Sedgwick and Rubin, in comparison to the work of feminists, particularly feminist sociologists, who had, she argues already established the constructed nature of gender and sexuality long before queer and Foucault were around. Such earlier and continued work develops a far more rigorous account of gender and sexuality, including heterosexuality, than has emerged from queer accounts:

> For while queer theorists seek to denaturalise heterosexuality, to reveal that it depends for its definition and privilege on its excluded 'other' ... they are relatively unconcerned about what goes on *within* heterosexual relations, with everyday practices and institutional structures that sustain a heterosexual and gendered social order. (39 original emphasis)

Without the presence of feminist ideas from the past and present, the modes through which gender and sexuality are conceptualised are impoverished. This is the starting point for Richardson who proposes that 'the rise of queer theory has resulted in a loss of conceptual space for lesbian/feminist approaches to sexuality and gender, which has significant consequences for both gender theory and politics' (21).

Therefore, for several contributors (including Jackson, Richardson and Garber) setting the record straight is very important. Garber constructs part of her chapter as three 'history lessons about the real contribution lesbian feminism has made':

> History Lesson, Chapter One: Contrary to received wisdom lesbian feminism was at its inception a social-constructionist project. ...
>
> History Lesson, Chapter Two: Again contrary to received wisdom, ample evidence shows that working-class-and-lesbians of colour were active in lesbian feminism and the women's liberation movement in the 1970s. ...
>
> History Lesson, Chapter Three: Identity politics is not necessarily essentialist, nor contrary to queer politics. (82–84)

Having a grasp of previous work and claims made by feminists, particularly radical and lesbian feminists, is seen as a vital element to moving forward with a genuine partnership between queer and feminist ideas and the work produced in the 1970s. Jackson, Richardson and Garber all identify feminist writings within the second wave that bear clear and unacknowledged similarities to arguments within queer accounts. In particular Adrienne Rich (1986) and her text on compulsory heterosexuality originally published in 1980 has clear parallels for Butler's (1990, 1993) more recent work on the regulatory matrix of heteronormativity. Richardson notes 'Although Rich does not explicitly mention the heterosexual/homosexual binary that is the focus of much queer theory, her work can be seen as an early attempt to disrupt (queer) the boundaries of sexual categories' (130). While other key feminist writers from the 1970s are acknowledged in Butler's *Gender Trouble* (1990), both Richardson and Jackson argue that the treatment of such texts is superficial. For example, both highlight that Butler acknowledges the debt she owes to Monique Wittig's work on the role of heterosexuality in constructing gendered hierarchies (1980), but does so without also acknowledging the form Wittig's argument took, namely a materialist analysis.

However, while the legacy left by previous work is important to Jackson, Richardson and Garber, there are differences regarding how this legacy should be treated. For Jackson, there is a need to retain the superiority of existing feminist arguments about the operation of gender and sexuality. Jackson sees little new or beneficial brought to the table through the queer arguments of Rubin, Sedgwick and Butler. This position is not maintained by most of the other contributors who do assert that there is something to be gained by queer inclusions in feminist debates. For Richardson the loss of conceptual engagement comes, in part, from within the temporal logic maintained in theoretical rhetoric, where coming later automatically equates to theoretical superiority: 'Where theoretical "inheritance" is acknowledged by queer theorists, the tendency has been to construct feminism as foundational, an 'originating source' from which queer theory has emerged' (29).

If debates between feminist and queer writings remain contained by who came first and later what will be lost is the benefit of engaging now with the overlaps that are possible. Richardson argues that inheritance or legacy is less important than engaging with the intersections between gender and sexuality: 'questions about intellectual "inheritance" go beyond asking whether or not adequate recognition has been given to the legacy of feminist ideas in the historical development of queer theory, towards a much broader focus on how feminism and queer theory might productively inform each other' (29). Therefore, it matters less who identified first the regulatory significance of heteronormativity on social and intimate relations, what matters is mapping its significance through analysis of its cultural, social, political and material presence.

Richardson's arguments are taken forward by other contributors to the book who reflect on their frustration in the divide that has been created between the 'proper' feminists of the 1970s and the writers of today who are both rejected by feminism and unwilling to be seen as feminist. Wilson sums it up well, when she describes her irritation with feminism (as a feminist):

> that 'it' seems to forever belong to a baby-boomer few who fought at its vanguard and, having earned the right to pass on wisdom, have become its only spokeswomen; that while students, and those on the 'Queer omnibus', may support equal pay, women's right to divorce and child-care initiatives, they would wince at being labelled with the 'F-word'. While feminism seems to belong to one generation, queer seems to belong to another: one respected but dated, the other cutting-edge and cool. (156)

Other contributors go further in their rejection of generational thinking and the need to maintain and acknowledge the legacy of previous work. Halberstam, controversially in terms of the metaphors used and claims made, warns of the danger of being trapped within an Oedipal version of legacy, as the older generation is seen as the holder of wisdom, knowledge and at times status, to be passed down to the correct younger generation. There is a disciplinary power within this, as it leaves the elder generation to dictate who shall become the new carriers (the dutiful daughters) to pass on such wisdom to and become the new voices of feminist politics:

> The pervasive model of women's studies as a mother-daughter dynamic ironically resembles patriarchal systems in that it casts the mother as the place of history, tradition and memory and the daughter as the inheritor of a static system which she must either accept without changing or reject completely. (103)

Working with the arguments of Sedgwick, Halberstam argues that 'by casting generations of feminism as somehow at odds, both young and old feminists engage in paranoid models of interaction' (104). Wilson notes too the disciplinary handcuffs generated by the dominance of memory and legacy recounted by the 'older generations' of both feminist and lgbt activism who feel betrayed in the refusal to acknowledge properly the memory and legacy of their work and perspectives. Within the claim of betrayal is a desire to remain the focal point from which feminist and lgbt arguments should be articulated. In essence the older generation is demanding their status as the voices of feminism and lgbt politics remain: 'The inflection of voice commands a respect for "herstories" individually recalled and insinuates worries about the distance from those writing the next chapter of feminism' (164). Like Garber, Halberstam also sees legacy and generational thinking occurring in lesbian politics and cultural expression, the difference is that what Halberstam notes is an active rejection of the symbols and politics of lesbian feminism in current 'boi' lesbian culture. In particular she critiques boi lesbian culture as limited in its political potential through simply being a rejection of previous models of lesbian identity associated with feminism without offering anything more beyond individualism and consumerism. In the rush to reject anything which may hint at feminist or gender politics, they reject any political aspect to their performance and become a nontransgressive lifestyle, so lacking in radical potential they can fit comfortably in the US TV schedule (for example The L Word). Halberstam's solution to the tension between transgender politics and feminist politics is not to move past them, into the individualism and ambiguousness of boi lesbian culture, but instead to work towards a 'merger of trans and feminist politics' (97). Significantly, she argues that this merger can only occur through forgetfulness. The future possibilities of new articulations of identity, culture, community and politics will not occur through establishing how such visions of possibility sit in relation to previous work – either as a rejection or acknowledgement of. What queer and transgender priorities can offer feminism is the value of 'resting a while in the weird but hopeful temporal space of the lost, the forgotten and the unmoored' (114).

Social theory is constantly changing, due to shifts in social and political contexts and because of the emergence of new ideas. How existing work is engaged with as new ideas emerge is an important issue. The questions that lie behind the contributions here are: how to give acknowledgement to existing ideas without being trapped in an overly deferential relationship to such work? Are there arguments, positions that need to be 'forgotten' in order to generate ideas, actions appropriate/useful to now? Not all the contributors answer the questions the same way; indeed the questions remain open at this stage. What we have is a wish to recognise varied bodies of work, but to do so less contained by when and how such ideas developed and to be open to new ways to cross fertilise ideas that maintain the importance and relationship between gender and sexuality and cultural and material relations. Political implications remain important criteria for judging whether such fertilisations are possible. If feminism has one legacy to take forward here it is the legitimacy of using political criteria as the marker for the validity of social theorising.

1
Bordering Theory

Diane Richardson

Introduction

Over the last decade and a half the term 'queer' has gained prominence both in the academy where its institutional growth has been rapid, especially in the arts and humanities, and in popular usage primarily, though not exclusively, as a form of self-description distinguished from naming oneself gay or lesbian. Such developments have provoked a great deal of critical debate and discussion about the possible consequences for the study of sexuality and gender, for political movements concerned with sexual politics, and for theoretical understandings of identity. In this chapter, I want to draw on some of these debates in considering the relationship between queer theory and feminism.

Despite an extensive feminist and burgeoning queer literature, examination of the influences of queer ideas on feminism and vice versa – though as I shall go on to argue probably more so the former than the latter – remains a relatively under-theorised area. This is all the more striking when one considers that queer theory emerged, in part, both out of and as a critical response to feminism, or at least certain forms of lesbian/feminist theorising (Weed and Schor, 1997). However, it is precisely because, as Stacey (1997: 62) puts it, 'Queer Theory has taken on a weighty, symbolic significance in debates about "developments" in Feminist Theory' that I believe we need a more careful and detailed examination of the dynamic ongoing relationship that exists between them.

One possible explanation for why there has been little systematic analysis of this relationship in the literature, is that in its theoretical approach queer resists definition and is characterised by indeterminacy, as Halperin remarks: *'There is nothing in particular to which it necessarily refers'* (Halperin, 1995: 62 original emphasis). Along with other queer writers such as Warner (1993), Halperin offers a definition of queer as a positionality 'vis-a-vis the normative'. Queer, he argues, is by definition 'whatever is at odds with the normal, the legitimate, the dominant' (Halperin, 1995: 62). This suggests that queer can be deployed in many different ways and in relation to any number of different areas. If we are to understand queer theory in this way as a fluid, mobile, non specific zone of enquiry that is resistant to being 'fixed', attempts to locate it in relation to other theoretical perspectives, in this case feminism, might seem likely to be beset with difficulty.

This said I would argue that, as McKee puts it: 'Queer is not an entirely empty signifier ...' (McKee, 1999: 237). It does have meanings and positional claims that are shared and recognised. That is to say, despite being constructed in terms of 'vagueness', it is possible to iden-tify patterns in how queer theory is practised in terms of what it theo-rises, the theoretical paradigms it deploys, and the disciplinary traditions where queer theory is most apparent. It is important that we acknowledge this in order to understand how queer shapes 'how and why particular knowledges, practices, identities, and texts are validated at the expense of others' (Sullivan, 2003: 47), more especially in con-texts where queer ideas appear hegemonic. This point is pertinent to one of the aims of this chapter, which is to consider how queer impacts on feminist thought and practice, in particular through the construc-tion of the theoretical investigation of sexuality as the 'proper' domain of queer studies.

Work that has focused specifically on the question of the relationship between queer theory and feminism has so far tended to do so primarily in the context of examining the role of feminist thought in the emer-gence and development of queer theory (e.g. Jagose, 1996; Stacey, 1997), as well as considering how queer theory might enrich feminism (e.g. Merck *et al.*, 1998) or, as some argue, threaten to make lesbian/feminist analyses seem redundant and the study of sexuality 'feminist free' (e.g. Jeffreys, 1994, 2003). Various writers have also provided a partial account of queer's relationship with feminism, as an aspect of their work on shifts in theorising sexuality and gender and in the political discourses of social movements concerned with sexual politics (e.g. Seidman, 1997; Richardson, 2000; McLaughlin, 2003).

A variety of feminist responses to queer theory can be observed in these analyses, reflecting different theoretical perspectives, ranging from pro-queer/feminists to feminists who are opposed to queer, with varying degrees of critical engagement with queer theory between these positions. We can, then, think of the relationship between feminism and queer theory as a complex dynamic of oppositions, intersections and contestations. Postmodern feminist theories of gender and sexuality have been taken up by queer theory in ways that blur the boundary between feminist/queer writers, Judith Butler's work being a prime example. It is within postmodern feminism, therefore, that queer and feminist theory may seem most obviously to intersect, although this is not necessarily without criticism or contestation (e.g. Grosz, 1995; Probyn, 1996; Berlant, 1997; Merck *et al.*, 1998).

Many feminists, however, are critical of queer for reasons that echo feminist concerns with postmodern theorising more generally (see, for example, Brodribb, 1992). A key aspect of such critiques has been that queer theory's deconstructionist approach to gender, and the postmodern critique of identity that is central to this, seems to threaten collective understandings and identities. These debates parallel those within feminism in the 1980s over the possible negative consequences for political organising in deconstructing the categories 'woman' and 'man'. In this context, the primary focus is that queer theory's questioning of the viability and political utility of sexual and gender identity categories render political action as lesbians and feminists difficult. This is one of the reasons that lesbian and radical feminist writers such as Sheila Jeffreys (2002) and Bonnie Zimmerman (1997) oppose queer theory on the grounds that it has not only 'disappeared lesbians', but also threatens to do the same to feminism. Thus, for example, Jeffreys claims that the postmodern and queer approaches to gender have led to the development of a form of 'gender' politics which is in clear opposition to, and serves to replace and render invisible, feminism (Jeffreys, 2003: 49).

The view that queer theory is damaging to the interests of feminism has been productive of an oppositional stance towards queer among many feminists. (As I will discuss further below, such a binary has also been reinforced by representations of queer theory that, as Walters (2005) also suggests, characterise it as opposed to a certain kind of feminist and lesbian theorising.) An important aspect of these critiques is the argument that the rise of queer theory has resulted in a loss of conceptual space for lesbian/feminist approaches to sexuality and gender, which has significant consequences for both gender theory and politics. Within materialist feminist accounts, for instance, gender is understood as a socially constructed product of patriarchal hierarchies (Jackson, 1999b); the *outcome* of material power differences (Wittig, 1981, 1992; Delphy, 1984). For those feminists who adhere to such analyses of gender relations, the political goal of challenging gendered power differences will, as a consequence, lead to the elimination of the idea of gender. Queer theory's deconstructionist approach to gender has a different aim, to disrupt and denaturalise sexual and gender categories in ways that recognise the fluidity, instability and fragmentation of identities and a plurality of gendered subject positions. In the emphasis on destabilising binary distinctions between women and men, as well as the heterosexual/ homosexual divide, gender as a concept appears to be retained. In other words, it is not gender *per se* that is problematised, but particular normative constructions of gender that presumes a certain set of interrelationships between sex, gender and sexuality (Martin, 1998). As Jackson (2005: 33) comments,'If Butler and her followers have a utopian vision, it is a world of multiple genders and sexualities, not a world without gender or heterosexuality.'

Although queer theory may appear to be reluctant to relinquish gender as a discursive web from which there can be 'no escape', the process of deconstruction *is* associated with a rejection of the assumption of stable and unified gender and sexual categories. Associated with this is a critique of 'identity politics'; the mobilistion around an identity such as 'woman' or 'gay' or black' as a basis for political action. In a lot of queer work, the focus is on disrupting gender and sexual binaries through actions that subvert identity and displace gender and sexual norms. This is a further source of tension between queer theory and feminism, as well as lesbian and gay and anti-racist movements. (A tension that echoes earlier debates within feminism, especially during the 1980s, over the issue of 'difference', prompted by black, working class, and lesbian feminist critiques of 'hegemonic feminisms' *and* the impact of postmodernist ideas and the problematisation of the category 'woman'.) While recognising the many different ways in which one can 'do gender', the complex and varied identities and meanings associated with the identity 'woman', and that women have different material interests amongst themselves, many feminist (and some queer writers) at the same time argue for the political utility of such gender categories in order to articulate and contest material inequalities.

This tension within and between feminist and queer theory can be understood as a pull between the disciplinary and enabling effects of gender and sexual categories. In Butler's work and that of many postmodern feminist and queer theorists, although both effects may be acknowledged, the focus is primarily on the disciplinary effects of discourse, rather than on 'any positive gains from our inhabiting the categories which are on offer' (Alsop *et al.*, 2002: 108). For some feminists this highlights one of the limitations of queer theory, its reluctance to recognise that identity categories can provide both a space for political action as well as frameworks by which we become intelligible to ourselves and others.

We have then interesting counter currents running through the relationship between feminist and queer theory. A primary focus in queer theory, as I have outlined, is the process of deconstruction and disruption of gender and sexual categories. Although feminist theorising incorporates such work, within feminism there are also theoretical positions that see doing away with gender as central to their project, not reimagining it (although feminists *have* done this). From such a perspective, queer theory may be critiqued on the grounds that it perpetuates the 'idea of gender'. At the same time, critics including queer theorists have argued that feminist practices may serve to reinforce and maintain binary gender and sexual categories. More specifically, that feminist movements (and lesbian and gay movements) can be seen as part of the social process that creates the illusion of the existence of stable and unified gender and sexual categories, even as they may claim the eradication of such categories as a primary political goal.

The implications of queer theory for political action and social change are themes that have also been taken up by feminists who regard queer theory in a more positive light, and consider the interstices between feminist and queer ideas as potentially productive. Socialist and Marxist feminist writers such as Elizabeth Wilson (1993) and Mary McIntosh (1993), for example, have in the past acknowledged queer theory as important for feminist theory; in particular by providing a critique of the heterosexual assumptions embedded in much feminist work. However they are critical of the emphasis within queer on the 'politics of transgression', making the point that this is unlikely to bring about social transformation. Some gay sociologists writing from a Marxist perspective (e.g. Kirsch, 2000) have similarly argued that while queer theory may bring useful theoretical insights, it also renders political action for social change problematic. Connected with this, queer theory has also been subjected to criticism for its focus on discourses and texts, in so far as this has led to insufficient attention to issues of structure and materiality. Feminists such as Stevi Jackson (1999b), Rosemary Hennessey (1994, and in this volume) and Janice McLaughlin (in this volume) call for material concerns to take greater prominence in queer theory and to re-examine queer concepts in the light of material as well as cultural dynamics.

Feminists, both proponents and opponents of queer theory, have also raised a number of questions related to the genealogy of queer theory. In particular, whether there has been sufficient recognition of the historical antecedents to queer theory and, related to this, how far queer theory can be seen as emerging out of earlier feminist and other theoretical work on sexuality and gender. A further associated area of debate concerns the extent to which queer theory and feminist theory can be thought to be more or less similar or different to one another. If similar, then where do the main areas of theoretical overlap and shared interests lie? If different, then can queer theory and feminist theory be understood as two separate fields of enquiry? If so, then are these two fields of study merely distinct from one another or are they counter posed?

This chapter will attempt to interrogate these questions, hopefully in a way that will allow for recognition of the possible intersections as well as the contestations between queer theory and feminism. My starting point, however, is to problematise this aim in asking what is the basis for the methodological distinction that is often made between them.

Theorising sexuality and gender

As a number of writers have noted, a number of social and political factors contributed to the emergence of queer theory and politics in the late 1980s and 1990s including the HIV/AIDS crisis and the impetus this provided for the formation of political alliances between lesbians and gay men, the rise of post-structuralist theory, and, as I shall go on to discuss below, 'sex debates' between feminists and associated critiques of lesbian/feminism by feminists (Phelan, 1994; Walters, 2005). In addition, queer developed as a critique of the politics of normalisation and assimilation that, since the 1990s, has become the dominant political discourse of lesbian and gay movements (Warner, 2000; Seidman, 2002). This is something queer shares with certain strands of feminism that are critical of these shifts (see, for example, Cooper, 2004; Richardson, 2005).

In the context of this discussion, however, it is important to situate the growth of queer theory within the context of the academy. The rise of postmodernism provided a supportive and fertile environment in which queer theories could flourish. However, the development of queer theory is also identified with a critical response to feminist theories of sexuality that were perceived as limited by an emphasis on gender (Jagose, 1996; Sullivan, 2003). To ask how feminist and queer theories interrelate is, therefore, to raise methodological and epistemological issues concerning the conceptualisation of gender and sexuality. Rubin's work from the early 1980s, in which she argued that although connected gender and sexuality 'are not the same thing' (Rubin, 1984: 308), has been particularly influential in these contemporary debates. Rubin's argument is centred on an understanding of sexuality and gender as two distinct areas of social practice. If the primary goal of feminist analysis is theorising gender then, according to Rubin, something more than feminist theory is required to 'fully encompass the social organisation of sexuality' (Rubin, 1984: 314). Rubin's critique of feminist theories of sexuality was particularly pertinent to those theories of gender developed by certain radical feminist writers, such as MacKinnon (1982), who argued that sexuality, as it is currently constructed, is constitutive of gender. From this perspective, sexuality is not theorised apart from gender; rather understandings of gender are located in terms of an analysis of sexual relations.

In making a methodological distinction between gender and sexuality, Rubin has since claimed that she was neither attacking feminism nor was she seeking to establish a new field of knowledge that would result in an intellectual division of labour between feminism and gay/lesbian/queer studies (see Rubin with Butler, 1998: 61). Nevertheless, her rationale is clearly motivated by what she identifies as epistemological concerns. According to Rubin, by the early 1980s feminist work on sexuality had established itself as an 'orthodoxy', a site of knowledge production about gender and sexuality that was privileged over other analytical approaches. (For a critical discussion of this view see Richardson, 2000.) Feminism is regarded as not merely insufficient, not the best analytical 'tool for the job', but as exerting disciplinary power to the detriment of scholarship on sexuality. In Rubin's own words, 'I was trying to make some space for work on sexuality (and even gender) that did not presume feminism as the obligatory and sufficient approach' (Rubin with Butler, 1998: 61). Echoing Rubin, the queer writer Eve Sedgwick argues that although sexuality and gender are completely intertwined with one another 'the study of sexuality is not coextensive with the study of gender' (Sedgwick, 1990: 27) and that, as a consequence, 'antihomophobic inquiry' and feminism can be usefully separated'.

In certain respects then the relationship between queer theory and feminism can be understood as a debate about the 'disciplinary turf' of the study of sexuality and gender. In this sense, it might be argued that any theoretical 'division' between the two is a rather tenuous one, a division constituted – at least in part – out of the material interests of those who invoke such theory borders and the political and historical contexts associated with the emergence of such interests. Arguably, this has primarily been seen as a contestation over theorising sexuality rather than theorising gender, which is somewhat ironic when one considers the profound influence that Judith Butler's work has had on theorising gender and the possible implications of this for feminist theory and practice. Queer theory is frequently constructed as productive of new (and better) forms of knowledge about sexuality, both as a consequence of bringing new methods/analytical tools to bear on the subject and also by focusing on areas of investigation considered to be poorly theorised by feminist and other work on the study of sexuality. This has led to claims that queer and feminism are now 'widely understood to be two fields of study', with the theoretical investigation of sexuality allocated to queer theory, and the analysis of gender to feminism (Merck *et al.*, 1998: 1). If this is so, then we might interrogate the relationship between feminist and queer by asking whether these two (presumed) fields of study are constructed by these debates as more similar than different or as relatively autonomous?

For many writers, both feminist and queer, this is a qualified separation, with emphasis on how the two are interconnected and can enrich each other (e.g. Butler, 1994; Martin, 1998). For others it represents a very real separating out of interests whether writing as feminists (e.g. Heller, 1997; Jeffreys, 2003) or as queer theorists (e.g. Halperin, 1995). There are, however, tensions in the view that queer is a radically new conceptual model and form of sexual politics, and the argument that to a large extent it has developed out of existing knowledges, including feminism (Turner, 2000). This has prompted criticisms of queer's tendency to construct itself as 'a vanguard position that announces its newness' (Martin, 1998: 11). For instance, Kirsch (2000:17) argues that the ' "newness" of Queer theory is not new, but has precursors in past theoretical debate'. In the following section, I will go on to consider these tensions through an examination of how feminist theorising intersects with queer theory.

Feminism is to queer ...

Within the literature, as I have already indicated, it is common for queer theory to be described as 'in opposition' to certain forms of lesbian/feminist theorising (Stacey, 1997; Walters, 2005). Nevertheless, there have been attempts by both queer and feminist writers to identify the links between them. For example, many writers have suggested that queer theory owes an intellectual debt both to lesbian and gay studies and to feminism. This would appear to be something that, to greater or lesser extent, feminists and queer theorists appear to agree upon. For some queer theorists this development is characterised primarily as one of queer emerging out of feminism. For example, in the introduction to an important early queer text *Fear of a Queer Planet* Warner states that '. . . feminism has made gender a primary category of the social in a way that makes queer social theory newly imaginable' (Warner, 1993: p. viii). Warner also acknowledges the historical importance of feminist work on sexuality, citing among others the work of Adrienne Rich (1980), Gayle Rubin (1984), Monique Wittig (1980/1992), as well as writers such as Eve Sedgwick (1990) and Judith Butler (1990), who in other contexts might well be represented as queer theorists. Interestingly, Warner claims that despite queer's aim to disrupt gender divisions, its relationship to feminism is gendered. Queer male theorists (as well as women who write about gay men and/or AIDS) he claims are strongly influenced by Foucauldian analyses and constructionist theory more broadly, whereas queer theory by women writers more typically refer to French feminisms and Anglo-American psychoanalytic feminism (Warner, 1993: pp. xxvi–xxvii).

In seeking to engage with feminist theory, Warner identifies similarities in terms of what he identifies as the key task of queer studies 'to force a thorough revision within social-theoretical traditions, of the kind being won by feminism' (Warner, 1993: p. x). By doing this, he argues that queer theory will enable sexuality to be recognised as a primary category for social analysis and social organisation in a way that parallels feminist theoretical work on gender 'when feminists began treating gender more and more as a primary category for understanding problems that did not initially look gender-specific' (Warner, 1993: p. xiv). Although Warner espouses the need for queer theory to find a 'new engagement' with various traditions of social theory that includes feminism, and recognises similarities between the two, the underlying tone is nevertheless one of feminism as a model that queer theory might usefully follow in developing its own critiques. Feminism is also positioned here as concerned with theorising gender as distinct from sexuality, in a manner that can be seen as working to establish the methodological autonomy of queer studies differentiated from feminism by their respective 'objects' of analysis. The risk in this splitting, I would argue, is that this may restrict rather than enhance our efforts to theorise the complex intersections between sexuality and gender.

Some feminist critics of queer theory argue that this represents a deliberate attempt to establish queer theory as an autonomous field of inquiry. Thus, for instance, Jeffreys speaks of queer theory's '*determination* to establish that the study of sexuality is a field of inquiry quite separate from and impervious to feminist theory (Jeffreys, 1994: 466 my emphasis).

As a consequence, she argues that a major concern for many lesbian/feminists is that the rise of queer theory will result in the study of sexuality becoming 'feminist-free'. From this perspective, attempts to establish queer theory as a new field of study can be interpreted as a colonising move to wrest disciplinary control over the subject area of sexuality, delimiting feminism to the study of gender (see also critiques by Wolfe and Penelope, 1993; Kitzinger and Wilkinson, 1994; Wilkinson and Kitzinger, 1996). However, it is important to recognise that for many feminists the study of sexuality is seen as intrinsically connected to analyses of gender, especially within lesbian and radical feminist accounts (Walby, 1990; Jackson, 1999b). Any such move, therefore, would represent a challenge to feminist theorising of *gender* as well as sexuality.

A number of queer theorists have acknowledged the input of feminist work into the development of queer theory. These include Seidman (1997) who, though he argues that queer theory has been primarily influenced by post-structuralism and psychoanalysis, especially the work of French writers, also acknowledges that many queer theorists draw on feminism as a 'conceptual resource.' Indeed, in terms of his own interest in making explicit the interconnections between queer theory and sociology, which he argues are 'barely acknowledged', Seidman identifies feminist sociology as a specific strand of sociological work that queer theory 'owes a great deal to' (Seidman, 1997: 94). The areas he specifically refers to include feminist critiques of the authority of science, and its claims to 'objectivity' and 'truth', the questioning of foundationalist and universalising views of knowledge, constructionist work on sexuality, and the destabilising of unitary concepts such as 'woman' and, albeit to a lesser extent, 'man'.

In addition to its theoretical contribution, Seidman also highlights the internal dynamics within feminism, as well as lesbian and gay movements, as significant for the development of queer theory and politics. What Seidman is, in part, referring to are the highly contested debates that emerged in lesbian feminism towards the end of the 1970s and early 80s in the United States, Canada, the United Kingdom, New Zealand and Australia, what some have since described as the feminist 'sex wars', over a range of issues concerned with sexuality, in particular butch/femme, bisexuality, pornography, sado-masochism and transexuality (Duggan and Hunter, 1995; Jackson and Scott, 1996). Interestingly, then, we have queer represented as 'coming out of feminism' both in terms of it having a theoretically enabling role and, more negatively, as a consequence of a critique of lesbian/feminism on the part of some lesbian/feminists (see also Butler, 1997a).

This is a view that appears to find a certain resonance with many feminist writers, both supporters of queer and its critics. Indeed, a common criticism made of queer theory, especially by sociologists and social historians (see, for example, Escoffier, 1990; Stein and Plummer, 1996; Weeks, 1998), is that it has paid insufficient attention to its own genealogy in ignoring earlier work in lesbian and gay studies, as well as feminist theoretical work in particular. Where theoretical 'inheritance' is acknowledged by queer theorists, the tendency has been to construct feminism as foundational, an 'originating source' from which queer theory has emerged.

Many feminist and some queer writers have been highly critical of this construction of feminism's relation to queer. Drawing on feminist criticisms of enlightenment Stacey (1997), for example, argues that queer theory's distinction from previous theoretical traditions are frequently couched in modernist narratives, surprisingly so given the extent to which queer theory is informed by postmodernism, with queer positioned as progressive relative to feminism. Despite her view of the relationship between queer and feminist theory as mutually productive, Martin (1998) nevertheless expresses similar concerns to Stacey in arguing that queer theory oversimplifies feminism. It does this, according to Martin, by reducing feminism to just one rather than many theoretical approaches and in conceiving gender as the subject of feminism and in negative terms, in terms of fixity in contrast with the fluidity of sexuality. This is evident, she claims, in the tendency for queer writers to construct queer theory as antifoundationalist through and against 'a fixed ground', that is often identified with 'feminism, or the female body' (Martin, 1998:1). Spurlin (1998) also contests that gay (male) studies and, by implication, queer theory has not sufficiently theorised its relation to feminism. One of the consequences of this, he argues, is that feminism – along with lesbian and gay studies – has often been constructed as both a 'master discourse' and a site of privilege (that queer contests) and as an originary force (that queer supersedes).

In this context, questions about intellectual 'inheritance' go beyond asking whether or not adequate recognition has been given to the legacy of feminist ideas in the historical development of queer theory, towards a much broader focus on how feminism and queer theory might productively inform each other. As I have already indicated, there have been attempts by both feminist and queer theorists to explore the links between the two in this way. Feminist writers have, in the main, tended to focus on identifying specific connections between queer and areas of feminist theoretical work. For example, Jackson (1996a, b), Hennessey

(1994) and Richardson (2000), among others, have highlighted the connections between queer theory and feminist critiques of heterosexuality. They argue that queer theory has a particular affinity with earlier lesbian and radical feminist work that contributed to the development of a deconstructive model of gender and (hetero) sexuality. It is clear that the materialist feminist Monique Wittig's (1980/1992) work, for example, has been influential in informing the early work of both Judith Butler (1990, 1993) and Michael Warner (1993). Queer theory has also been informed by Adrienne Rich's (1980) groundbreaking work on 'compulsory heterosexuality' that, in highlighting the socially and economically constructed nature of heterosexuality, represented an early attempt to denaturalise heterosexual relations, an aim that queer has more recently claimed.

These interconnections, I argue, have not been sufficiently interrogated by either feminist or queer writers. In her work, Rich made the link between heterosexuality as a social institution and the oppression of women, challenging the assumption that 'most women are innately heterosexual' and suggesting that ' heterosexuality may not be "a preference" at all, but something that has had to be imposed, managed, organized, propagandized, and maintained by force' (Rich, 1980: 20). She went on to describe some of the factors which 'coerce' women into heterosexuality, including the unequal position of women in the labour market, the idealisation of heterosexual romance and marriage, and the association of heterosexuality with the idea of 'normality'. (Butler (1990) also invokes the idea of a compulsory order of heterosexuality though in her case this is conceptualised in terms of cultural norms.) Central to Rich's critique is a concern with challenging binaries that she identifies as restricting our ability to determine the meaning and place of sexuality in our lives. She claims,

> We have been stalled in a maze of false dichotomies which prevents our apprehending the institution (of heterosexuality) as a whole: 'good' versus 'bad' marriages; 'marriage for love' versus arranged marriage, 'liberated' sex versus prostitution; heterosexual intercourse versus rape; Liebeschmerz versus humiliation and dependency. (Rich, 1980: 31)

Although Rich does not explicitly mention the heterosexual/homosexual binary that is the focus of much queer theory, her work can be seen as an early attempt to disrupt (queer) the boundaries of sexual categories. Rich put forward the notion of the 'lesbian continuum', which challenged the restriction of the definition of lesbianism to those who had had or desired genital sexual experience with another woman. For Rich, the term lesbian included a broad range of social practices between women and she seemed to assume that 'lesbianism was a propensity common to all women' (Jackson, 2005: 20). Not only did this disrupt hegemonic understandings of lesbianism, it also challenged conceptualisations of 'the erotic', as Rich herself points out in describing what she means by lesbian existence and a lesbian continuum:

> As the term 'lesbian' has been held to limiting, clinical associations in its patriarchal definition, female friendship and comradeship have been set apart from the erotic, thus limiting the erotic itself. (Rich, 1980: 22)

Although contemporary feminist and queer writers would no doubt be quick to pick up on the idea of 'false' dichotomies referred to in the first quote, it is clear that in using the idea of a continuum Rich's work can be seen as disrupting dominant discourses of sexuality by destabilising sexual binaries; by conceptualising the category lesbian as a broad social category rather than as sexual preference, and by contesting the view of lesbian existence – both as unnatural desire and 'alternative lifestyle' – as a marginal or less 'natural' phenomenon. There are, then, some significant overlaps in Rich's writing and that of queer theorists. That said, in other respects Rich can be read as opposed to queer. The critique made by Butler (1990) and other queer writers of feminism's potential to reinforce gender binaries and imply universal and unified sexual categories could also apply to Rich's work. Thus, for example, in terms that are reminiscent of Jeffreys' more recent claim that queer denies and erases the specificity of lesbian experience, Rich states that:

> In defining and describing lesbian experience I would hope to move toward a dissociation of lesbian from male homosexual values and allegiances. I perceive the lesbian experience as being, like motherhood, a profoundly *female* experience, with particular oppressions, meanings, and potentialities we cannot comprehend as long as we simply bracket it with other sexually stigmatized existences. (Rich, 1980: 22)

Alongside Rich's notion of the lesbian continuum, the development of concepts such as woman-identified woman and political lesbianism (see Radicalesbians, 1973 [original dissemination 1970]; Leeds Revolutionary

Feminist Group, 1981) can also be seen as representing a radical challenge to the heterosexual/homosexual binary by 'queering' the boundaries between the two. One might see 'queer', for example, functioning in similar ways to the term 'political lesbian'. Identification with these categories is not based on sexual preference as a source of shared identity. In both cases there is a (partial) dissociation with sexuality in that one does not have to consider oneself to be lesbian/gay to be a political lesbian/queer. They might both be thought of not so much as identities, but as discursive positions open to all which, in their 'openness', are potentially disruptive of the heterosexual/ homosexual divide. Other writers have similarly questioned the originality of queer in terms of the activist practices of queer politics, pointing out that similar practices have a long history within feminism (Jeffreys, 2003).

Some queer writers would contest this, arguing that rather than queering boundaries such radical feminist work invoked new boundaries. However, I would argue that in certain respects lesbian/feminist theories of the 1970s, as well as more contemporary feminist work, might be constructed as 'queer' or at least sharing what queer claims to be 'new' in its approach. For example, queer theorist Steven Seidman highlights how queer theory is suggesting that 'the study of homosexuality should not be a study of a minority', but a study of those 'knowledges and social practices that organize "society" as a whole by sexualizing – heterosexualizing or homosexualizing – bodies, desires, acts, identities, social relations, knowledges, culture, and social institutions' (Seidman, 1996: 13). Is this so very far from Rich's attempts to theorise heterosexuality and lesbianism, as well as more contemporary feminist work on (hetero) sexuality?

Both feminist (e.g. Richardson, 1996; Jackson, 1999b; Ingraham, 2005) and queer (e.g. Butler, 1990, 1994; Sedgwick, 1990; Warner, 1993, 2000) writers have challenged constructions of heterosexuality as natural and universal and queried the heterosexual/homosexual binary. Like queer theory, which aspires to be a general critical social theory rather than a theory of queers, a great deal of feminist work on sexuality has similar epistemological aims, in interrogating the impact that ignoring or excluding heterosexuality has had on the development of social theory (see, for example, the edited collection, Richardson, 1996). As I have argued elsewhere, both feminist and queer work on sexuality 'invite a radical rethinking of many of the concepts we use to theorise social relations' (Richardson, 1996: 2). It is also clear that in both feminist and queer theory sexuality is understood not as a 'private issue', not just about what we refer to as our 'sexual lives', but as central to the social organisation of the 'public' world and to the conceptual frameworks we deploy to make sense of the social worlds we inhabit. The hetero/homosexual binary is conceptualised as something that is encoded in a wide range of social institutions and practices not normally thought of as connected with sexuality such as, for example, housing, urban planning, health services and care of the elderly (Warner, 1993); labour markets, educational opportunities, leisure pursuits and travel (Richardson, 1997).

Related to this, it is important to acknowledge not only the continuing significance of earlier feminist work for queer theory, but also that of contemporary feminist writers. Over the last ten years or so, feminist theorising on heterosexuality (see, for example, Wilkinson and Kitzinger, 1993; Segal, 1994; Richardson, 1996; Jackson, 1996a, b, 1999b; Ingraham, 1996, 2005) has offered a critical analysis of heterosexuality as identity, practice and institution, and argued that in all of these respects heterosexuality is not a natural, normal, universal, transhistorical phenomenon. In addition to identifying some of the discourses and practices that constitute it as a social institution and norm, they also critique the way in which heterosexuality is often understood in monolithic terms (e.g. Segal, 1994; Richardson, 1996; Smart, 1996). For instance, acknowledging the heterogeneity of heterosexuality, feminist work has highlighted how single mothers can represent the 'heterosexual other' (Lawler, 2000). Such an approach is potentially useful to those queer theorists who have been critical of the focus on the heterosexual/homosexual binary within queer studies for failing to adequately address these kinds of questions. Thus, for example, Sullivan cites Cohen's (1997) work which suggests that a broadened understanding of queer would highlight how 'heterosexuals have multiple subject positions' and are not 'situated socially, politically, economically in the same way' (Sullivan, 2003: 49).

Debates about sexual citizenship are another site of potential productive engagement between queer and feminist theory. Since the 1990s, a rights-orientated assimilationist agenda has become the dominant discourse within contemporary sexual politics in the United States, Canada, Australasia, the United Kingdom and elsewhere in Europe (D'Emilio, 2000). Within such discourses lesbian and gay men are represented as oppressed minorities seeking access to core institutions such as marriage, family and the military, as 'good' citizens who want to be included and share in the same rights and responsibilities as heterosexuals. A number of feminist writers (e.g. Phelan, 2001; Cooper, 2004) have critiqued these shifts towards what I have referred to elsewhere as the rise of a neoliberal politics of normalisation (Richardson, 2005) in ways that have informed (and been informed by) those offered by queer theorists (e.g. Bell and Binnie, 2000; Warner, 2000).

Despite a number of obvious areas of potential engagement, the detailing of how queer debates either are or could be informed by especially contemporary feminist work is not all that apparent in the literature. This is indicative, I would argue, that queer has not sufficiently theorised its relationship to feminism and that, to date, this has been constructed primarily in terms of lineage. Having considered how feminist work might oppose, contest *and* inform queer theory, I will now go on to consider the influence of queer ideas on feminism.

Queer is to feminism ...

As I have suggested in the previous section, within recent feminist and queer literature there has been some acknowledgment of what queer shares in and with feminism. This can be understood, in part, as a response to the way in which queer has been seen as 'oppositional' to feminism. Whilst some feminists have reinforced this view (Jeffreys, 1994, 2002), others have contested certain alleged differences, drawing attention to possible similarities between the two (see, for example, Richardson, 2000; McLaughlin, in this volume). It can also be explained in terms of the charge that queer theory has ignored its historical antecedents which, as I outlined in the previous section, has encouraged both feminist and queer writers to identify areas of overlap between queer theory and earlier feminist work. However, as I suggested at the beginning of this chapter, there has been far less attention to the question of how queer ideas might inform and shape feminism.

Examples of what can be construed as negative engagement include the work of feminist writers who have been highly critical of queer theory and politics. Earlier I indicated that some lesbian and radical feminist writers have expressed concern about the disciplinary control that the developing field of queer studies may exert over the study of sexuality and, for some, analyses of gender. They argue that queer theory is often expressed in terms explicitly oppositional to feminism, especially lesbian and radical feminism (Kitzinger and Wilkinson, 1994; Wilkinson and Kitzinger, 1996). As a consequence, the development and increasing proliferation of queer theory is seen as posing a threat to both lesbian/feminist theory and politics and to the lesbian/feminist subject (Wolfe and Penelope, 1993). Jeffreys (1994, 2003), whose work I have quoted earlier, also makes this argument. Interestingly, however, it is *precisely* for these reasons that she argues that feminists ought to engage critically with queer studies.

A more positive engagement with queer requires us to ask how the development of queer theory might enrich rather than impede feminist theory? A potentially productive relationship can be identified in a number of key areas. First, in the development of critiques of the homosexual/heterosexual binary, which focus on how understandings of sexuality inform the social in ways that are often ignored in social and political theory. A further important contribution that queer theory has made to feminist understandings has been the detailing of how homosexuality and heterosexuality serve to define each other (e.g. Dollimore, 1991; Fuss, 1991a). More specifically, in highlighting how homosexuality is at the heart of heterosexuality, which is both sustained and threatened by the sexual other. That said, I would like to see greater acknowledgement that this aspect of queer can in some senses be linked to ideas developed much earlier by sociologists such as, for example, Goffman (1963), who in his important study of stigma highlighted how the discrediting of certain individuals and groups simultaneously reinforces the 'normality' and 'usualness' of other individuals/ groups.

Second, and related to this, is the development of critiques of normative assumptions about sexuality and gender, and the regulatory function of normalising techniques of control. As I have indicated earlier, both of these are aims that are shared by feminists engaged in theorising (hetero) sexuality some of whom, along with queer theorists, have been critical of heterosexist assumptions within social theory, including feminist work. For instance, feminist theories which attempt to explain the origins of women's oppression for assuming the universality and normality of heterosexuality (Jackson, 1996a; Richardson, 1996).

If we can see this as indicating possibilities for methodological convergence between queer and feminism, we can also understand how it may have contributed to the development of divisions between them and the idea of their operating as two separate fields. As Butler (1994; 1997a) has argued, that queer theory is understood as a separate domain from feminism is indicative of how deeply identified feminism is with normative, heterosexist assumptions. I would add that this is also suggestive of how particular knowledges within feminism, in this case the work of feminists who theorise the interrelationship between gender and sexuality, are evaluated at the expense of others (see, for example, Stacey, 1997; Richardson, 2000; McLaughlin in this volume).

A third area where engagement with queer theory may be helpful to the development of feminist theory is in identifying the need for critical frameworks that problematise universalising understandings of sexuality's relationship to gender. The relationship between sexuality and gender has been theorised in different ways by feminist writers (see Jackson in this volume). While recognising the importance of this earlier work, I would argue that the articulation of new ways of thinking about how sexuality and gender are interrelated is one of the main tasks facing both feminist and queer theory. More specifically, a major challenge for future work is to elaborate frameworks that allow more complex analyses of the dynamic, historically and socially specific relationship between sexuality and gender, as well as the gendered and sexualised nature of their interconnections.

The fourth area where queer theory has been identified as offering (possible) theoretical insights is through its expansion of the concept of 'difference' in ways that enable theorisation of the interarticulations of power between sexuality, gender, race and class. Walters (2005: 11), for example, argues that queer 'can make both theoretical and political space for more substantive notions of multiplicity and intersectionality'. However, at the same time she cautions that there are potential risks for feminism if in this process gender is not 'complicated', but becomes 'merely ignored or dismissed' within queer theory.

The fifth and final area I have identified where queer theory has had a part to play in feminism revisioning some of its theoretical assumptions is in relation to the sex/gender binary. The analytical separation of sex and gender was an important aspect of earlier feminist work, in which gender was understood to be the cultural interpretation of biologically given 'sex'. Queer theory critiques this distinction between sex and gender that Oakley (1972), in what became a feminist classic, and others sought to establish. As a deconstructive strategy, it aims to denaturalise understandings of both gender *and* sex, contesting the notion of sex as pregiven and foundational although some queer theorists have disputed this (see, for example, Grosz, 1994). This disruption of the sex/gender binary has been identified by some feminist writers as being one of the most important contributions of queer theorists to feminist theory (e.g. Martin, 1998). At the same time, we need to balance this with the recognition that similar arguments have been advanced within postmodern feminism (Nicholson, 1994), in radical feminist work, in particular that of French materialist radical feminists such as, for example, Delphy (1993), and in earlier work by social psychologists such as Kessler and McKenna (1978; see also Kessler and McKenna, 2000; McKenna and Kessler, 2000).

Conclusion

In this chapter I have argued that there has been little detailed analysis of the relationship between queer theory and feminism, which has often been characterised as an oppositional dynamic with queer theory represented as the 'answer to previous theories of sexuality' (Stacey, 1997: 60) and, I would add, gender. It is clear that there are significant differences between certain strands of feminism and queer. An important zone of contestation, as I have noted, is that the elimination of the very idea of gender reflects the theoretical perspective of many feminists, which contrasts with the queer project of the deconstruction of gender (and sexual) categories that is productive of a plurality and multiplicity of genders. A further important difference is also connected to materialist analyses of gender. A primary focus for feminist writers has been on how (hetero)sexuality is related to the maintenance of male domination and gender hierarchies, whereas within queer theory attention has been on the ways in which 'heteronormativity' functions to privilege and sustain heterosexuality and exclude sexual 'others'. Gender, it seems, is often displaced in queer theory's discussion of heterosexuality. Even Butler, who is concerned with theorising gender, appears to have little interest in discussing material inequalities between women and men or that heterosexuality might be related to male dominance. As Jackson (2005) also notes, this is all the more remarkable when one considers that her work has been significantly influenced by that of materialist feminists such as Wittig. One might also point to a lack of attention to materiality in queer theory in a different sense, in arguing that the focus on cultural norms often fails to address questions of how these norms are constituted and why they prevail.

While recognising the importance of such differences for both theoretical and political practice, what I have also tried to do in this chapter is to explore interconnections. I am suggesting that in future a more careful and systematic examination will enable dialogue between queer theory and feminism that moves us beyond a concern with genealogy. To extend our theoretical understandings of both gender and sexuality we need to consider the relationship between feminism and queer not so much in terms of binaries such as before/after and either/or, but rather as an ongoing interaction that allows for possible intersections, as well as oppositions and contestations.

2
Heterosexuality, Sexuality and Gender
Re-thinking the Intersections

Stevi Jackson

For most feminist, lesbian, gay, queer and other critical thinkers, it has become axiomatic that gender and sexuality are social rather than natural phenomena and that the relationship between them is a matter for analysis and investigation. Yet in wider social arenas the idea that both gender difference and the realm of sexuality are ordained by nature still has considerable purchase on commonsense reasoning. Indeed its hold may be increasing. While queer theorists were busy troubling heterosexuality, deconstructing the hetero–homo binary and emphasising the fluidity and instability of sexuality, biological determinism was gaining ground – even within gay communities and among campaigners for homosexual rights (see Whisman, 1996; Rahman and Jackson, 1997). In the form of its latest, most fashionable incarnation, evolutionary psychology, it has become ubiquitous in popular representations of science.[1] We have also seen theories of female and male brains (see Fausto-Sterling, 2002), gay brains (LeVay, 1993) and the increasing medicalisation of sexuality (Marshall, 2002; Moynihan, 2003). The effect of this trend is to locate gender and sexuality ever more firmly in biology, in the realm of the natural sciences, and to sideline the social and the cultural as mere modifiers of pre-given evolutionary, genetic, neurological or physiological patterns and processes.

Reclaiming the ground for social and cultural theorists entails not only direct critique of biological determinism, but also unpicking the commonsense assumptions at the heart of what passes for scientific fact. What particularly concerns me here is the assumed immutable link between gender and (hetero)sexuality, which is deeply embedded in our culture, indeed in the very language with which we think about gender and sexuality. This is most evident in the relationship of gender and sexuality to a third term: 'sex'. That the words 'sex' and 'sexual' can denote both the distinction between women and men ('the two sexes', the 'sexual division of labour') and erotic activity ('having sex', 'sexual fantasies') is no chance effect. 'Sex' is what makes women and men different and it is what that difference is *for*; reproductive, heterosexual sex (*the* sex act) is thought of as the mythic origin and purpose of sex differences. Thus 'normal' masculinity and femininity and 'normal' sexual desire find their expression through heterosexuality.

A social understanding of gender and sexuality does more than merely revealing that the 'normal' is normative rather than natural; it can also demonstrate that gender and sexuality are themselves constructions and are each far too complex for so neat a functional integration between them. One of the great strengths of social and cultural analysis is that it can tease apart the ties that connect gender and sexuality and reveal the multiplicity of strands from which they are woven and which, in turn, weave gendered and sexual relations into the wider social fabric. Queer theory has, of course, contributed to this project; some of its canonical texts sought to disentangle sexuality from gender and reveal the contingency of their interrelationship (e.g. Butler, 1990; Sedgwick, 1991). I would argue, however, that to understand more fully how the interconnections between gender, sexuality and heterosexuality come to be naturalised as taken for granted features of social life, attention needs to be paid to aspects of the social that are rarely addressed by queer theorists. For while queer theorists seek to denaturalise heterosexuality, to reveal that it depends for its definition and privilege on its excluded 'other' (Fuss, 1991b; Sedgwick, 1991) they are relatively unconcerned about what goes on *within* heterosexual relations, with the everyday practices and institutional structures that sustain a heterosexual and gendered social order.[2] These issues have more often been addressed by feminists working within the social sciences (see, e.g. Wilkinson and Kitzinger, 1993; Richardson, 1996; Holland *et al.*, 1998; Jackson, 1999b).

Informed by a feminist sociological perspective, this chapter re-examines the intersections between gender, sexuality in general and heterosexuality in particular. Any analysis of these linkages will depend upon how we define gender, sexuality and heterosexuality and the sense in which we understand them as socially constructed. Hence conceptual clarification constitutes an essential first stage of my argument. Moreover, it is also necessary to acknowledge that contemporary debates have a history, which I will briefly survey, and that this history informs my own feminist and sociological perspective. In the final section of the paper, building upon an earlier version of these arguments (Jackson, 2005) I begin to explore some ways of tackling the complexity of the interconnections I am addressing. I am not proposing solutions to the problems I identify, but hope to setting an open agenda for future debate and investigation.

Priorities and definitions: gender, sexuality and heterosexuality

I have, in the past, argued for the logical priority of gender over sexuality in shaping their interrelationship (see Jackson, 1999b; 2005). There were two main reasons for this. Initially I wished to challenge the undue emphasis given to sexuality by feminists and non-feminists alike within Western culture. I therefore contested those psychoanalytic arguments that reduce gender difference to the direction of sexual desire (e.g. Mitchell, 1982) as well as forms of feminism that reduce male domination to men's appropriation of women's sexuality (e.g. MacKinnon, 1982; Jeffreys, 1990). Second I have suggested that without gender categories we could not categorise sexual desires and identities along the axis of same-gender or other-gender relationships, as heterosexual, bisexual or homosexual/lesbian. I would still defend these positions, but a few caveats are needed. In the first place, these two arguments by no means exhaust all the ways in which gender and sexuality are interrelated. Furthermore, even where I do accord priority to gender, I nonetheless see gender and sexuality as *inter*-related, thus accepting that sexuality has effects on and implications for gender as well as vice-versa. Finally, and crucially for the discussion I will pursue here, the picture shifts when it comes to considering gender's relationship with heterosexuality rather than sexuality in general, not only because heterosexuality is a privileged, institutionalised form of sexuality but because institutionalised heterosexuality encompasses more than erotic sexuality. What I am suggesting, then, is the relationship between gender and heterosexuality is of a different order from that between gender and sexuality.

Part of the problem we have in thinking through the connections between gender, sexuality in general and heterosexuality in particular is that we do not all mean the same thing by these terms and are often talking about different objects at different levels of analysis. The language we use is imprecise, slippery and its meaning shifts with context. For example, the term 'heterosexuality' can denote a mode of erotic attraction or an institution involving wider social relations between women and men. 'Sexuality' itself is sometimes understood primarily in terms of the hetero–homo binary, or the straight, gay, lesbian or bisexual identities deriving from it, while others take it to encompass a fuller range of desires, practices and identities. 'Gender' can mean the division or distinction between women or men, whether this is seen as primarily a bodily difference or a social hierarchy, but also refers to the content of gender categories, conventionally defined as femininity or masculinity.

I tend to opt for the broader senses of these terms because to narrow them down risks losing sight of significant portions of social life – although keeping them broad causes other problems, in that a great deal of sociocultural complexity is thereby collapsed into a single concept. I use the term gender to cover both the division itself and the social, subjective and embodied differences that give it everyday substance. What is absolutely fundamental to gender if we are to see it as fully social (rather than as founded on a pre-existing natural difference) is the fact of gender division itself and the categories it produces. I define gender as a hierarchical social division between women and men embedded in both social institutions and social practices. Gender is thus part of the social order, but this is not all it is. It is also a cultural distinction, largely taken for granted, but given meaning and lived out by embodied individuals who 'do gender' in their daily lives, constantly producing and reproducing it through habitual, everyday interaction (Kessler and McKenna, 1978; West and Zimmerman, 1987).[3] There is another curious feature of gender, of course: the binary division of gender is a persistent and resilient feature of social and cultural life, incredibly difficult to shift, yet it co-exists with a considerable degree of latitude regarding lived masculinities and femininities, even increasing tolerance (slight, but discernible) towards those who cross the divide. So while gender is a binary division, the categories it produces are not homogeneous. This heterogeneity is in part attributable to other social divisions or distinctions – of class, ethnicity, nationality and so on – which intersect with gender, but this is not the whole story. It may be, as Delphy (1993) suggests, that one of the defining features of gender is the co-existence of variability in its content with the intractability of gender categories themselves.

It should be clear from the above that I see gender as an entirely social and cultural phenomenon, in no way resting on a pre-existing biological base. So-called 'biological sex differences' cannot be taken for granted as given, since the recognition and classification of them are themselves social acts (Kessler and McKenna, 1978; Delphy, 1993). If gender is used to denote all aspects of the distinction and division between women and men (and boys and girls) then some of the ambiguities of the term 'sex' can be avoided. 'Sex' can then be reserved to denote carnal or erotic acts, with 'sexuality' as a broader term referring to all erotically significant aspects of social life and social being. Sexuality is not, therefore, reducible to the heterosexual–homosexual binary – although this is an important aspect of its social organization – but of the multitude of desires and practices that exist across that divide.

I am thus making an analytical distinction between sex and sexuality on the one hand and gender on the other. While some make the case for the irreducibility of the former to the latter in order to create a space for the theorisation of sexuality *per se* (Rubin, 1984; Sedgwick, 1991), I do so in order more effectively to theorise their interrelationship. Without an analytical distinction between them, we cannot effectively explore the ways in which they intersect; if we conflate them, we are in danger of deciding the form of their interrelationship in advance. Yet, while analytically separable, gender and sexuality are empirically interconnected (Gagnon and Simon, 1974). If we ignore the empirical linkage between them there is a danger of abstracting sexuality from the social. Sexual practices, desires and identities are embedded within complex webs of non-sexual social relations (Gagnon, 2004), most, if not all, of which are gendered.

It is here that one of the biggest difficulties confronts us: sexuality and gender may be interrelated but they are rather different and not directly comparable social phenomena. Sedgwick argues that 'the whole realm of what modern culture refers to as "sexuality" ... is virtually impossible to situate on a map delimited by the feminist defined sex/gender distinction' (1991: 29). I am in agreement with Sedgwick's queer project in that sexuality, as she says, exceeds male–female difference and 'the choreography of procreation' (1991: 29). My position, however, is that sexuality and gender differ because the former is a sphere or realm of social life while the latter is a fundamental social division. While my view of sexuality is not dissimilar to Sedgwick's my understanding of gender dffers.

In the broad sense in which I am using the term sexuality it encompasses all erotically significant aspects of life – for example, desires, practices, relationships and identities. The concept of 'sexuality' thus refers to a rather fluid field since what is sexual in the sense of erotic is not fixed but depends on what is defined as such. Biological determinists of course do not have this problem – they know what is sexual. For those of us interested in the social construction and implications of sexuality, however, it is necessary to take seriously the idea that what makes an act, a desire or a relationship sexual are the meanings invested in it (see Gagnon and Simon, 1974). These meanings are contextual and variable and hence sexuality has no clear definitional boundaries – what is sexual to one person in one context may not be to someone else or somewhere else.

It could be objected that gender is a matter of social definition too – and so, in a sense, it is. As social division, however, it is also a ubiquitous feature of social life. Gender is taken by Sedgwick to define 'the space of differences between men and women' (1991: 29). As she points out (1991: 28), gender categories are generally understood as co-constructed and relational. Seen more sociologically, as categories produced by social division rather than 'difference' they are more: they are hierarchical categories associated with inequalities of labour and resources; they pervade all aspects of sociality, locating men and women differently in virtually all spheres of life. Social divisions are not always binary, and not always sharply defined, but these are particular features of gender, dividing members of society into two discrete categories. Many aspects of gender may be more fluid and variable, less definable, but the division itself has a certain incorrigible facticity that is difficult to elude.

Precisely because gender pervades all aspects of social life, sexuality is no exception. Thus while, as Sedgwick claims, we cannot map sexuality directly onto gender, we can and should explore the variety of ways in which sexual desires, activities and relationships are gendered. In so doing, however, the distinction between sexuality as a sphere of social life and gender as a social division should be kept in mind. If we compare sexuality and gender with work and social class perhaps this will be clearer. Work is a sphere of life and not in itself a social division, yet its social organisation gives rise to class, which is a social division. Sexuality is a sphere of life, which need not necessarily be associated with social division, but as currently socially ordered, it is associated with both gender and the social division between homosexuality and heterosexuality.

What is more comparable with gender in this sense, then, is the binary divide and social division between heterosexuality and homosexuality. Thus we produce greater conceptual congruence with gender by pluralising sexuality – speaking of 'sexualities' rather than 'sexuality'. This move, however, is not usually made with that intent, but rather with the aim of recognising diversity in sexual identities and practices within as well as between heterosexuality and homosexuality (see, e.g. Plummer, 1985). Moreover, while it might offer us a set of categories relatable to gender categories it produces other problems. In the first place it directs attention away from the broader scope of sexuality (singular) as a field of study and sphere of life and limits explorations of the gender–sexuality linkage to the ways in which gender is related to sexual 'identities'. Secondly, and importantly, if heterosexuality becomes conceived as simply one of a number of sexualities, albeit a hegemonic one, this might prevent us from seeing that heterosexuality in its institutionalised form entails more than sexuality.

Heterosexuality is a key site of intersection between gender and sexuality, and one that reveals the interconnections between sexual and non-sexual aspects of social life. As an institution heterosexuality is, by definition, a gender relationship, governing relations between women and men, ordering not only sexual life but also domestic and extra-domestic divisions of labour and resources. As I have noted elsewhere (Jackson, 1999b), it entails who washes the sheets and whose wage pays for them as well as what goes on between them. Thus heterosexuality is not precisely coterminous with heterosexual sexuality, even though it serves to marginalise other sexualities as abnormal and deviant. Indeed compulsory heterosexuality is so effective precisely because of its institutionalisation as more than merely a sexual relation. Yet it is not a monolithic entity: it is both sexual and asexual, publicly institutionalised yet often experienced as private and intimate, maintained through everyday practices yet so taken for granted that it appears unremarkable. Thus while heterosexuality is thoroughly gendered, conceptualising how it is gendered as a complex of institution, ideology, practice and experience is far from straightforward.

So where does all this leave us? If, as I have argued, sexuality as a field of enquiry and a sphere of social life entails more than the homo–hetero binary, then it is crucial to retain a means of analysing the ways in which all facets of sexuality and all sexualities may be gendered. Since all aspects of social life, sexual and non-sexual, are also gendered, then we need to be able to think about how this gendering process is related to heterosexuality without deciding the issue in advance. If heterosexuality as an institution entails more than specifically sexual relations, we should consider whether the term should be confined to the actualities of social relations between heterosexual couples (in and out of marital and monogamous relations) or should be extended to cover wider aspects of social life (cf. Ingraham, 1996). The ways in which we define gender, sexuality and heterosexuality thus have implications for the ways in which we theorise their intersections and the comparative weight given to each. Before considering these further, however, there is another source of potential disagreement and confusion in play here that requires further exploration – differences in the ways in which the social or cultural construction of gender and sexuality are understood.

The complexity of social construction

'Social constructionism' is a rather clumsy term, perhaps because there is no single perspective laying claim to it, but rather a cluster of differing approaches deriving from varied theoretical roots.[4] These focus on different aspects of gender and sexuality informed by differing conceptualisations of social processes – hence there are differences in both what is seen as socially constituted and how that social constitution is envisaged, in both the object of analysis and the appropriate methodology brought to bear on it. If we are to avoid narrowing our field of vision and the risk of missing some of the multiple strands linking gender, sexuality and heterosexuality we cannot afford to be too theoretically purist. Rather we should appreciate, albeit critically, the diverse insights that competing perspectives have to offer and build upon these. It is not merely that 'social constructionism' comprises multiple perspectives but that social construction itself is a multi-layered, multi-faceted process, requiring attention to a number of levels of social analysis.

In my recent work I have been thinking in terms of four intersecting levels or facets of social construction (Jackson, 1999a; 2000; 2001): the structural, at which gender is constructed as a hierarchical social division and heterosexuality institutionalised, for example, by marriage, the law and the state; the level of meaning, encompassing the discursive construction of gender and sexuality and the meanings negotiated in everyday social interaction; the level of routine, everyday social practices through which gender and sexuality are constantly constituted and reconstituted within localised contexts and relationships; and finally, at the level of subjectivity through which we experience desires and emotions and make sense of ourselves as embodied gendered and sexual beings.

I am not, however, proposing a total theory of social construction wherein all these levels are welded together as a seamless whole. Such an endeavour would be ill advised and likely to produce another form of reductionism. Moreover, it is difficult, if not impossible, to focus on all these levels at once. We do, however, need to be aware that when we concentrate on one facet of social construction we have only a partial view of a multi-faceted process. It is this framework that informs what follows, and I will return to a more detailed consideration of how it might be applied to the interconnections between gender, sexuality and heterosexuality once

I have placed current debates in historical context. This history is primarily a feminist one, since it is feminists for whom there is most at stake in emphasising the connections between gender and sexuality.

Feminism, gender and (hetero)sexuality

In the 1970s feminists began to challenge the male privilege encoded into conventional heterosexual relations, attacking double standards of morality, questioning masculine definitions of sex and exposing sexual coercion and violence. Underpinning most feminist arguments was a commitment to challenging the idea of 'natural' differences between women and men in their sexual as well as their wider social lives. This work laid the foundations for a radical critique of heterosexuality, which was to emerge at the end of the decade, but at this stage hetero-sexuality was rarely identified as the specific object of analysis.[5] In consequence some connections were not always thought through so, for example, work on housework was seldom related to that on specifically sexual hetero-relations (see Jackson, 1999b).[6] The connections between different elements of heterosexuality were later made explicit by, among others, Adrienne Rich (1980), for whom compulsory heterosexuality both kept women *in* (within its confines) and kept them *down*, subordinated. Yet Rich did not offer an entirely convincing account of the construction of gender and sexuality. Although 'women' can be understood in her account as a socially constituted subordinate group, traces of essentialism remain in her assumption of a common womanliness uniting us all on the 'lesbian continuum'. While she exposed heterosexuality as a coercive imposition, she thereby seemed to imply that lesbianism was an innate propensity common to all women.

Other early accounts posed a far more direct, indeed causal, connection between the social construction of gender and sexuality. Catherine MacKinnon (1982), for example, argued that sexuality should occupy the same place in feminism that labour does in Marxism. Thus just as the social organisation of capital and labour produces economic class, so gender is a product of men's appropriation of women's sexuality. While this argument had the virtue of establishing gender as a product of the social rather than a natural order, it over-privileged sexuality as the ultimate origin of women's oppression. Other aspects of gender inequality, including those implicated in the social organisation of heterosexuality, disappear from view or are rendered secondary.

At the other end of the spectrum were those who dissociated the study of sexuality from the study of gender, such as Gayle Rubin (1984), whose perspective had more in common with what would later be defined as queer. Explicitly constructed against McKinnon's and others' emphasis on sexuality as a site of women's oppression – which she saw as 'sex negative' – Rubin's account focused on the oppression of sexual 'minorities', their exclusion from the 'charmed circle' of normative, monogamous heterosexuality. This analysis should be read in the context of her earlier work, which tied gender very closely to reproductive sexuality through the idea that every society 'has a sex/gender system – a set of arrangements through which the biological raw material of human sex and procreation is shaped by human social intervention' (Rubin, 1975: 165). While Rubin's move away from biological foundationalism and her analytic uncoupling of gender from sexuality represent positive shifts, she went too far in denying the empirical connections between gender and sexuality. She leaves us with no means of analysing the hierarchical social division between women and men and the institutionalisation and practice of heterosexuality (other than as privileged norm), or of exploring the gendering of the various desires and practices she defends (see Jackson, 1996a). In replacing 'sex-negativity' with a pro-sex or pro-pleasure position she is in danger of putting much of sex and sexuality beyond the reach of social analysis and critique; it becomes re-naturalised as a good thing in itself.

More promising accounts of gender and sexuality were produced by French materialist feminists in the late 1970s and early 1980s. These feminists saw the social division between women and men as analogous to a class relationship: just as there can be no bourgeoisie without the proletariat, conceptually and empirically there could be no 'women' without the opposing category, 'men'. As Wittig puts it: 'there are no slaves without masters' (1992: 15). Gender or 'social sex' is the product of a hierarchical social relationship and heterosexuality entails the appropriation of women's labour as well as their sexuality (see, for example, Delphy, 1984; Wittig, 1992; Guillaumin, 1995; Leonard and Adkins, 1995).[7] Here gender and sexuality are related in that gender division gives rise to the homosexual–heterosexual divide as well as the categories 'women and men' (Questions féministes collective, 1981), but neither women's subordination nor heterosexuality as an institution are reduced to sexuality *per se*.

Materialist feminists, however, subsequently became irreconcilably divided over the issue of political lesbianism, to which Monique Wittig's analysis of heterosexuality was central (see Wittig, 1992; Jackson, 1995; 1996a). For Wittig, the heterosexual contract founded the category 'woman', leading her to argue that lesbians, as fugitives from that contract were 'not women' (1992: 32). Wittig became a standard bearer for those who saw lesbianism as the only truly radical source of opposition to male domination. France was not an isolated case. In Britain, opinions polarised around a paper produced by Leeds Revolutionary Feminists, 'Political lesbianism: the case against heterosexuality', in which heterosexual feminists were denounced as 'collaborators' engaged in 'counter-revolutionary activity' (1981: 6–7). Moreover the British political lesbians, unlike their French equivalents, focused on heterosex *per se* rather than heterosexuality as an institution entailing the appropriation of women's bodies *and* labour. In according sexuality a privileged place in accounting for women's subordination they were closer to theorists like MacKinnon than the French materialists – hence the continued focus of some of their number, particularly Sheila Jeffreys (1990; 2002), on the sexual exploitation of women.

The furore surrounding political lesbianism effectively derailed debate on heterosexuality. In the 1980s, on both sides of the Atlantic, the terrain of disputes over sexuality shifted to the so-called 'sex wars' between libertarian and anti-libertarian feminists, centring on such issues as pornography and prostitution. As a result, there was something of a hiatus in debates on heterosexuality itself until the 1990s, with the resurgence of feminist debate and the emergence of queer theory. The former continued to emphasise male dominance in hetero-relations, as well as the privileging and institutionalisation of heterosexuality, but in the context of the 1990s the debate was less acrimonious and more productive, with the critique of institutionalised heterosexuality kept distinct from the condemnation of heterosexual feminists and greater attention given to disentangling the relationship between heterosexuality as institution, practice and identity (see Kitzinger and Wilkinson, 1994; Richardson, 1996). Many feminists were also engaging with queer theory, including its critical stance on sexual and gendered identities and its emphasis on destabilising the binary divisions between women and men and hetero and homosexualities.

While there are considerable differences within and between feminism and queer, both contributed to a renewed questioning of the ways in which heterosexuality, gender and the heterosexual/homosexual divide are routinely normalised. One of the key texts in orienting debate in the 1990s was, of course, Judith Butler's *Gender Trouble* (1990), which can be seen as both feminist and queer and which helped set the queer agenda. Butler put the interrelationship between gender and heterosexuality firmly back on the political the map through the idea of the heterosexual matrix within which sex, gender and sexuality were caught up together.[8] Her interest, however, was primarily in gender difference and sexuality in the sense of the direction of desire. Hence heterosexuality was explored primarily in terms of its normativity, and only this aspect of its institutionalisation received much attention. While recognising that gender was both regulatory and coercive in its imposition, she did not attend to gender as a hierarchy or the way in which heterosexuality is implicated in the maintenance of that hierarchy, despite her debt to Monique Wittig. Wittig's materialism disappears in Butler's queer reading of her.

My argument is that an effective critique of heterosexuality must include both heteronormativity and gender hierarchy (see Jackson, 1999b), since both are intrinsic to heterosexuality and the latter is essential to a feminist analysis of it. Moreover, such a critique needs to be broad enough in its scope to include those aspects of the social often absent from theoretical analysis of gender and sexuality: social structures; the socially situated contexts of everyday gendered and sexual lives and the material conditions under which our sexualities are lived. I therefore want to turn my attention to an analysis of heterosexuality that does attend to these questions and one which, for me, remains one of the most significant contributions to be made in the 1990s: Chrys Ingraham's discussion of 'the heterosexual imaginary' (1996).

Heterosexuality, gender, heterogender

Ingraham's thesis is that heterosexuality should displace gender as the central category of feminist analysis and is the most persuasive and consistent challenge to the primacy of gender that I have encountered. Ingraham, like Butler, is influenced by Wittig's analysis of heterosexuality, but from a less queer, more sociological perspective and with a stronger purchase on French materialist feminism. She therefore defines heterosexuality as an institution that regulates far more than our erotic lives. The object of her analysis is the 'heterosexual imaginary',[9] which masks the ways in which gender has consistently been defined from a heteronormative perspective. Drawing attention to the construction of 'women' and 'men' as mutually attracted 'opposite sexes', she argues that sociologists (including feminists) have failed to see the heterosexual ends to which this gender divide is directed.

As Ingraham points out, the definitions of gender employed by feminist sociologists indicate that it is a binary 'organizing relations *between* the sexes' (1996: 186; her emphasis). She goes on to suggest that heterosexuality 'serves as the organizing institution and ideology ... for gender'

(1996: 187) and is implicated in the operation of all social institutions at all levels of society, from family to workplace to the state. She asks,

> Without institutionalized heterosexuality – that is, the ideological and organizational regulation of relations between men and women – would gender even exist? If we make sense of gender and sex as historically and institutionally bound to heterosexuality, then we shift gender studies from localized examinations of individual behaviours and group practices to critical analyses of heterosexuality as an organizing institution. (Ingraham, 1996: 187)

The question posed here cannot be conclusively answered, but personally I find it easier to imagine gender without institutionalised heterosexuality than vice versa. Yet I take Ingraham's point that heterosexuality is *an* organising principle of many aspects of social structure and social life, and an important one. For example, it is possible to relate all gendered aspects of work and employment to heterosexuality. But does this give heterosexuality primacy? Are gendered labour markets and wage differentials heterosexual in themselves or are they simply related to the social organisation of heterosexual family life? Is it heterosexuality that orders, even constructs, gender rather than the other way around? The problem here is that it is possible to argue links from either direction and that causal or logical priority is difficult to determine. Defining heterosexuality so broadly that it encompasses all aspects of gendered relations, and then collapsing heterosexuality and gender into one term – heterogender – does not, for me, represent an adequate solution to the problem of conceptualising their interrelationship. While gender and heterosexuality are so closely entwined that it is not easy to unravel their intersections, we need to retain the capacity to do so. Hence it seems necessary to maintain an analytical distinction between gender, as the hierarchical relation between women and men, and heterosexuality, as a specific institutionalised form of that relation.

Thus despite my sympathy with Ingraham's perspective I am uneasy with her conclusions. This in part reflects the object of her polemic, clear in the quotation above: studies of gender concerned only with 'localized examinations of individual behaviours and group practices'. This may reflect the US context in which she is working – for while it is the case that British and European sociologists sometimes study gender only in such local settings or treat it simply as a variable, there is a strong tradition on this side of the Atlantic of analysing gender as a major social division (see, for example, Delphy, 1993; Walby, 1997). Thus when we talk of gender in terms of relations between women and men, we do not generally mean only local, personal, or face to face, relations but wider social relations – as we might talk of class relations. It is therefore not absolutely necessary for heterosexuality to displace gender in order to see that both are institutionalised, structural features of our society and that, as such, they are closely connected.

Ingraham's argument certainly provokes us to think about the ways in which heterosexuality may order gender relations – as well as vice-versa. However, something has slipped out of our grasp in this analysis: sexuality in the wider sense of erotically significant desires, practices, relationships and identities. It is left floating somehow separate from the gender–heterosexuality relation although clearly in some way implicated in it.

Rethinking the intersections

How, then, might we begin to explore in more detail the complex of intersections between gender, heterosexuality and the broader field of sexuality? I will sketch out possible approaches to this question by returning to the four interconnected levels of social construction I identified earlier. I offer here only a bare outline, and an evolving exploration, of how such an analysis might proceed (see also Jackson, 2005). The purpose of my approach is to highlight the complexity of the picture that emerges when different facts and levels of the social are taken into account. The ways in which the intersections between gender sexuality and heterosexuality are manifested vary within and between levels, are not always unidirectional and the linkages are stronger at some points than at others.

The impact of social structures in shaping our gendered and sexual being is frequently ignored – Ingraham's analysis of heterosexuality being one of the few notable exceptions. The concept of social structure is now out of favour with those who envisage the social in terms of fluidity and mobility (Urry, 2000; Adkins, 2002). Yet it should be evident that certain social patterns persist. Gender division has not gone away despite changes in the ways that gender is lived (Walby, 1997); heterosexuality remains effectively normative despite the increased visibility of alternative sexualities (Jackson and Scott, 2004); it remains enshrined in social policy (Carabine, 1996) despite the rights granted to non-heterosexual couples. Here we have one of the strongest connections within the web of gender, sexuality and heterosexuality: institutionalised heterosexuality is by definition gendered and the heterosexual contract is a powerful mechanism whereby gender hierarchy is guaranteed. However, it is still wise to keep gender and heterosexuality analytically distinct, not only to facilitate further exploration of the ways in which they sustain each other but also because this specific linkage cannot be assumed to have a determining effect on all other points of connection at all other levels of the social. For example, we cannot deduce from it the ways in which a heterosexual couple negotiate gendered and sexual practices in their daily lives.

Structural constraints do, however, impinge on everyday life, enabling and/or constraining our patterns of existence. In this respect we should think about the ways in which sexual (erotic) practices, identities and desires are enmeshed with non-sexual aspects of social structure. For example, attention has been drawn to the ways in which a normatively heterosexual society accommodates queer practices as lifestyle choices within commodity capitalism (Evans, 1993; Hennessy, 2000) and to the ways in which heterosexual sex is also commodified as style (Jackson and Scott, 1997). The structural enabling of sexual lifestyle choices is certainly not equally available to all (Hennessy, 2000), but is facilitated or inhibited by class, ethnicity and gender. Forms of cultural capital may also mediate access to particular sexual spaces and as well as affecting perceptions of sexual conduct. For example, working class women who are too obviously sexual are more likely to provoke public distaste, even disgust, than middle class women with independent lifestyles (Skeggs, 2003). The forms of cultural capital available to us also provide resources for making sense of our sexual lives and for fashioning sexual selves (Skeggs, 2004), which may in turn impact upon other facets of social construction, on meanings, practices, and subjectively constructed identities.

Where questions of sexual and gendered meanings are concerned there are a variety of complex intersections to be teased out. At the level of society and culture as a whole, gender and sexuality are constituted as objects of discourse and through the specific discourses in circulation at any historical moment; these discourses serve to distinguish male from female, to define what is sexual, to differentiate the 'perverse' from the 'normal' and masculinity from femininity (cf. Foucault, 1979). Here there is room for, and evidence of, fluidity and change – yet this exists alongside the persistent naturalising of gender and sexuality. Meaning is also deployed within, and emergent from, the routine, everyday social interaction through which each of us makes sense of our own and others' gendered and sexual lives. Here we can see how certain of the discourses available within our culture become hegemonic, informing the 'natural attitude' (Kessler and McKenna, 1978) whereby most of the population, most of the time, takes for granted the existence of 'men' and 'women' as given categories of people who 'naturally' form sexual liaisons with members of the 'opposite' gender. Here we are constantly 'doing gender' in the sense of attributing it to others, rarely noticing the variety of cultural competences and complex interpretational processes this entails (West and Zimmerman, 1987). Thus gender and normative heterosexuality are constantly reaffirmed, but it is also here that their meanings can be unsettled or renegotiated, although we need to be aware of how easily such challenges can be neutralised and accommodated back into the 'natural attitude'.

At the level of meaning we can see how gender and sexuality constantly intersect, where the construction of gender difference is bound up with the assumption of gender complementarity, the idea that women and men are 'made for each other'. Hence the boundaries of gender division and normative heterosexuality are mutually rein-forced. However, as Kessler and McKenna (1978) suggest, the attribution of gender is the primary one, at least at the level of everyday interaction. That is to say, we 'do' gender first: we recognise someone as male or female before we make any assumptions about heterosexuality or homo-sexuality; we cannot logically do otherwise. Moreover, the homosex-ual–heterosexual distinction depends upon socially meaningful gender categories, on being able to see two men or two women as 'the same' and a man and a woman as 'different'.

The homo/hetero binary, however, by no means exhausts the gendered meanings of sexuality. The idea, still widely prevalent, that men and women are naturally different extends to their supposed sexual desires and proclivities – producing all the stereotypes with which we are so familiar. Even though these are changing, it is the degree of difference and the forms of difference that are changing – not the idea that there *is* a difference. Meanwhile, self-help manuals for het-erosexual couples continue to promote the idea that male and female sexuality are naturally different and we must learn to live with it (see, for example, Gray, 1996). Interestingly ideas about difference can serve to justify heterosexual desire *and* homosexual or lesbian attraction – eschewing heterosex does not entail de-gendering sex, but negotiating different ways of eroticising gender.

Commonsense meanings of gender and sexuality reflexively order and are ordered by our quotidian routines. They are thus continually produced and reproduced at the third level of social construction, that of everyday practices. Here too gender, sexuality and heterosexuality interconnect, but in complex and variable ways not easily reducible to simple causal connections. In their daily lives women are frequently identified and evaluated in terms of their sexual availability to men and their presumed 'place' within heterosexual relationships as wives and mothers – this is evident in everything from interaction on the street to the sexualisation of women's labour (Adkins, 1995) and men's resistance to equal opportunities policies (Cockburn, 1993). Hence gendered assumptions here seem to be informed by heterosexual ones. But this does not apply in the same way to men. The sexualisation and hetero-sexualisation of women is a means by which men habitually establish women as 'other' and themselves as simply the norm. Where manliness is specifically called for it can be demonstrated in relation to heterosex-uality and a gay man may find his claims to masculinity imperilled by his sexuality. Yet this is only one among many means of validating masculinity. A man can be a man by virtue of physical or mental prowess, courage, leadership abilities and so on (Connell, 1995; 2000), whereas womanliness is almost always equated with (hetero)sexual attractiveness and (heterosexual) domesticity. Here then there is a marked asymmetry whereby women's gender is more tightly bound to and defined by sexuality than that of heterosexual men.[10] When think-ing specifically about how heterosexual sex confirms femininity and masculinity, gender asymmetry reappears in a different form. As Janet Holland and her colleagues found in investigating the experience of first heterosex, having sex may make a boy a man, but it does not make a girl a woman (Holland *et al.*, 1996). What confirms masculinity is being (hetero)sexually *active*; what confirms femininity is being sexually *attractive* to men. As a result young women's desires remain more constrained than those of young men (Holland *et al.*, 1998; Tolman, 2002).

These asymmetries may be everyday reflections of the gender inequality that has historically been fundamental to institutionalised heterosexu-ality. Since heterosexuality entails not only sexuality, but also non-sexual gendered practices this will be evident in its everyday enactment. Each heterosexual couple 'does' heterosexuality as much through divi-sions of labour and distributions of household resources as through specifically sexual and reproductive practices. And here, of course, they are also doing gender since, despite the late modern emphasis on togetherness and equity in hetero-relations, the evidence suggests that it is still women who do most of the domestic work necessary to keep the household running and most of the emotional labour necessary to maintain the relationship itself (VanEvery, 1996). It is in the everyday negotiation of housework and relationship work that the existing heterosexual and gendered order can either be reconfirmed or resisted – as well as in the more specifically sexual aspects of the couple relationship.

This raises the question of how we come to be the embodied gendered and sexual individuals who enact these practices, but who nonetheless have the capacity to renegotiate gender divisions and resist dominant constructions of sexuality. The theorising of subjectivity has been dominated by psychoanalytic approaches in which gender and sexuality are too closely entwined to be separated. I prefer a rather different approach, based on the concept of the social self, initially developed by G. H. Mead (1934) and underpinning the account of the social construction of sexuality later produced by Gagnon and Simon (1974). The self is not a fixed structure but is always 'in process' by virtue of its constant reflexivity. Such a perspective allows us to think of subjectivity as a product of socially located biographies in which our past and present lives are in dialogue; it is not only the past that shapes the present, but the present significantly re-shapes the past in the sense that we are constantly reconstructing our memories, our sense of who and what we are in relation to the sense we make of the present. The cultural resources we draw on in the process of making sense of ourselves are of course historically specific, enabling us to understand the ways in which particular modes of self-construction and self-narration become available at different historical moments in specific social locations (Plummer, 1995; Whisman,1996).

How might we apply this to gender and sexuality? Here too, there are grounds for arguing for the primacy of gender attribution in that the moment we are born we are ascribed a gender (Kessler and McKenna, 1978). While heterosexual assumptions may play a part here, as is evident with those born intersexed, it is the difference itself that seems to matter here (see Kessler, 1998). It is this difference, one of the first social categories a child learns, that forms the foundation for the ways in which we locate ourselves within a gendered sexual order and make sense of ourselves as embodied, gendered and sexual beings. From this perspective, a gendered sense of self precedes awareness ourselves as sexual (see Gagnon and Simon, 1974; Jackson, 1999b).[11] As soon as we turn to heterosexuality, however, the picture becomes more complicated, because children come to understand non-sexual aspects of heterosexuality – families, mothers and fathers, for example – way before they gain access to specifically sexual scripts or discourses. This becomes 'everyday knowledge' available for reconceptualisation, as sexually significant once children become sexually aware. Gendered, sexual selves continue to be reflexively renegotiated or reconfirmed throughout our lives and how they continue to interconnect as we go about our daily lives within a gendered, heterosexually ordered social world.

Conclusion

Attempts to counteract biological or evolutionary explanations of gender and sexuality tend, in popular understanding, to be cast in terms of a simplistic nature–nurture opposition. Clearly a social understanding involves a great deal more than mere 'nurture', and we need to make the most of what a more complex understanding of the social offers. While this complexity is possibly less immediately appealing to commonsense understanding than biological explanations, the perspectives I have drawn on do at least have more purchase on everyday social life than the more abstract, more culturally focused theorisations generally associated with queer.

In exploring the complexity of sexuality and gender, how we define our field of enquiry matters a great deal. In particular, I have argued that we cannot regard gender, sexuality and heterosexuality as phenomena of the same order, mapping easily on to each other. In particular, we cannot afford to reduce sexuality to the heterosexuality–homosexuality axis, or any other means of classifying sexualities, or reduce heterosexuality to sexuality alone, to one form of sexuality among others. In teasing apart these intersections I have drawn on some ideas from queer theory and insofar as I wish to challenge the connections that bind gender and sexuality into the 'heterosexual matrix' (Butler, 1990) my project converges with theirs. However, I have also argued the need to pay attention to aspects of the social that generally fall outside the scope of queer – particularly social structure and everyday social practices and have argued for a more sociologically grounded understanding of the self. Furthermore I have suggested that a more sociological understanding of the ways in which sexuality intersects with non-sexual social relations affords a fuller understanding of heterosexuality. On my definitions, some patterns or directions of intersection emerge.

I am suggesting then, that we take as the defining feature of gender the fact of gender division itself as a social division and cultural distinction – although it can and does encompass more than this. As a social division, and a very fundamental one, gender infuses all spheres of social life. Sexuality is a sphere of social life, like any other (such as work, for example) and like any other it overlaps and interconnects with other areas of the social (including work) and like any other it is thoroughly gendered. One of the ways in which it is gendered is through the heterosexual–homosexual binary and here it reacts back on gender, reinforcing gender divisions. But sexuality is gendered in a host of other ways and here the connections in each direction are more variable and difficult to map. Yet while there are certainly *inter*connections here, I would still maintain that gender, because it is a social division, shapes sexuality more profoundly than vice versa. So gender remains logically prior to sexuality in the broader sense of the term.

Heterosexuality presents a very different case, since it is pivotal to both gender and sexuality. It is impossible to conceive of an aspect of heterosexuality that is not gendered since it is defined by gender difference. Conversely, gender is ordered in terms of heterosexuality. Thus the connections between heterosexuality and gender are much tighter and much more reciprocal than the links between gender and sexuality, precisely because it is not only sexual, because there are aspects of institutionalised heterosexuality that are not sexual. Yet its sexual aspects are also important in defining what establishes and constitutes a viable heterosexual couple and the expectations/obligations that flow from this. It is in relation to the specifically sexual that other sexualities are defined as perverse or marginal and also, as queer theorists maintain, that the homosexual other in turn confirms heterosexuality's normative status (Fuss, 1991b).

There is clearly a great deal more work to be done in exploring these connections further and, since the connections I have drawn derive from particular definitions of the field they are contestable precisely at that point. Any alternative definitions of gender, sexuality and heterosexuality would yield rather different maps of their intersections.

Notes

1. This perspective underpins innumerable television programmes purporting to inform us of the 'scientific truth' of human sexuality as well as animal behaviour and is usually presented as uncontested fact rather than a highly controversial theory. Of particular relevance here is the way in which this approach links gender to the inevitability of heterosexuality, seeing a range of supposed differences between women and men as ultimately reducible to the reproductive imperative: the 'need' to pass on our genes to the next generation. For further discussion and critique see (Cameron, 1997/98, Segal, 1999, Rees, 2000 and Rose and Rose, 2000).
2. Since most of the founding statements of queer were produced not by sociologists but by philosophers (Butler, 1990) or literary scholars (Dollimore, 1991; Sedgwick, 1991) they cannot be expected to prioritise sociological analysis. Some queer theorists frame their arguments in terms of feminist

debates (Butler, 1990), others, even some who define themselves as feminist such as Sedgwick (1991), do not focus on gender relations as a primary concern.

3. 'Doing gender' in the sense I mean it here owes less to Bulter's (1990; 1993) notion of performance and performativity than to the ethnomethodological and interactionist traditions (Garfinkel, 1967; Goffman, 1976, 1977; Kessler and McKenna, 1978; West and Zimmerman, 1987).

4. These include Marxism, phenomenological and interactionist sociology, post-structuralism and postmodernism, all of which have been engaged with and developed by feminist, lesbian, gay and queer theorists. For an earlier discussion of how these perspectives have informed feminist debates on heterosexuality see Jackson 1996a.

5. I am aware that I am summarising a huge volume of work in a few sentences here. For a more detailed discussion of this early work see Jackson and Scott, 1996.

6. There were some notable exceptions, for example Charlotte Bunch (1975a, cited in Ingraham, 1999).

7. The works cited here are all collections including work that dates back to the late 1970s and are the best English language sources on this group of theorists. Earlier English translations of these writings are of variable quality, some were published in sources that are not now easy to find and do not always represent the most significant of these authors' contributions. Note also that Delphy was alone among the original materialist feminists to use the term 'gender' – the others talked of 'sex'; because they did not accept the sex–gender distinction, or the importation of an Anglophone concept. Delphy prefers 'gender' since it marks out a social rather than a natural category (see Delphy, 1993). The term 'genre', in the sense of 'gender' is now, however, becoming more common in France, especially among sociologists.

8. I do not want to enter into an extended discussion of Butler here since I have done so elsewhere (Jackson, 1999b), but simply want to locate her early work as a key turning point in theorising the interrelationship between gender and sexuality and to acknowledge her contribution.

9. As will probably be clear, the concept of the imaginary being deployed here derives from Althusser's analysis of ideology, particularly that ideology constitutes our imaginary relation to our real conditions of existence. While Ingraham's analysis borrows a vocabulary from structural Marxism, it is not, in my view, a wholly Althusserian argument.

10. Men whose masculinity is in doubt may share the fate of women: gay men are susceptible to being defined by, reduced to, their sexuality and an 'effeminate' man may well find his sexuality in question.

11. I am not suggesting that children are intrinsically asexual (or intrinsically sexual either). Rather, the distribution of sexual knowledge within our society and the definition of children as asexual innocents means that their access to crucial elements of adult sexual knowledge is restricted. While children now become sexually knowing earlier than in the recent past, the pattern remains and shapes the ways in which children become sexual and also contributes to the social construction of childhood (see Jackson and Scott, 2000, 2004 for further elaboration of these ideas).

3
The Return of the Material
Cycles of Theoretical Fashion in Lesbian, Gay and Queer Studies
Janice McLaughlin

Introduction

The antagonism between some queer and feminist authors is well known. Writers such as Judith Butler (1990), Gayle Rubin (1993), Eve Sedgwick (1990) and Carol Vance (1992) challenge feminist writers, with different levels of hostility, for viewing sexuality only through a gaze of gender and patriarchy. They argue that feminists ignore alternative forms of identity and pleasure in favour of a concentration on male oppression and female victimisation. While Butler pursues these criticisms in order to generate new feminist perspectives, for writers such as Sedgwick and Rubin, their arguments lead to the conclusion that there is a need to move beyond feminism. Meanwhile feminists such as Elizabeth Glick (2000), Sheila Jeffreys (1994; 2003), and Martha Nussbaum (1999b) accuse these same queer theorists of being elitists who are unwilling to concern themselves with what happens outside the academy, the novel or the film. They see the queer perspective as a prime example of the turn in theory away from the reality of the material world and towards a concern with cultural activities and career success (Stanley and Wise, 2000; Wilson, 1993).

In particular areas of the academy queer ideas have acquired significant status. This status is witnessed in the institutional setting of some of the central queer writers, the amount of PhD work being carried out within it and the tendency to place 'queer' in the title of any book or journal article examining sexuality, particularly lesbian and gay sexuality. The dominance of queer agendas is not wholesale; it is stronger in the arts and humanities than in the social sciences. It also appears more established in the United States (read Ivy League) than the United Kingdom, a factor some critics have used to validate their attack. More recently criticisms of queer agendas have gathered pace, including work from writers who have been associated with the development of queer ideas (de Lauretis, 1994; Seidman, 1997). A significant focus within these criticisms is queer theory's treatment of material issues and its conceptual approach to understanding the significance of material relations (Fraser, 1997a; Hennessy, 1995). Conferences and special editions of journals have appeared questioning its dominance in lesbian and gay studies, followed by calls for a return to the ideas and political concerns discarded in the rush to embrace performativity and transgression (Jackson, 1999a; Merck *et al.*, 1998).

This chapter examines the feminist and queer critiques of each other in order to explore the influence of particular contexts in the production of theoretical positions and critiques. What is argued is that the way queer theory emerged through its critique of feminism and the way some feminists focus on attacking it are the products of certain rituals of academic debate and cycle. Theoretical debates move through cycles of what is thought interesting, new and appropriate. How these cycles take place influences not only when ideas reach prominence, it also influences how ideas are articulated. In many ways this is an obvious, perhaps even banal point, however it is this style of debate that generates the belief that these two bodies of work are in opposition and in the process limits the opportunity to establish new types of analysis and understanding.

The notion that ideas that are labelled either queer or feminist are discrete and in opposition is a by-product of norms of academic ritualistic debate oddly rooted in enlightenment models of theoretical development; odd given the explicit rejection of enlightenment models of knowledge generation and production within both feminist and queer writings. Back in 1993 Michael Warner argued that queer theory is about the 'queering of existing theory rather than the production of theory about queers' (quoted in Richardson (2000: 40)). When feminists set up women's studies departments in the 1970s and 1980s an explicit aim was to generate new ways of thinking and linking theory to practice. The continued enactment of academic ritualistic debate (perhaps heightened in the United Kingdom under the gaze of the Research Assessment Exercise and its regulatory measures of performativity, which enforce disciplinary separation and evaluation of work) suggests that the aimed for destabilisation has not occurred; it highlights the limited success of both queer and feminist writings and activities in challenging the rules of the game. The theoretical labelling and name calling that has developed within some exchanges between feminist and queer writers is disabling as it forms barriers to working through how material and discursive processes inform each other. These labels hide the rich work going on examining the intersections between material and discursive relations that can only be understood and thought through by stepping outside the boundaries created by some forms of queer and feminist styles of debate and argument. The chapter concludes by arguing that theorists within both feminist and queer perspectives need to move on from trying to find out who is wrong and instead concentrate on contributing to the work engaging with the intersections between material and discursive processes. Such multi-disciplinary and innovative work does exist and is hidden by the rhetoric of hostility and opposition between feminist and queer ideas. Transnational feminist debates are briefly examined as one particularly fruitful example of such work.

Sticks and stones

Queer writers, including those who identify as feminist, have consciously set out to either challenge or to completely reject feminist arguments about the centrality of gender inequality in generating sexual identities and exploitation, drawing on the forthright criticisms made of lesbian and radical feminism by writers such as Susie Bright (1984) and Pat Califia (1981) in the early eighties. Rubin and Sedgwick are amongst the strongest critics of feminist explanations for the role of sexuality in gender relations in society. Both charge feminist writings with working within a narrow framework for understanding the significance and operation of sexuality and within this women's ability to have agency as sexual actors. Sedgwick's assertion is that 'The study of sexuality is not coextensive with the study of gender; correspondingly, antihomophobic inquiry is not coextensive with feminist inquiry' (1990: 27). She identifies a number of inadequacies and problems in the analysis of sexuality within radical feminist work. First, that sexuality is seen as operating as a function of gender relations, denying that the symbolic and individualised meanings that people may attribute to sexuality can revolve around other processes. Second, that feminist approaches to sexuality have betrayed a homophobic response to gay male desire. In particular, she castigates feminist accounts that contrast gay male desire as more permissive, masculine and superficial in comparison to lesbian spirituality and connection (an approach she associates with Adrienne Rich (1986)). Third, that by analysing lesbian experiences of oppression through the feminist fixation on gender, feminists fail to acknowledge the shared oppression lesbians face with gay men and other sexual minorities, which revolves around sexuality rather than gender. Fourth, that the 'anti-sex' approach towards pornography and sado-masochism (S/M) takes feminism back to 'the most repressive nineteenth-century bourgeois constructions of a sphere of pure femininity' (ibid.: 37). Finally, the legitimacy of 'trans-gender role-playing and identification' is denied by feminist accounts that attribute butch–femme relationships and identities to replications of male oppression and hierarchy.

Rubin's essay (1993) 'Thinking Sex: Notes for a Radical Theory of the Politics of Sexuality', first published in 1984, takes a similar position arguing that feminist approaches to sexuality are exclusionary and ultimately highly conservative. Rubin argues that the radical feminist framework robs lesbian sexuality of any meaning other than as a marker of feminist and gender solidarity. Rubin and other writers such as Cheshire Calhoun (1995), Biddy Martin (1992) and Joan Nestle (1987) suggest that the only form of lesbian sexual expression allowed in this framework is monogamous, non-penetrative, long-term lesbian relations. The cost of producing such a template is to generate a notion of sexuality and identity that is fixed and, crucially, essentialist. Martin argues that the reasons for lesbian feminists generating such rules are understandable as 'a defence against the continued marginalization, denial and prohibition of women's love and desire for other women' (1992: 98). The problem is that the strategy has had too high a cost, excluding forms of pleasure and expression in the name of securing a singular lesbian identity. Like Sedgwick, Rubin argues that feminism should not be seen as the privileged site for the analysis of sexuality: 'The realm of sexuality also has its own internal politics, inequalities and modes of oppression' (Rubin and Butler, 1998: 100). This call to push feminist analyses to the side is fundamental to queer arguments about sexuality. Rubin (1993) argues that analysis of the 'sex/gender system' has taken gender to be the dominant factor and has viewed sex as irrelevant or only as a product of patriarchy. This has led radical feminism to mistakenly view male homosexual practice as a product of male power and an important factor in the oppression of women.

Rubin supports the feminist claim that sexuality is important to the oppression of women, but challenges radical feminism for viewing all forms of sexual expression as a symptom or product of male power and privilege. Carol S. Vance makes a similar point, arguing that feminism, in its focus on sexual danger, has become embarrassed to speak of sexual pleasures; sexuality has became the source of 'unremitting victimization'

(1992: 5). In the work of both Vance and Rubin, as well as other queer writers, feminist anti-pornography campaigns and hostility to S/M are seen as symptomatic of an approach to sexuality with little scope for pleasure, experimentation and fun (Christina, 1990). As should become clear later, while it is not always stipulated, it is radical feminist arguments and campaigns that lie at the heart of queer displeasure with feminism.

Partly in response to the claims made above, feminists have been at the forefront of criticisms of queer ideas. There are a variety of feminist criticisms of queer theory, what they share is an assertion that queer ideas fail to address reality and material processes. Writers such as Rosemary Hennessy (1995) and Stevi Jackson (1999a) argue that the material issues that are or should be the concern of feminists cannot be responded to via the priorities of queer transgressive politics (Wilson, 1993; Matisons, 1998). Cultural analysis is not enough of a response to material processes and inequalities (Bordo, 1993; Gamson, 1998). Susan A. Mann argues that in all the analysis of difference, class has become an 'invisible ghost' (2000: 495). Feminists wishing to retain a material focus argue that the 'cultural' turn requires that feminism abandons 'analyses of the material conditions of women's lives and the denial of any systematic inequalities – patriarchal, capitalist or racist' (Jackson 1999a: 5). This at a time when we 'inhabit a global context characterised by extremely stark and worsening material inequalities' (ibid.: 5). At the same time by denying the validity of identity politics, queer and postmodern perspectives take the ground from which women can challenge the sources of oppression and exploitation. They have 'denied women the possibility of constructing political identities from which to name their oppression' (ibid.: 5). Various feminists argue that rejecting the importance of subject status is only appealing to those in a position to voluntarily give it up: 'one cannot deconstruct a subjectivity one has never been fully granted. ... In order to announce the death of the subject one must first have gained the right to speak as one' (Braidotti, 1994: 141). The uncertainty and fluidity that queer writers see hidden by the confining illusion of coherency, matches the indeterminacy women suffer by being denied subjecthood. For this reason feminists argue that uncertainty is not necessarily a liberating experience for women (and other marginalised groups). Lynn S. Chancer argues that the loss of a notion of the sovereign self will only leave women 'quite familiarly powerless, filled with self-doubt, unable to assert the ethical necessity and certainty of anything' (1998: 26). Denise Riley (1988) notes that 'ain't I a fluctuating identity' does not have the same resonance as Sojourner Truth's original plea.[1]

Queer concentration on the playfulness and fluidity of individual transgressive behaviour and representation fails to connect to the material contexts within which such activities appear and are defined as play. The prioritisation of representational analysis, and within this the concentration on research which studies modes of representation rather than modes of living, leads to an unwillingness to connect the development of alternative sexual practices with their historical and material roots. For example, queer discussion of the playfulness of S/M is unwilling to discuss the source of the symbols of that play – patriarchy, capitalism and fascism. By being unable to move beyond individual acts of transgression and representation, queer theory separates these acts 'from their location in political and economic systems' (Clark, 1991: 22). Nussbaum (1999b) proposes that queer theory is unable to make such connections because its proponents refuse to take any normative stance that might enable them to make claims about good and bad sexual practice or cultural experimentation. Glick argues that queer politics offers and fails to deliver a strategy of 'fuck our way to freedom' (2000: 19).

Queer theory begins with a critique of hierarchies of normality within sexual laws, only to go on to create its own sexual hierarchy where 'queer is good, queerer is better, but queerest is best of all' (Lloyd, 1999: 195). Queer talk of the joy of fluid and playful identities does not include awareness of the material and social inequalities, which enable some more than others to have the space in which to experiment (Fraser, 1995). Critical feminists ask who is in a position to be read as queer. In an article challenging claims by straight writers to be queer or 'queer straights' Annette Schlichter points out that even though queer approaches call for decentring the self, many queer writings concentrate on the transgression and queerness of the individual. Indeed in the accounts critiqued by Schlichter it is the writers' own transgression that seems to fascinate, an activity which is both self-centring and concealing of what enables the straight to obtain and claim the privilege of queer. The queer straight presents nothing more than a 'queer aspiration' which is an 'individualist and voluntarist endeavour' made lacking in risk via the hegemonic position of their retention (and indeed celebration) of straightness and the status of queer theory as a 'form of cultural capital in the academy' (Schlichter, 2004).

Feminist critics have linked the development of the contemporary sexual multiple identities celebrated in queer accounts to their economic context, in particular the role of new markets and arenas of commodity exchange (Delphy, 1993). Put broadly, if you have more than one identity you are going to need more products. Jackson (1995) sees a shying away from exploring male, white and middle class dominance in the playing out of sexual roles, desires and identities. When queer analysis does talk of institutional and material processes, the nature of their influence remains vague and primarily discursive. Without a thorough engagement in the material contexts within which representations and enactments occur we lose 'sight of the ways in which gender and heterosexuality are structurally deeply embedded in the social order, with important material consequences for our lives' (Richardson, 2000: 39). If an analysis of sexuality is going to take on board 'the distribution of wealth, resources, and power' it will have to 'address more than discourse' (Jackson, 1995: 153).

Robin Rowland and Renate Klein refer to feminist postmodern writing as 'disengagement theory' (1996: 13). Judith Squires warns of a 'loss of hope, of utopian vision' (1993: 3) and 'political paralysis' (ibid.: 9). Nussbaum famously described Butler as a 'collaborator with evil' (1999b). This collaboration is by default rather than wilful intent. Butler's 'disdainful abstractness' (ibid.) leaves her less able to identify and challenge the material and violent forces damaging many women's lives; particularly outside the protected environment of liberal Western academia. The collaboration Butler is said to be guilty of includes collaboration with the 'male agenda that dominates the field' (Jeffreys, 1994: 461). For Liz Stanley and Sue Wise (2000) those feminists working with queer ideas represent a form of institutionalised 'feminist Theory' that has become equivalent to 'malestream' social theory, more concerned with its rules of engagement and argument than with generating politically useful ideas. In the process Theory has become 'the preserve of specialist groupings of academics' rather than of 'feminists in general' (ibid.: 266). For a body of ideas so concerned with deconstruction and interrogation, it seems odd that little reflection occurs over Theory's purpose or approach. Without this reflection the work has become increasingly abstract and opaque; its only relevance is to those wishing to pursue an academic career. It is an area where academic stars dominate, in a prestigious network of prizes, elite conferences and institutions and media attention. All of this produces a form of Theory disjointed from the real world, unable to engage with the matters that count. The kind of differences focused on in such work are not the kind that matter; differences relating to experiences of violence, poverty, genocide, and economic re-structuring are left to the side (or in the words of Stanley and Wise put on 'theoretical ice' (2000: 269)), while questions of culture and representation dominate

Queer theorists challenge feminist writers for their unwillingness to explore sexuality outside of a concern with oppression and exploitation; feminist writers accuse queer writers of forgetting the reality of

oppression and exploitation. When queer ideas first came to prominence there was something attractive about breaking out of the apparent confinement of lesbian feminism and patriarchy, nevertheless the
cost has been the casual discard of wider political and economic agendas
that require engagement with lives and experiences beyond the linguistic. What this suggests is a need to move beyond the choice presented
between a concern with the real or the discursive, however the above
debate is presented as if this is not possible and instead the concerns of
feminism and queer theory are presumed to be insurmountably
opposed. This chapter proposes that this opposition is a product of the
contexts within which the arguments have been made and presented
and is therefore not necessarily true. The choice being demanded by
some queer and feminist writers is a product of styles and conditions of
argumentation, rather then a political or theoretical necessity. The
choice imposed is problematic because, as will be discussed later, the
notion of conflict and opposition ignores the important work seeking
new vital ways in which to work with material concerns that acknowledge the role of discursive and representational processes in their production. Queer arguments cannot obtain greater relevance and political
significance without a genuine engagement with material issues, while
feminists concerned with matters that count, need to acknowledge the
greater complexity involved in talking of such matters due to queer arguments about the presence of discursive and linguistic processes within
material relations. Before discussing modes of engagement, which do
bring together the discursive with the material, the contexts that generate the illusion of opposition are discussed.

Styles and conditions of argumentation

The emergence of theoretical approaches and the style they take are
influenced by the conditions around them. Ideas do not exist in a
vacuum; their popularity and their substance are linked to the wider
political and economic context. In this section the influences on the
emergence of both queer ideas and their feminist critics will be
discussed. It is important to do this to establish the role of social and
political context in playing a part in the status of different ideas and also
how such contexts play a constructive role in shaping the nature of
different ideas and their engagement with other work.

Institutional, political and social context

When queer theory began to make its mark in the early 1990s in
academic circles various contexts helped it appear appropriate and

timely. In particular three academic and political processes underway at the time opened up new agendas for theoretical interrogation and thereby generated the space for queer ideas to develop. The first was the challenge to identity politics within lesbian and gay activism and studies. The politics of the gay liberation movement and lesbian feminism were rejected for producing a 'straight jacket' of hierarchical, exclusionary and fictional identity (Seidman, 1997). Queer ideas both contributed to this critique and provided an alternative agenda of identity play and fluidity. The second context was the switch from women's studies to gender studies in much of the academy. This shift reduced the centrality of feminist ideas to debates on sexuality and opened up analyses to include issues such as masculinity and heterosexuality (although heterosexuality, for example Rich's notion of compulsory heterosexuality (1986, first published 1980), was examined within feminism in the 1970s). The final context was political events, for example, the social and political revolutions in Eastern Europe. These events helped generate and fuel the critique of absolutist/global ideologies and opened up the space for ideas talking about local power relations and resistance. Marxist analyses of economic regulation and material inequalities were replaced by debates about the role of representation and language in identity regulation. Queer theory's call for play, in uncertain times suspicious of ideological positions, couldn't help but appear more interesting than a concern with global issues (Winter, 1997).

Queer responses to changing contexts have expanded the valid areas of analysis within feminisms, gender studies and lesbian and gay studies. However, there are tendencies within some of this work that are less welcome. Name-calling has replaced genuine analysis of both feminist and Marxist ideas. It has been too easy to conceptualise any ideas associated with the past as absurd, out of date, and simply wrong. Those boring radical feminists and deterministic Marxists – what were they like? In Rubin's paper she argued that sexual conservatism had achieved a 'temporary hegemony over feminist analysis' (1993: 28) and as a result of this,

> A good deal of current feminist literature attributes the oppression of women to graphic representations of sex, prostitution, sex education, sadomasochism, male homosexuality, and transsexualism. Whatever happened to the family, religion, education, child-rearing practices, the media, the state, psychiatry, job discrimination, and unequal pay? (Ibid.: 28)

While acknowledging that this approach is not representative of all feminism, at various points she equates lesbian and radical feminism to a version of sexual conservatism that would be at home in the Vatican. She slips between being specific about particular feminists and feminist ideas, and broader generalisations such as 'The women's movement may have produced some of the most retrogressive sexual thinking this side of the Vatican' (ibid.: 29). Given the paper was written during the height of John Paul II's reign as Pope, this is a serious and ultimately offensive accusation, with little substance or attempt at grounding in specific analysis or evidence. Shifts in social, political and economic context require the generation of new ideas, however when whole bodies of work get mislaid or stereotyped there is a danger of forgetting that change is never absolute, continuities in material relations and social inequalities still exist; that there are ideas of merit amongst rejected works and that such works influence those texts that present themselves as their replacement.

The greater space now being given to criticisms of queer ideas can be linked to further changes in social and political context. The protests and collective movements formed against the inequalities generated by global capitalism have placed economic issues back at the centre of activist agendas, albeit informed by some of the strategies of queer politics. The heightened presence of terrorism, and the questionable wars against it, direct us to debate the causes that lie behind it and how far states should go in the protection of their 'citizens' and power. The linked apparent rise in fundamentalism, including evangelical Christian movements, are challenging how we respond to and theorise questions of cultural difference and social justice. In the United Kingdom and many other Western countries changes (linked to the economic fundamentalism of neoliberalism) in the labour market, employment and education do not seem to be reducing many of the inequalities between men and women (particularly for working class women and women from black and ethnic minority communities (Equal Opportunities Commission, 2005)). The global anti-capitalism movements, the issues that lie behind state terrorist activities, the rise of fundamentalist groups and the inequalities between different groups point to the continued role of economic processes in shaping local and global relations (Grewal and Kaplan, 1994). New or perhaps newly remembered/noticed contexts are shifting some people's attention back to patterns of economic as well as linguistic exchange.

Trump cards

A trump card is a claim or statement that acts as a silencer of other arguments, it is articulated in such a way that it presumes it overrides all other statements or positions. The trump card of critics of queer theory is the material, for queer theory it is a combination of essentialism and economic determinism. It is easy for a claim to talk about real processes, material inequality, and the actual body to operate as a trump card. When reality is used as a trump card to speak of discourse is itself evidence of a complicity in inequalities; this is the logic Nussbaum and Jeffreys in different ways expel in their criticisms of queer ideas and particular writers. In Nussbaum's article accusing Butler of collaboration with evil she argued that Butler's arguments are wrong because 'Hungry women are not fed by this, battered women are not sheltered by it, raped women do not find justice in it, gays and lesbians do not achieve legal protection through it' (1999b). On one level Nussbaum has a point, but the danger in her use of such examples is that the presentation of such figures is in place of genuine engagement with the detail of the argument. The implicit conclusion is that to defend deconstructionism or transgression is to defend privileged positions while denying the tools of improvement – collective interest in generating awareness of patriarchy or global capitalism – to others. This argument is also present in Teresa L. Ebert's critique of Butler and others:

> Pleasure and desire can be the overriding concern only for the classes of people (middle and upper) who are already free from economic want and have the means to pursue or, more specifically in commodity cultures, to consume the means of pleasure. (1993: 8)

Again, possibly this is true, but Ebert is moving towards the dangerous position of defining for others where and in what their interests lie, that working class women are not concerned with or participants (or perhaps should not be) in commodity cultures. This assumption can be challenged using Beverley Skeggs's (2001) work, Skeggs discusses the uses of particular forms of consumption and pleasure amongst working class women in the articulation of a particular class identity, for these women representation and pleasure do matter and are informed by material issues and consumption choices. This level of analysis and recognition is missing in the arguments of Nussbaum and Ebert; instead we are told that a concern with language and discourse, particularly when articulated in a complicated way, is academic elitism. An accusation of elitism replaces an analysis of the text and argument.

The queer response to being asked to acknowledge the importance of the material produces its own trump card: it's all a matter of interpretation. When asked to be concerned with material issues in relation to the body, Butler asserts that she is, but she doesn't want to deny the inescapable 'reality' that any claim to materiality is 'both marked and formed by discursive practices' (1993: 3). Materialisation is a linguistic act. Any attempt to identify the material, particularly as a structure of relations that underpin the cultural, cannot fail to be interpretative. When someone makes a claim to something structural that acts as a foundation to cultural or linguistic processes, the queer theorist can point out that words are being used to identify the real body, class dynamic, or institutional structure and that therefore a linguistic act has taken place. This response continues to prioritise the linguistic realm as the creative force in social, political and material relations, which in comparison appear to have little presence beyond the words used to symbolise them.

If injecting interpretation into material accounts is not enough to reject feminist concerns, then such concerns are equated by queer writers to essentialism or economic determinism. Radical feminists are trapped in biological myths of the body and Marxist feminists are trapped in historical materialist myths of the dominance of the economic in shaping social relations. Neither myth is a fair representation of past or contemporary work within work associated with either radical or Marxist feminism. Richardson (2000) rejects the essentialist tag on radical feminism for failing to acknowledge the complexity of the work generated by writers such as Rich or Catherine MacKinnon. Queer theory, Richardson argues 'over estimates the extent to which earlier generations of lesbians and gays and feminists believed in essential identities, rather than viewing sexual and gender identities as 'necessary fictions' for the purposes of protest and political recognition' (2000: 45). Momin Rahman and Anne Witz (2003) reject the determinist tag put on Marxist and materialist feminist ideas because it reduces the work of writers such as Christine Delphy (1984) and Heidi Hartmann (1978) to a crude form of economic Marxism that conceals the broader material and social analyses undertaken. Such a representation, they argue 'facilitates her [Butler] argument that the full realm of the social is under-theorized or under-apprehended within Marxist materialism and its feminist variations' (2003: 249).

Within the rules of academic dialogue, still rooted in enlightenment models of knowledge production, in order to set themselves up as the voices of a new important framework, queer theorists have spent a great deal of time pointing out what is wrong with other ideas currently out of fashion, in particular feminism. At times this critique has fallen into the trap of stereotype and has paid little attention to specific texts and arguments. As Jackie Stacey notes 'radical feminists are dismissed as essentialist, lesbians are all assumed to be radical feminists, socialist feminists are assumed to be uninterested in sexuality, and liberal feminists are seen as naïvely reformist' (1993: 52). As feminists have responded often they have approached queer ideas in a similar way, as witnessed in Nussbaum's attack on Butler, replacing analysis of the arguments with accusations of cowardice and elitism. When Jefferys argues that 'Many lesbians, perhaps the vast majority of lesbian feminists, feel nothing but hostility towards and alienation from the word queer and see queer politics as very specifically masculine' (1994: 460), she creates an opposition between queer ideas and feminists which is a product of her claim rather than a pre-existing reality. The cycle of theoretical trends rules out collaboration because one has to present one's ideas as so much better and current than those of 'yesterday'.

Theoretical cycles

Finally, the debates between queer and feminist writers have been influenced by the way in which modes of theoretical thought move through cycles of challenge, recognition, institutionalisation and critique. This cycle is shaped by the need to set up support and approval within institutions, generate conference circuits, and capture publishers, future postgraduates and the media's attention. There are certain rules that come with setting up a new framework and a cycle that develops from it that go through the following stages. Before proposing what these rules are it should be acknowledged that the development of ideas and debates is more complex and contingent than this may suggest. Nevertheless, there is an undercurrent framed by academic contexts that influences how new ideas emerge and entangle with existing work and which ultimately has the potential to domesticate the challenge of the new and acts as a barrier to developing intersections between different bodies of work. The rules look something like this:

1. An existing body of work is identified as dominating, exclusionary, narrow, and no longer appropriate for current times;
2. A new body of work develops marking its territory by indicating the failings of what came before;
3. Academic Chairs/stars appear in prestigious universities with equally prestigious offices;
4. Publishers/Journals/Conference organisers seek to provide venues for the articulation of these new ideas and stars;
5. The rhetorical presentation of past ideas as just wrong continues apace, the representations become increasingly stereotypical and based on vague knowledge of the texts/period/writers ridiculed;

6. A growing proportion of postgraduate work is done from within the framework;
7. Criticisms begin to appear of the framework for being dominating, exclusionary, narrow, and no longer appropriate for current times;
8. So the cycle begins again.

Like Women's Studies before them, Lesbian and Gay Studies and Queer theory have been influenced to varying degrees by this form of cycle. Theory, as does any other commodity, changes with the fashion; queer theories simply became more fashionable than feminism. Its 'hip' image and the star status of its proponents may say more about the commodification of ideas than it does any theoretical quality or superiority. Stanley and Wise argue that the current academic stars of feminist Theory are produced by 'intellectual fashion, ritualistic "company we keep", referencing practices of academic audiences, the status accorded to particular institutions and those who work in them, and the vagaries of media fame' (2000: 273). Teresa de Lauretis, one of the writers associated with first using the queer term to symbolise a particular perspective, perhaps said it best when she commented:

> As for 'queer theory', my insistent specification lesbian may well be taken as a taking of distance from what, since I proposed it as a working hypothesis for lesbian and gay studies in this very journal, has very quickly become a conceptually vacuous creature of the publishing industry. (de Lauretis, 1994: 297)

The repeated attacks on feminism – rarely acknowledged as being about a narrow version of radical feminism – helped its fashionable criteria. Particular figures such as MacKinnon and Andrea Dworkin have become the straw figures (although rarely read) of queer theory attacks on dowdy feminism. While Martin believes that there is much of value within queer theory, she is concerned with the way the opposition between feminism and queer theory is projected. She notes that 'celebrations of queerness rely on their own projections of fixity, constraint, or subjection onto a fixed ground, often onto feminism or the female body, in relation to which queer sexualities become figural, performative, playful, and fun' (1998: 11).

The criticisms of queer theory and the call for material issues to take centre stage are in danger of falling into the same cycle. In particular the criticisms are in danger of stereotyping queer ideas (in the same way queer writers stereotyped feminist ideas); it is the same authors (Butler overwhelmingly) who appear over and over again as proof of their inadequacy. Contemporary advertising, film and popular music are experiencing/suffering nostalgia with the past. There is a danger that the call for a return to material issues by reclaiming the work of material and radical feminism could fall into a nostalgic fascination with the activities and ideas of the 1970s. Going back to this work is important, what is at issue is how this 'return' occurs so that it allows for acknowledgement that what queer theory identified as a need – that is to work with the contingency of identity and claims to the 'real' – cannot occur by only going back. Some current articles are saying little more than 'Wasn't it great when we talked about women and didn't blush?' 'Wasn't it great when feminist writing was connected to the street and talked to real people?' 'Wasn't it great when the revolution was still possible?' Challenging queer theory's stereotypical version of the past with an equally stereotypical representation is not useful; it freezes time and refuses to acknowledge that contexts have changed.

Intersections

A simple return to past feminist agendas and concerns is not possible or advisable because old certainties are not appropriate to uncertain times. Politics and identity have fragmented as new patterns of life and inter-action develop. New forms of coalition and connection are made possible in new types of global and local activism. Cultural experimentation is part of the agenda of protest politics, exemplified in the anti-capitalist protests where humour and parody are central strategies. Questions of identity and experiences of fluidity and multiplicity are part of daily life. Confusion and flux surrounds social values and expectations. These processes can be experienced as liberating as queer theorists argue; however they can also be experienced as threatening and confusing. Anxiety and doubt are part of women's lives as they carve out a sense of self and future. Feminist theorising has a responsibility to capture these dynamics in women's lives and provide ways of making sense of them:

> To take responsibility is to firmly situate ourselves within contingent and imperfect contexts, to acknowledge differential privileges of race, gender, geographic location, and sexual identities, and to resist the delusory and dangerous recurrent hope of redemption to a world not of our making. (Flax, 1992. 460)

Sara Ahmed *et al.* argue that feminism must find a language that can allow it to understand and respond to 'the multiply determined bodies, spaces and histories "women" assume and occupy' (2000: 11). Previous certainties cannot be regained, because the world within which feminism exists has changed. Feminism must 'refuse to (re)present itself as programmatic, *as having an object which can always be successfully translated into a final end or outcome'* (ibid: 13 original emphasis). The present moment 'is a space in which we can speak of our uncertainties about what are or should be feminist agendas, rather than assuming that such uncertainty necessarily involves a loss or failure of collectivity' (ibid.: 13). The present moment is one which demands an international, and therefore complex and varied, response. Global patterns of neoliberal trade and capitalism, economic and political migration, nationalism and fundamentalism, require new or altered models of political and social justice. Angela McRobbie talks of the 'positivity' embedded in acknowledging certain forms of failure in feminist politics and proposals, in ways that echo the contribution of Halberstam here, that the future for feminism lies within understanding that it has 'passed away' (2004: 515). For McRobbie acknowledging the failure of existing models of socialist and radical democracy may offer the opportunity to develop ideas that work with those of Butler and that allow for a model 'for the expansive transformation of the current global system towards global justice' (ibid.: 505).

Susan Lurie (Lurie *et al.*, 2001) argues that 'flawed feminisms' may offer new possibilities of alignments with other groups and strategies of resistance. The founding subject of feminism may have turned out to be an exclusionary fiction, but the multiple subjects with transient identities who have taken her place can form new coalitions with a broader politics that brings together questions about the material with issues of cultural recognition and experimentation. Feminist sociologists are at the forefront of such attempts seeking to 'induce feminist constructionism to work with a sociologically more adequate reconceptualisation of the social as a more fully integrated realm of symbolic and material practices' (Rahman and Witz, 2003: 254). Such attempts do not however, simply look back to the material analyses of Marxist or material feminism, but instead call for queer influenced ways of thinking about the material in ways that are not limited by materialist modes of analyses. For Rahman and Witz writers such as Susan Bordo (1998) and Hughes and Witz (1997) are developing constructionist informed approaches to engaging with material processes that go beyond the economic and encompass aspects such as the body.

Syntheses of feminist and queer ideas are possible and occurring. Writers such as Himani Bannerji (1995), Hennessy (1993a) Jackson

(1995) and Skeggs (2001) seek to explore the generation of identity, difference and subjectivity, in the contexts in which they are produced. What these works offer is wider historical and social investigation than often present in queer analysis. They also offer a more sustained concern with the role of language, cultural relations and individual activities in patterns of resistance and regulation than presented in some forms of material and radical feminist analysis. What the approach of writers exploring the relationship between representations, discourses, identity and material processes indicate is that beneath the rhetoric of a divided agenda, a shared one is already being forged. The focus of materialist feminists is the lack of attention paid within queer theory on the institutional forces that are at play in the regulation of identity and material realities (Jackson 1999a). An awareness of institutions requires greater focus on the constraints on exploring different forms of sexual identities, rather than a celebration of the fluidity of forms of desire and identification (Gamson, 1998). Hennessy here and elsewhere (1995) argues that without a form of historical materialist analysis capable of recognising the material practices involved in the regulation of sexuality, any analysis becomes irrelevant.

The most sustained fusion between cultural/linguistic concerns with material/economic contexts is occurring within transnational feminism. Transnational feminism examines the contemporary interactions between global economics, nationalism and national movements and gendered and sexualised identities and inequalities. Cultural values are understood as the product of particular economic, political and social contexts. The role of global patterns of economic and cultural change in the production of varied subjectivities and harm is a prominent theme. Blackwood (2005) describes 'transnational sexualities' as insisting 'on the recognition that particular genders and sexualities are shaped by a large number of processes implicated in globalization, including capitalism, diasporic movements, political economies of state, and the disjunctive flow of meanings produced across sites' (2005: 221). It considers the multiple boundaries Inderpal Grewal and Caren Kaplan highlight as creating new patterns of 'scattered hegemony' and hybridity that modernist notions of the West and Non-West, centre and periphery and postmodern notions of postcolonialism do not fully capture (Grewal and Kaplan, 1994). New hybrid and hegemonic forms of subjectivity are connected to 'cultural production in the fields of transnational economic relations and diasporic identity constructions' (Grewal and Kaplan, 1994: 15).

Of particular importance in feminist transnational work is the analysis of boundaries. Connections are made between experiences of being caught in the shifting, bloody boundaries of global politics and the boundaries between and within bodies and discourses. Crucial to this work and only getting recognition now after her death (recognition visible in her appearance in several chapters here) is Gloria Anzaldúa. Anzaldúa described borders as

> the places that are safe and unsafe, to distinguish *us* from *them*. A border is a dividing line, a narrow strip along a steep edge. A borderland is a vague and undetermined place created by the emotional residue of an unnatural boundary. It is in a constant state of transition. The prohibited and forbidden are its inhabitants. (1999: 25 original emphasis)

Growing up and living in the border between Mexico and the United States as a lesbian Chicano woman, Anzaldúa was aware of the cultural and social relations, which emerge from being positioned within different boundaries. The alien becomes so culturally, economically and politically on each side of the boundary. Experiences of boundaries cannot be solved by a search for home, at the same time as Anzaldúa questioned the dominance and exclusivity of American culture, as a lesbian feminist, the Chicano culture presented its own forms of denial and limitation for her. Aspects of her identity, which did not fit within dominant articulations of Chicano culture, could not be revealed if she stayed at home. Other transnational feminists have echoed this point. Irene Gedalof (2000) argues that home is a dangerous metaphor for women because their identity and bodies are often violently appropriated both within the home and within disputes over national and ethnic authenticity within boundaries and territory. Staying within one home does not reflect the multiplicity of boundaries most of us travel through, particularly those whose identities do not fit dominant norms. This feeling of homelessness can be a harsh experience: 'Alienated from her mother culture, "alien" in the dominant culture, the woman of color does not feel safe within the inner life of her Self' (Anzaldúa, 1999: 42).

What this work exemplifies is the need, missing in much of the work associated with queer theory, to connect the pain of identity construction and destruction to the economic and political contexts in which it takes place. In queer arguments homelessness can come across as a fluid and pleasurable experience, to treat identity as transient, experimental and individual. In transnational feminism homelessness is a metaphor used with greater care, out of recognition that it equates to real experiences as well as to a symbol of flux and movement. Here it stands for the pain and confusion that exists where material, economic and collective relations place one outside of collective communities.

Conclusion

Feminists are correct to challenge the arguments and politics of queer writings for their too easy dismissal of feminist work and the need to stay tuned to the material world outside of the academy. However, in moving on from the narrowness of certain queer agendas feminist writers must recognise that the contexts we need to engage with outside the academy are different and that some of the previous certainties contained within Marxist, socialist and liberal feminism will not derive a political agenda that is useful and appropriate. From within the work of materialist and transnational feminism ideas are developing which are connected to outside the academy, are working with the experiences of displaced and marginalised groups, are concerned with the materially embedded 'reality' of the production and destruction of particular identities (and lives), and are open to collective visions of politics and change. This work offers intersectional ideas which are not precious about past ideas or grounded in claims to certainty and universality about the arguments they present to capture the social, cultural and political dynamics under examination. This work fits neither into the neat categories of queer feminism nor into previously existing categories of radical, lesbian or Marxist feminism, but this is no bad thing. If theoretical debate can move past asserting which body of work got it right we may be able to engage in multiple debates that explore the complexity of matters that count.

Note

1. Riley is playing on the speech made by the anti-slavery campaigner Sojourner Truth in 1851 at the Women's Rights Convention in Akron, Ohio where she challenged the white audience by asking 'Ain't I a Woman'. Although the exact wording of the speech is disputed the symbolism of her question became an integral part of Black American feminism in the 1970s.

4
On the Evolution of Queer Studies
Lesbian Feminism, Queer Theory and Globalization
Linda Garber

As lesbian/gay and queer scholars have developed and embraced queer theory over the past fifteen years or so, the field has made inroads in the academy as it has created new avenues and languages for discussing the machinations and representations of genders and sexualities. The very need to make plural those last two nouns hints at the fundamental shifts and profusion, even at the level of language, caused by the meeting of women's and gay/lesbian studies with the larger post-structuralist project that has suffused the academy in recent decades. A great deal has been gained – no less in institutional acceptability than in provocative intellectual exchange. As a lesbian studies scholar, I think also about what has been, if not entirely lost, then buried or misrepresented. The casualty immediately obvious to many lesbians is the culture and poli-tics in which I came of age, lesbian feminism. Formulated in the United States in the 1970s, lesbian feminism was (and remains, though less potently) a multi-issue movement at whose core lies the belief in lesbianism as itself a material, political expression of radical feminist politics. For all its manifest and often rehearsed faults, not least the pri-oritizing by some of an insular counterculture over substantive political activism by the mid-1980s, there is also much we should remember and that contributed to queer theory itself. As scholars in the United States embrace the study of queer cultures around the world,[1] we would do well to remember the lessons of both lesbian feminism and queer theory, in part because lesbian feminism's influence on activists and scholars remains evident in many countries even as queer theory's influ-ence has spread around the globe. And yet, as US queer studies turns its attention to the global and postcolonial (a growing trend of cultural studies in the United States more broadly), the field seems to be replaying earlier sexist exclusions, reminiscent of errors and omissions committed by the first wave of 'gay studies' scholars in the US academy in the 1970s.

Queer theory, which rose with both the development of post-structuralist theory and the co-sexual gay/lesbian activism responding to the AIDS pandemic in the 1980s, has tended to repudiate any connections to lesbian feminism and the larger identity politics in which it takes part. But clear similarities, amid perhaps more obvious differences, illustrate ties between them. Judith Butler's analysis of gender performativity and drag resonates with lesbian-feminist analyses of feminine drag as symptomatic of patriarchy, with the lesbian-feminist ideal of gender subversion through androgynous behaviour and appearance, and with Adrienne Rich's notion of compulsory heterosexuality.[2] Queer gender-fuck echoes lesbian-feminist androgyny. Post-structuralist 'phallogocentrism' reframes an earlier feminism's 'patriarchy'. Queers' disruption of 'heteronormativity' extends lesbian feminists' political choice of lesbianism.[3]

In the 1980s, as US lesbian feminism sagged under the weight of its own internal debates (over racism, separatism, sex) and under attack from a newly co-sexual queer movement that began to supplant it, like many activist and academic lesbians I found myself caught between two competitive ideologies each vying for my allegiance. I had come out as a lesbian through my feminism in 1984 and been mentored, in part, by several (self-proclaimed or de facto) dyke separatists. I educated myself in matters of race, class, sexuality and gender through a handful of women's studies classes and the resources of (largely lesbian-feminist) women's bookstores, which led me to feminist, anti-racist and lesbian political activism. As a 'baby dyke' I was raised, as it were, by women (and some 'wimmin') who believed in the healing power of crystals, the transformative power of women's innate peaceful nature, and the sexual superiority of women over men – in short, New Age-leaning, activist lesbian chauvinists. Even when I was sceptical of the beliefs and practices surrounding me, lesbian feminism and its counterculture was an educational and nurturing place to be.

But by the late 1980s the cosy incubator of the lesbian-feminist counterculture was cracking open under various pressures – from angry lesbians of colour, righteous sex radicals, and (once I hit graduate school in 1987) post-structuralist critics who made a good point or two even as they seemed to go a little overboard in excesses of verbal play and vitriolic anti-lesbian-feminist rhetoric. I never fully embraced either camp – a word I choose advisedly, since they quickly took up positions pitched against one another, battling over terminology, activist praxis, fashion and bookstore shelf space (that is, over hearts, minds, and expendable income). In the terms of the debate at the time, I was meant to align myself with my 'generation', which was presumed to be queer. Both a precocious lesbian feminist and over time a reluctant but intrigued queer intellectual, I wound up a defender of my lesbian-feminist heroes while attempting to be an ambassador of one camp to another at meetings of the National Women's Studies Association and the Modern Language Association, in graduate seminars, and in the women's bookstore where I worked.

As I thought and wrote about this issue throughout the 1990s, I realized that what was construed in the United States as a generational debate seemed to turn on the virtual absence in the conversation of working-class-and-lesbians of colour and their writings. However, their words and activism make most clear the link between queer theory's US lesbian history and its present. Especially in works published in the 1980s, working-class-and-lesbians of colour tend to assert identity while creating it anew, shifting the ground of its meaning from essential characteristic to multiple possibilities. In particular, the writings of politically engaged poets – such as Pat Parker, Judy Grahn, Audre Lorde, and Gloria Anzaldúa – have led me to think of this postmodern identity politics as an 'identity poetics'.

A writer like Anzaldúa, for example, mobilizes categories – race, gender, sexuality – that have been essentialised by both claimants and assailants, but she does so in combinations that defy overgeneralization and stasis. She writes in the poem 'To live in the Borderlands means you' that belonging neither to one group nor to another, living in the borderlands means being 'caught in the crossfire between camps' (Anzaldúa, 1999: 216–7, l.3); 'You are the battleground / where enemies are kin to each other' (ibid.: ll.28–29) she writes; 'To survive the Borderlands / you must live *sin fronteras* / be a crossroads' (ibid.: ll.40–42). Acknowledging the various aspects of her identity, Anzaldúa claims all and none at the same time. In 'To Live in the Borderlands,' she concentrates on ethnicities; elsewhere, she focuses on the multiplicity of her sexual and gendered positions in combination with her national and racial identities:

As a *mestiza* I have no country, my homeland cast me out; yet all countries are mine because I am every woman's sister or potential lover. (As a lesbian I have no race, my own people disclaim me; but

I am all races because there is the queer of me in all races.) I am cultureless because, as a feminist, I challenge the collective cultural/ religious male-derived beliefs of Indo-Hispanics and Anglos; yet I am cultured because I am participating in the creation of yet another culture ... (Anzaldúa, 1999: 148)

Not only does she forego the pigeonhole of one identity per category, the categories themselves alternate in prominence depending upon context, in both senses stretching beyond the model of Woolf's 'As a woman I have no country'. Though Anzaldúa proclaims no allegiance to queer theory – and her rebuff of lesbian feminism's claim to her suggests she would resist any appropriation to a movement defined by others – her ideas seem partly in tune with queer theory, even as they sprang from lesbian-feminist and Chicano politics.[4] It is telling that in work Anzaldúa produced in 1991 she called herself 'queer' alternately with 'dyke' and 'lesbian'. During this time, identity remains crucial in her world view, but it is fluid and contingent.

Strategic essentialisms

As I pursued the connections and miscommunications between queer theory and lesbian feminism in my research in the 1990s, the essentialist/ constructionist debate kept coming up.[5] Something peculiar emerges in even the most clearly social-constructionist theory: the strategic impor- tance of proclaiming identity as a basis for political activism, that is, the need for an occasional 'deployment' of essentialism, in Diana Fuss' term (Fuss, 1989: 32). In the introduction to *Queering India*, Ruth Vanita asserts the necessity of deploying identity categories, against post- structuralist queer objections:

> It is significant that it is usually those who have already obtained most of their basic civil rights and liberties in first-world environ- ments who object to the use of these terms [*gay* and *lesbian*] in third- world contexts. ... [T]he choice of terms has crucial consequences for lesbian and gay movements in urban India ... The Indian press and media have overall represented gay organizations and their demands for human rights in a supportive way, thus making terms like *gay* and *lesbian* accessible to urban bilingual populations whose opinions are crucial in determining who gets civil rights and who does not. (Vanita, 2002: 5)

Fuss makes a similar case from a theoretical vantage point:

> In the hands of a hegemonic group, essentialism can be employed as a powerful tool of ideological domination; in the hands of the subaltern, the use of humanism to mime (in the Irigarian sense of to undo by overdoing) humanism can represent a powerful displacing repetition. The question of the permissibility, if you will, of engaging in essentialism is ... framed by the subject-position from which one speaks. (Fuss, 1989: 32)

Though employing different terms, Fuss describes the strategy Vanita supports 'in third world contexts'.

Scholars working in and on the United States since the early 1990s have been less likely than Vanita to endorse (or Fuss to allow for) the use of terms that seem to them dated, fixed or culture-bound. Activist scholars in the United States generally acknowledge that movements are built on the foundations of earlier activists' efforts, most notably the 'Civil Rights movement that ["Black folks"] created that just rolled up to your door', as Bernice Johnson Reagon (1983) put it in 1981. The transition from lesbian-feminist to queer (on the streets and in the academy) instead played out as a bitter conflict and is recalled as an utter rejection. Understanding the genealogy of our movements, activist and academic, as connected and overlapping, rather than purely as action leading to acrimonious reaction, requires a reexamination of the tenets of and participants in lesbian feminism in the 1970s and '80s. In short, a US history lesson, here offered in three brief instalments.

A brief lesson in recent US lesbian history

History lesson, chapter one: Contrary to received wisdom, lesbian feminism was at its inception a social-constructionist project. In the late 1960s and early '70s there were two strains of lesbian-rights activism, essentialist and existentialist. 'Essentialists', who usually called themselves 'gay women', believed they were born homosexual and that their problems came from society's attitudes toward homosexuality; they were more likely to be aligned with the gay liberation movement than the women's liberation movement. Lesbian feminists, who said they 'existentially' chose lesbianism, argued that the problem is society's attitudes toward women, and that lesbians are at the political vanguard as they suffer the extreme of that sexism (Faderman, 1991: 189, 204–5). In 1972, Charlotte Bunch wrote in the lesbian-feminist newspaper *The*

Furies, 'Lesbianism puts women first while the society declares the male supreme. Lesbianism threatens male supremacy at its core. When politically conscious and organized, it is central to destroying our sexist, racist, capitalist, imperialist system' (Bunch, 1975b: 29). In the 1970s, lesbian feminists confronted the heterosexism of the liberal feminist women's movement and the essentialism (and sexism) of the gay liberation movement with the declaration that any woman could and all women should choose to be lesbians. The early lesbian-feminist manifesto 'The Woman-Identified Woman' asked, 'What is a lesbian?' and answered with a rhetorical flourish illustrative of Fuss' explanation of the deployment of essence: 'A lesbian is the rage of all women condensed to the point of explosion' (Radicalesbians, 1973: 240).

History lesson, chapter two: Again contrary to received wisdom, ample evidence shows that working-class-and-lesbians of colour were active in lesbian feminism and the women's liberation movement in the 1970s. Nevertheless, lesbian feminism has been misconstrued as an entirely white movement. This is due in part to the prominence of white women, though that has been often erroneously reduced to the status of a few, such as Mary Daly and Adrienne Rich, as being either emblematic of or leaders of lesbian feminism. The pointed critique of racism in the movement raised by lesbians of colour lends further credence to the misconception; however, many of those lesbians of colour, Anzaldúa among them, were levelling their charges from within the movement itself. (The same could be said of queer theory, whose public face is predominantly white, and at least some of whose critics of colour come from within the movement.[6])

Chela Sandoval explains that women of colour were both active within and 'at odds with' white feminism 'from the beginning of what has been known as the second wave of the women's movement' (Sandoval, 1991: 4). Judy Grahn describes the diversity of the women involved in the women's and lesbian-feminist movements on the west coast as early as 1969, including Black lesbians, Asian American lesbians, 'Jewish radical Lesbians', and women 'from the European folk "marginal culture" known variously as lower class, working class, white trash' (Grahn, 1985: p. xviii; Seajay, 1990: 25). In a critique of bell hooks, Cheryl Clarke states simply that 'a considerable number of [lesbian feminists] are black' (1984: 153). The Combahee River Collective Statement, issued in 1977 by a group of Black feminists and lesbians who had been meeting and organizing since 1974, points out that 'Black, other Third World, and working women have been involved in the feminist movement from its start, but both outside reactionary forces and racism and elitism within the movement itself have served to obscure our participation' (Combahee River Collective, 1983: 272–3). At least 17 periodicals by and for women of colour were publishing in the 1970s (Kranich, 1989: n.p.).

Sandoval argues that women of colour are erased by typologies of 'white hegemonic feminism' because women of colour often have operated 'between and among' the organizations and strategies of resistance commonly associated with the white feminist movement (Sandoval, 1991: 13–14). In other words, in the telling of the story of lesbians 'as lesbians' in the 1970s, working-class-and-lesbians of colour active within and around lesbian feminism have been given short shrift because they were not only and always talking about sexuality. In so limiting the picture of lesbian activism and community, we miss the story behind the multicultural lesbian and feminist explosion of the 1980s in the United States, which was developing throughout the previous decade. Tiana Arruda, a Latina lesbian-feminist bookstore collective member and activist, summed up the problem when she recalled that the watershed 1981 publication of *This Bridge Called My Back: Writings by Radical Women of Color* was 'the end' result of years of activism by working-class-and-lesbians of colour, 'not the beginning' (1992).

History lesson, chapter three: Identity politics is not necessarily essentialist, nor contrary to queer politics. The original meaning of 'identity politics' formulated by the Combahee River Collective is in keeping with a postmodern sense of identity as fluid and contingent – what Audre Lorde referred to as her multiple 'selves' (Lorde, 1978: 62). The Combahee manifesto explains that the group's politics stemmed from the fact that 'no other ostensibly progressive movement has ever considered our specific oppression as a priority or worked seriously for the ending of that oppression' (1983: 275). Conspicuous from today's vantage point is the lack of an essentialist notion of identity. The manifesto distinguishes between perceived identity as a pretext for oppression and one's sense of self: 'As Black women' – the identity/ pretext – 'we find any type of biological determinism a particularly dangerous and reactionary basis upon which to build a politic' (Combahee River Collective, 1983: 277). Like the Combahee River Collective, Lorde understood the importance of defining one's own identity in this hostile context. 'If we don't name ourselves, we are nothing', she told an interviewer in 1980. 'As a Black woman I have to deal with identity or I don't exist at all. I can't depend on the world to name me kindly, because it never will. ... So either I'm going to be defined by myself or not at all. In that sense it becomes a survival situation' (Hammond, 1980: 19). Prominent lesbian feminists of colour in the United States throughout the 1980s clearly understood and wielded the provisional essentialisms that post-structuralist critics would later theorize.

These three historical lessons have largely been lost on the (dare I say?) mainstream of queer theory. Especially in the early days of establishing the field as distinct from lesbian and gay studies, there was a tendency to oversimplification and glib (or vitriolic) dismissal of lesbian feminism and identity politics. Among the worst offenders was the anthology *Sisters, Sexperts, Queers*, published in 1993, which repeatedly asserted a stereotypical view of lesbian feminism so one-dimensional that the book's editor (and contributing author) later described it as 'overly critical of lesbian feminists' excesses and insufficiently apprecia-tive of some of their contributions. It also tended to homogenize the legacy of lesbian feminism, which was far from seamless and mono-lithic' (Stein, 1997: 4). The phenomenon reached mainstream audiences through the public personalities of 'two notoriously un-1970s lesbians', Camille Paglia and Susie Bright, who according to Karman Kregloe and Jane Caputi have 'in common ... their willingness to blame any "lack," real or spurious, in lesbian lives not on the blights of heterosexist culture but on the stultifying influence of lesbian/feminism' (Kregloe and Caputi, 1997: 137).

Working-class-and-lesbian of colour poets

The lesbian-feminist branch of the family tree that forms queer culture's genealogy is evident, though, in the writings of working-class-and-lesbian of colour activist-poet-theorists. Because she is so widely read, Audre Lorde's writing provides one of the clearest examples. Lorde's is a poetics of location, of constructed lesbian heritage. She takes a firmly rooted, multiply located stand based on an identity forged through multiple differences. In this sense, Lorde both draws on the poetics of lesbian feminism and prefigures the politics of postmodernism. In her multiple self-positioning as 'Black lesbian feminist warrior poet mother', she stands historically and rhetorically at the crux of the so-called generation gap between lesbian-feminist and queer-theoretical notions of identity.

Much has been made by critics of Lorde's 'postmodern' stance on identity. In '*Zami* and the Politics of Plural Identity,' Erin Carlston (1993) offers an astute reading of the novel as a proto-theory of 'positionality'. Thomas Foster (1990) places Lorde's poem 'School Note' in the textual company of such postmodern luminaries as Derrida,

Gramsci, Harding, Kristeva and Lyotard. And, in fact, Lorde's insistence on her multiple selves – her many public declarations and poetic expressions – speak to a postmodern sensibility. Her poem 'Between Ourselves' rejects the temptation 'of easy blackness as salvation' (Lorde, 1978: 112–14). She positions herself as perpetually shifting location, simultaneously occupying seemingly contradictory spaces when she writes in 'School Note,' 'for the embattled / there is no place / that cannot be / home / nor is' (Lorde, 1978: 55, ll.21–5). In the first stanza of 'Sister Outsider' (Lorde, 1978: 106), Lorde explores the past when differences seemed insurmountable: 'in a poor time / never touching ... / never / sharing' (ibid.: ll.1–5). In the second stanza she describes the present, when by contrast 'we raise our children / to respect themselves / as well as each other' (ibid.: ll.8–10). In the third and final stanza, she captures the ever-present, productive contradiction: 'now / your light shines very brightly / but I want you / to know / your darkness also / rich / and beyond fear' (ibid.: ll.14–20). Over and over she insists on the string of identifiers that proclaim her 'Sister Outsider', a figure Donna Haraway (1990, originally published 1985) would term emblematic of a postmodern, cyborgian sense of self.

But Audre Lorde was a lesbian feminist; she said so again and again – in her famous interview with Adrienne Rich, in her essay 'Age, Race, Class, and Sex,' in the title of 'Man Child: A Black Lesbian Feminist's Response' (Lorde, 1984). She offered a diffuse definition of lesbianism to interviewer Karla Hammond in 1981, citing Barbara Smith's 'Toward a Black Feminist Criticism' (1982, originally published 1977) and echoing Lillian Faderman's and Adrienne Rich's famously lesbian-feminist definitions. Literary critics frequently discuss Lorde along with Grahn and almost always with Rich, two of the poets whose names are most closely associated with lesbian feminism.

Does Lorde's avowed and recognized lesbian feminism mean that her work does not share an affinity with queer theory? Definitely not. Does that affinity negate her lesbian feminism? Not at all. These are questions possible only from an either/or perspective. I hesitate before terming Lorde 'both/and,' however. She so incisively criticized the limits of hegemonic categories, so forcefully exposed the racism of white women's studies and activism, that I am tempted to call her 'both/and/neither'. Queer critics who turn to Audre Lorde's work use her multiple positioning, the moral/political force invoked by the particular locations she inhabits, and her widespread influence on lesbian and feminist politics and theory to shore up their constructivist position, and to oppose what they see as lesbian feminism's naive essentialism. The queer move of laying claim to Lorde is used against lesbian feminism, at least to the extent that her lesbian feminism is downplayed. In the process, Lorde's own fluid subject position is denied by claims to her allegiance that have little to do with her historical context or contributions to theory.

Signs of hope

Throughout the 1990s I worried a great deal about the misrepresentation of lesbian feminism and activist-poet-theorists like Lorde in the genealogical narrative of queer theory (perhaps in itself a contradiction in postmodern terms). Since then a few experiences have made me more hopeful. The first was the millennium Dy$_2$ke March in San Francisco in June 2000. By that time, queer politics had clearly ascended at the expense of lesbian feminism, at least in San Francisco. I was puzzled, then, at the announcement of a gender-separatist queer event. A 'woman-only' 'dyke' event seemed an anachronism, but the young women running things embraced the notion and its feminism wholeheartedly. Of course, in San Francisco in 2000 'dyke' and 'woman' were construed a bit differently than they were by the Furies Collective in 1972; according to a lesbian angry at the change, in 2003 the organizers officially opened the Dyke March to 'all who want to celebrate the woman within themselves' in an attempt to satisfy the transgender community ('Letters', 2003). Nevertheless, the march remained a recognizably women's event, though cheered on from the sidelines by gay men, whose presence would have been unheard of and unwelcome in San Francisco in the 1970s.

The synthesis of lesbian-feminist and queer sensibilities was most clearly symbolized in the neon-bright Queer Nation-style stickers (circa 1990) that appeared everywhere at the march. The bold slogans ranged from the contemporary (*Digital Queer, Tranny Dyke*) back through the 1980s sex wars (*Leather Dyke*) to some old favourites from the 1970s (*Woman-Loving Woman, Vagitarian, Sappho*). The booming sound system was decked with posters picturing a woman dancing on a casket beneath the very-seventies caption 'Death to the Patriarchy'. The exuberant gathering seemed to hold something for everyone in the very diverse crowd. (The melding of styles and messages almost made me wonder whether I was hallucinating; at the time, I was literally putting the finishing touches on a book manuscript about connections between queer theory and lesbian feminism.) In fact, the event was a sort of identity poetics on parade, right down to the featured speakers at the rally: two poets, one African American, one white, both working-class identified.

Around the same time as that synergistic Dyke March, I noticed a slight shift in my lesbian/gay studies classes, particularly among young lesbian students. In a lesbian literature seminar at a large state university, I assigned Adrienne Rich's 'Compulsory Heterosexuality and Lesbian Existence'. Political-theoretical essays of this sort were new to most of the students, and only one, a transfer student from a small liberal arts college, had read the essay before. After a spirited class discussion, she hung back to thank me for giving her permission to appreciate Rich's insights. Puzzled, I asked what she meant. She told me that in a feminist theory seminar at her old school, the essay had been introduced derisively; well reasoned critiques and queer dismissals of Rich and lesbian feminism had been rolled into a sort of smear campaign before students ever read the essay. I was reminded of Bonnie Zimmerman's observation that the oppositional stance of many queer theorists has meant that 'increasingly, young women learn about lesbian feminism through parodic representations of it' (Zimmerman, 1997: 163). To hear my student tell it, Rich's essay was assigned in her earlier class primarily as a mechanism to discredit lesbian feminism in favour of post-structuralist theory. I was encouraged that by the time she took my seminar, the student felt enough removed from the debates to reevaluate Rich's essay in its historical context, able to grasp its contributions while aware of its limitations. This may be a sign that lesbian-feminist ideas can once again be considered at face value, that the early need for queer theory to establish itself against its lesbian-feminist forerunners has past.

More recently in a class on US gay and lesbian literature, I explained lesbian feminists' basic rationale for connecting lesbianism and feminism. A young queer student simply remarked, 'Cool!' For her, even farther removed from the competitive grounding of queer theory than my earlier student had been, feminism, lesbianism, and her own 'boi-dyke', drag king identification could coexist without apparent conflict. At age 20, she entered queer community and gender studies far enough beyond 'post-feminism', the sex wars, and Queer Nation to be able to assimilate useful insights without the bias that seemed to me to have indelibly marked the field.

Potholes on the road to global queer studies

As it begins to be acceptable in the United States to entertain the best of lesbian feminism in creative dialogue with queer theory, it remains to be seen whether the old, necessary feminist project of fully integrating women into scholarship and curriculum will be carried forward as the newer, global project of queer studies hits full stride. The signs so far are not particularly encouraging. Developing a course on queer cultures in Asia, I was disappointed to find that nearly all of the book length studies and most anthologies on same-sex love in China, India and Japan concentrate on men. A detailed examination of key authors writing in English about queer cultures in Asia illustrates the extent and significance of the widespread exclusion of lesbian material in global queer studies. I argue that the development of a relevant and comprehensive global queer studies requires, among other things, the use of tools developed in women's and lesbian studies, two fields which queer theory has frequently ignored. I am calling for a global queer studies that is attentive to both sexuality *and* gender, to gay men, (and bisexual and transgendered people), *and* lesbians.

To be sure, feminism has had an impact on global queer studies. For one thing, scholars now account for their inattention to love between women in history rather than presenting love between men unproblematically as the sole subject of study. For example, Chou Wah-shan explains in *Tongzhi: Politics of Same-Sex Eroticism in Chinese Societies,*

> The major issue when writing Chinese *nü* (female) *tongzhi*[7] history is the historical denial of women as sexual subjects. It is primarily a gender issue, not only an issue of sexual orientation. Traditional Chinese society denied and controlled the public expression of female sexuality. Because of women's inadequate public space and the male control of literacy, together with a patriarchal family-kinship structure in which women have little space for economic and social independence, there have been few historical records of woman–woman sexuality. (Chou, 2000: 38)

Research into women's sexuality in Asia not surprisingly turns out to have the same basic problem as lesbian history in the United States and Europe: sexist patriarchy. Historians provide reasons for the lack of evidence about love between women (men's control of literacy, publishing and archiving) and for the possibility that women's sexual options were more limited than men's (women's lack of personal freedom and consequent isolation from one another in homes controlled by husbands and fathers).[8] By contrast, in Japan there is a vast literature dating back at least to the seventeenth century of *nanshoku*, the love of men for men, and *wakashudo* (or *shudo*), the 'way of youths', that is, the path of men loving adolescent males (or adult men affecting the style of adolescent males) (Pflugfelder, 1999: 24–7, 34).[9]

Research into women's sexuality often must depend upon texts written by men, raising questions about its reliability. 'Lesbianism in Imperial China', the appendix to Bret Hinsch's *Passions of the Cut Sleeve: The Male Homosexual Tradition in China* (1990), draws on traditional, that is, male produced and canonized, texts. Nevertheless it provides provocative glimpses of ancient terminology for and narratives about sexual practices between women. Perhaps tellingly, though, while one of the stories Hinsch recounts is about marriage between women, the other is the apparently ages-old and cross-cultural prurient story of lesbian sex as foreplay for heterosexual intercourse. Carla Petievich foregrounds her study of *rekhti*, premodern Urdu poetry narrated in a woman's voice, with a discussion of the genre's problematic male writers. She asserts the importance of preserving and studying *rekhti* because of its unique insights into women's lives and sexuality; for example, *rekhti* makes use of two now obscure terms for a female narrator and her female beloved, *dogana* and *zanakhi* (Petievich, 2002: 53). At the same time, Petievich points to questions about the genre's linguistic credibility. While *rekhti*'s male writers and performers claimed to represent and speak in the idiom of the socially elite women of the eighteenth- and early nineteenth-century Mughal Empire, scholars believe the form's diction is adapted from conversations among 'women of ill repute' (2002: 48). The example of *rekhti* brings into focus the frustrating combination of scarce historical evidence and unreliable male point of view on women. Petievich concludes:

It may be tempting for the feminist reader of *rekhti* to see in it a private world where women, obliged to live in seclusion, resist gender oppression by discovering rich emotional and erotic possibilities with one another. ... We cannot look to *rekhti* for insight into what it means for women, living together, to develop a literature of same-sex eroticism. Intellectual honesty requires that we look there instead for insight into what it means for men, who keep women secluded and socialize with other men, to invent a parody of their own idealized love literature, and to perform it for other men while impersonating women. (Petievich, 2002: 56)

While Petievich warns against reading too much into the lesbian possibilities of *rekhti*, Jennifer Robertson's study of the twentieth-century Japanese all-female theatre review Takarazuka emphasizes how the 'official story' attempts to quell rumours and investigation of love between (frequently cross-dressing) women (Robertson, 1998: 41–6).

Such roadblocks make sense of Chou's call to 'look through the margins, gaps, discrepancies, ruptures, and breaks, and be sensitive to secrecy, masquerades, and the silence of women's voices' – among other things, to make assumptions about the intimate attachments likely formed between women secluded into sex-segregated communities (Chou, 2000: 38). In a similar vein, Vivien Ng speculates about early twentieth-century feminists in China who formed the all-female Mutual Love Society, led by the cross-dressing, 'dashing' Qiu Jin (Ng, 1997: 200). Ng's final word on the subject, that perhaps it is enough 'to reclaim the bonded nature of their emotional lives' without establishing 'beyond a reasonable doubt' their sexual intimacy (Ng, 1997: 204), harks back to the lesbian-feminist ideas of Adrienne Rich and Lillian Faderman.

Faderman famously posited in *Surpassing the Love of Men* that 'Lesbian' describes a relationship in which two women's strongest emotions and affections are directed toward each other. Sexual contact may be a part of the relationship to a greater or lesser degree, or it may be entirely absent. By preference the two women spend most of their time together and share most aspects of their lives with each other' (Faderman, 1981: 17–18). Her groundbreaking 1981 study of 'Romantic Friendship and Love between Women from the Renaissance to the Present', a classic of lesbian history, relies on the definition. Around the same time (1980), in 'Compulsory Heterosexuality and Lesbian Existence', Rich proposed 'the term *lesbian continuum* to include a range – through each woman's life and throughout history – of woman-identified experience, not simply the fact that a woman has had or consciously desired genital sexual experience with another woman' (Rich, 1986: 51). Even earlier, in 1971, Rich called for 'Re-vision – the act of looking back, of seeing with fresh eyes' as 'an act of survival' for women who must 'understand the assumptions in which we are drenched' in order to know ourselves. 'A change in the concept of sexual identity is essential', she wrote, 'if we are not going to see the old political order reassert itself in every new revolution' (Rich, 1979: 35).

Questioning the limitations of Foucault's 'homosexual'

Michel Foucault's Introduction to *The History of Sexuality* was published in the heyday of lesbian feminism (1976 in French; 1978 in English), but it would be another decade before his genealogy of homosexuality would gain wide currency in a postmodern US academy. Now, some fifteen years into queer theory, Chou's, Ng's (Faderman's, Rich's) common-sense calls for lesbian historical imagination coexist with the Foucauldian call to account for historical specificity. While Foucault considered 1870 the 'date of birth' of 'the psychological, psychiatric, medical category of homosexuality' (Foucault, 1978: 43), in Asia the notion was adopted somewhat later. Pflugfelder dates the earliest coinage of parallel terms and concepts in Japan, for which 'Meiji sexologists relied heavily on the research of their Western colleagues', to the 1890s, with the standardized medical term '*doseiai* or "same-sex love", but the term did not emerge in popular discourse until the 1920s. Pflugfelder notes that only then was 'an explicit parallel [drawn], for the first time in the record of Japanese erotic discourses, between male–male and female–female sexualities' (Pflugfelder, 1999: 248).[10] Given his book's focus on the period 1600–1950, Pflugfelder explains his study 'is thus properly regarded as a study of how male–male sexuality was constructed in masculine discourse' (Pflugfelder, 1999: 14). Hinsch makes the same case about China (though curiously he uses the term 'homosexual' anachronistically even as he explains why presentism must be avoided):

> Instead of a 'homosexual tradition', it might be more accurate to speak of the 'male homosexual tradition'. Unlike modern Western society, which sees male homosexuality and lesbianism as related, the Chinese viewed them as completely separate forms of sexuality. A Chinese woman reading about the history of homosexual men would not have drawn a parallel with female sexuality. Consequently, what I say about the 'homosexual' tradition in China applies only to men. (Hinsch, 1990: 6–7)

The exportation of the western concept of homosexuality is certainly one reason why 'many societies foster the homophobic myth that homosexuality was imported into their society from somewhere else', as is common in India (Vanita and Kidwai, 2000: p. xxiii; see also Thadani, 1996: 6–8). At least three volumes on same-sex love across the centuries in India – Ruth Vanita's *Queering India*, Vanita and Saleem Kidwai's *Same-Sex Love in India*, and Giti Thadani's *Sakhiyani* – refuse to draw strict Foucauldian boundaries around the historical invention of homosexual identity, both for political and scholarly reasons. Vanita acknowledges 'the tendency of queer theorists to avoid using terms like *homosexual* to refer to persons or relationships in earlier periods of Euro-American history or in places other than the first world today' (Vanita, 2002: 1). In *Same-Sex Love in India*, Vanita and Kidwai counter with textual evidence that 'support[s] examining representations of female and male homoeroticism together' drawing on the *Kamasutra, Puranic* and *Katha* literature and folk tales (Vanita and Kidwai, 2000: p. xviii) and invoking parameters for 'same sex love' that are reminiscent of Faderman's earlier definition of 'lesbian':

> A primary and passionate attachment between two persons, even between a man and a woman, may or may not be acted upon sexually. ... In most cases where such attachments are documented or represented in history, literature, or myth, we have no way of knowing whether they were technically 'sexual' or not. Nor does it seem particularly important to try to establish such facts, especially since ideas of what is sexual and what is not change with place and time. ... What matters is not the precise nature of the intimate interaction but the ways that such lifelong attachments are depicted and judged. (Vanita and Kidwai, 2000: pp. xiii–xiv)

In addition, Thadani, Vanita, and Kidwai all state explicit political justifications for their organizing strategies and use of terminology. Thadani, a founding member of the Sakhi Lesbian Archives in New Delhi, states plainly in the introduction to *Sakhiyani: Lesbian Desire in Ancient and Modern India*, 'My use of the concept of lesbian is a political choice, as it foregrounds erotic and sexual desire between women' (Thadani, 1996: 9). She considers the 'postmodern understanding' of lesbian desire 'limited' and refers to both lesbian feminism and Rich's 'compulsory heterosexuality' as touchstones for her work. Based on their research in India, Vanita and Kidwai call into question the judgement of 'Historians of love between men [who] have tended to relegate love between women to footnotes or epilogs, sometimes claiming that the two experiences were entirely unrelated and sometimes that scarcely any material is available on the subject' (Vanita and Kidwai, 2000: p. xvii).

Whether Vanita and Kidwai's and Thadani's assessments are fair to the apparently scrupulous research of historians like Pflugfelder and Hinsch, the separation of gay men and lesbians, and especially the relegation of women to far less space than men, in studies of contemporary queer communities is more clearly problematic, given the linkage of male and female homosexuality in medical and popular discourses in Asia by the 1920s. In *Male Homosexuality in Modern Japan*, Mark McLelland reveals the continuing separation of gay men and lesbians today in Japan in actual bars, community publications and websites, if not in other types of discourse. However, McLelland's choice to focus on men to the exclusion of women seems to have at least something to do with the twin factors of author interest and access. McLelland's research includes interviews with Japanese gay men whom he met through advertisements he placed on gay websites. Few men responded to ads in which McLelland explained that he was a researcher, but he found success with ads saying that he 'wanted to make Japanese gay friends' (McLelland, 2000: 16). His access to Japanese gay men's social culture via the Internet resulted in an overrepresentation of *gaisen*, the Japanese term for men interested in foreign men, one of several 'types' of sexual expression at play in Japan (McLelland, 2000: 16, 126). McLelland became aware of Japanese lesbian websites (McLelland, 2000: 156) but did not pursue them as research leads, either because he was not interested or would not have been welcome, or both. Chou does not divulge how he met his three hundred-plus interview contacts in Hong Kong and mainland China; his initial study included 40 men and 20 women, and he does not specify the ratio of men to women in the remaining majority of his informants (Chou, 2000: 8). While Vanita, Kidwai and Thadani are important exceptions, other editors and authors of books about India, such as Hoshang Merchant's *Yaraana: Gay Writing from India* and Jeremy Seabrook's *Love in a Different Climate: Men Who Have Sex with Men in India*, stick strictly to men, without comment on their choice to do so.

Conclusion

Whatever geographical region is under study, queer scholarship can attend to interlocking questions of inclusion, sexism, historicity, boundaries and nationalisms raised over the last thirty-plus years in the development of women's studies, lesbian feminism, gay studies, queer theory and postcolonial studies. It is possible, and I would argue both beneficial and responsible, to integrate the new insights of emerging fields without discarding the still useful contributions of their forerunners, which often bear unacknowledged similarities in ideas, if not in languages, objects of study, or specific goals. At the same time, we face the same-old difficulties of bringing multicultural lesbian studies to the (now international) academic table that we have had since the advent of 'gay studies' over thirty years ago. At least some of the new global queer studies is blending the best of both lesbian feminism and queer theory, whether pursuing co-sexual queer studies or taking responsibility for choosing not to do so. Re-visioning with post-structuralist sophistication, in the various forms that combination can take, seem our most hopeful path for an ongoing, vibrant future of research and activism.

Notes

1. The Center for Lesbian and Gay Studies at the City University of New York has featured international programmes prominently since the late 1990s, with a major increase in such programmes in 2003, the year that CLAGS started the Institute for Tonghzhi [queer Chinese] Studies. CLAGS also sponsors a project called the International Research Network (information available at http://www.irnweb.org/). For a few prominent examples of anthologies in global queer studies, see Hawley, 2001; Patton and Sanchez-Eppler, 2000; Cruz-Malavé and Manalansan, 2002.
2. In fact, Butler uses the term 'compulsory heterosexuality' in *Bodies That Matter* without citing Rich (Butler, 1993: 18).
3. Drawing connections between Judith Butler's work and her lesbian-feminist predecessors is no doubt likely to provoke spirited defences of one or the other by her/its partisans, given the theoretical differences that do of course exist and the vitriolic debates between the two camps. I have elaborated on the topic in *Identity Poetics: Race, Class, and the Lesbian-Feminist Roots of Queer Theory* (2001), which builds on other like minded work (including Heller 1997; Farwell, 1996; Zimmerman and McNaron, 1996).
4. For Anzaldúa's reflections on her participation in the lesbian-feminist and queer movements, see Anzaldúa, 1999; Perry, 1993: 20, 33–4; and Keating, 1993: 106.
5. While it reached a fever pitch across the disciplines in the 1980s, the essentialist/constructionist divide was still raging in the quarrels between US lesbian studies and queer studies in the early 1990s, with some lesbian feminists voicing derisive suspicions of 'postmodernism' and some queer theorists dismissing lesbian feminism as hopelessly essentialist. The extremes are on view in virtually any of Sheila Jeffreys' works, representing the anti-queer lesbian-feminist position (1993; 1994) and in Arlene Stein's zealously queer work of the period (1992; 1993).
6. See, for example (Holland, 2003).
7. Chou explains that '*Tongzhi* is the most popular contemporary Chinese word for lesbians, bisexuals, and gay people. [It is] a Chinese translation from a Soviet communist term, 'comrade', which refers to the revolutionaries who shared a comradeship. ... [It] was appropriated by a Hong Kong gay activist in 1989 for the first Lesbian and Gay Film Festival in Hong Kong ... as the organizer was keen to employ an indigenous representation of same-sex eroticism. ... Within a few years, it became the most common usage in Hong Kong and Taiwan, though the English term 'gay' is still commonly used, sometimes interchangeably with *tongzhi*' (Chou, 2000: 1–2).
8. In addition to Chou, on China see B. Hinsch, *Passions of the Cut Sleeve*, especially the introduction and appendix. On Japan, see G. M. Pflugfelder, *Cartographies of Desire*, especially the introduction and beginning of chapter 1; S. Miller, ed., *Partings at Dawn: An Anthology of Japanese Gay Literature*, p. 12;

and M. McLelland, *Male Homosexuality in Modern Japan*, especially the introduction.

9. Pflugfelder explains that the Japanese character 'way' (*do*, or *michi*) connotes 'a certain spiritual or ethical nuance, although not one that connected it exclusively with any particular religious tradition. ... While Buddhism (*butsudo* or shakudo), Shinto (the 'way of the gods'), and Confucianism (*judo*) all constituted 'ways', so did such secular pursuits as calligraphy, poetry (*kado*), the martial arts (*budo*), flower arrangement (*kado*), and the tea ceremony (*sado*). Broadly speaking, we may conceive of a 'way' as a discipline of mind and body, a set of practices and knowledge expected to bring both spiritual and physical rewards to those who chose to follow its path' (Pflugfelder, 1999: 28).

10. Robertson notes that *doseiai* was coined at the turn of the twentieth century as a term for 'passionate, but supposedly platonic, friendship between females, although sexologists found it difficult to distinguish friendship from homosexuality among girls and women'. The *–ai*, 'often translated as agape', which was considered the feminine form of love, contrasts with erotic love attributed to men (Robertson, 1998: 68). Pflugfelder discusses only the later, lasting definition of *doseiai* as homosexual, both male and female. In his introduction he references several articles by Robertson and his own forthcoming essay about female–female sexuality, ' "S" is for Sister: Schoolgirl Intimacy and "Same-Sex Love" in Early Twentieth-Century Japan', in B. Molony and K. S. Uno, eds, *Gendering Modern Japanese History* (Cambridge: Harvard University Press) (Pflugfelder, 1999, 14–15n.22).

5

Boys will be … Bois?
Or, Transgender Feminism and Forgetful Fish

Judith Halberstam

My whimsical title for this chapter references two sets of discussions which will, sometimes for better and sometimes for worse, help me to re-frame what has become a rather tired argument about whether transgender men and women can and should be feminist, whether feminists have helped or hindered transgender activism, and how feminism might build upon the utopian potential of transgender embodiment. The first part of my title 'Boys will be … . Bois' engages with the rigid and persistent identity politics that have emerged along-side a more open-ended discussion of the impact and meaning of trans-genderism within postmodernism. By referring to the new trend for androgynous lesbians to side-step both feminism and transsexual poli-tics in order to produce boi-culture,[1] I suggest that the new 'bois' give the impression of polyvocality, fluidity and radical politics but actually they tame the exciting potential of a merger of trans and feminist poli-tics. The new boi culture is an outcome, in many ways of a traditionally Oedipal process by which one generation supersedes the last by casting it as traditionalist and anachronistic. In this first section, I seek to find different models for generational struggle and I ask about the future of queer cross-gender identification. The second part of my title refers to a bold recent book by Joan Roughgarden, *Evolution's Rainbow*, which recasts the Darwinian narrative of evolution by giving alternative inter-pretations of intermediate genders, cooperative behaviour and competi-tive struggle in the animal world (Roughgarden, 2004). Arguing, Donna Haraway style, that researchers project narratives like 'survival of the fittest' onto phenomena that could as easily be interpreted according to other narrative templates, Roughgarden allows us to see friendship

systems between animals where other researchers have only seen competition; she replaces Darwin's theory of 'sexual selection' with a concept of 'social selection' and she rejects 'the primacy of individualism' in
favour of cooperative development. Roughgarden's interpretations of
creatures that change sex, engage in same-sex erotics or switch sex roles
are refreshingly original and they reveal the extent to which contemporary theories of human cross-gender identification are limited by their
commitment to dreary and unimaginative accounts of the body, the self
and diversity. In this section I situate Roughgarden's theories of species
diversity in relation to debates about feminism, history, generationality,
transgenderism and memory by looking at two recent films which fore-
ground forgetting and transgenderism as part of a comic rendering of
alternative temporalities.

Ever since 1979 when Janice Raymond described a 'transsexual
empire' within which, she claimed, female-to-male transsexuals used
medical technology to infiltrate women's space and appropriate 'female'
creativity, feminism and transgenderism have been pitted against one
another in mortal battle.[2] The contestation over the meaning of gender
variance within feminism that Raymond's text exemplifies has a long
history that is worth re-examining reaching back to sexology and the
beginning of the women's movement. In the 25 years since the publication of *The Transsexual Empire*, the terms of the enmity between feminism and transgenderism have shifted somewhat and yet a core of
mutual suspicion continues to animate debates between transgender
and feminist scholars about the politics of gender flexibility (Raymond,
1994). Some transsexual theorists like Sandy Stone have taken the
language of 'empire' from Raymond and have discussed transsexuals
and transgenders as colonized bodies struggling for some form of self-
determination in a world dominated by gender binarism (Stone, 1993).
Some feminist scholars like Bernice Hausman have updated Raymond's
analysis and accused transgenders not of futuristic fantasies of male
motherhood but of anachronistic desires for gender essentialism
(Hausman, 1995). The terrain has been greatly complicated more
recently by the surge in visibility of female-to-male transsexuals and
other masculine transgender forms like 'bois'.

Early histories of female masculinity

While the history of female masculinity that I and others have traced is
not the history of transgenderism tout court, contemporary struggles
over the meaning of gender transivity within feminist and queer

communities cannot be understood without this history of gender variance and the female body. Gender variance before the nineteenth century might have been read in relation to the violation of social roles or marital ritual but it was not necessarily cast as an identity (Foucault, 1980; Garber, 1992). By the end of the nineteenth century, all signs of masculinity in women had come to be associated with the medical condition of inversion, with some kind of psychological disorder and, significantly, with feminist aspirations (Chauncey, 1989); and the general sense of freakishness or ugliness that the masculine woman had conveyed prior to this time was now pinned down to an aberrant sexual desire emanating from severe cross-gender identification.

Once the masculine woman became clearly identified with sexual inversion, her role in European culture changed immensely. At certain moments the masculine woman in modernism comes to signify the ills of modern life itself: the coarsening of female beauty, the breakdown of separate spheres and the devolution and degeneration of the species (as in D.H. Lawrence's short story, *The Fox*). She also represents a catastrophe in nature itself, the untoward consequences of the Great War and the alienation of self that is so much a hallmark of modern literature. In eccentric accounts of gender like those produced, for example, by turn of the century philosopher, Otto Weininger, the masculine woman, paradoxically, also figures as a powerful female character type who has renounced her own flawed and damaged femininity. The enigmatic nature of the masculine woman in the first part of the last century then makes her into a perfect icon of modernity – she combines in one body the force of power and abjection, she is both phallic and obviously castrated; she is a riddle that neither psychoanalysis nor sexology can adequately solve.

Between 1890 and 1920 in England, notions of working class and ruling class male masculinity underwent huge shifts and changes.[3] Large-scale shifts in demographics, in immigration, in national discourse and in sexuality and gender definitions brought to visibility diverse expressions of minority male masculinities. New laws prohibiting male homosexuality were instituted even as sexological studies struggled to articulate the naturalness of homosexual instinct (Cohen, 1993). These new social, legal and medical definitions of normative and non-normative masculine expressions of desire coincided furthermore with the ravages of the First World War and a noticeable decline in British colonial power. So while male masculinity as it had been formulated in relation to colonial rule and national identity came under intense scrutiny, the development of sexological discourses of inversion contributed further to the unravelling of dominant conceptions of the masculine by allowing for the possibility of a non-male masculinity (Bederman, 1995).

During the First World War, the insights of sexology had profound implications as hundreds of male soldiers returned from the front suffering from various forms of a debilitating hysteria and, at the same time, hundreds of women either took over masculine jobs at the home front or petitioned to drive ambulances at the front. Since male femininity had been tied so definitively to homosexuality, male hysteria was a particularly troubling neurosis and since female masculinity had been tied so definitively to female homosexuality, the participation of women in masculine occupations gave cause for concern about the impact of these new occupations on 'female character' and on the 'woman question' in general. Otto Weininger (1906), a controversial Jewish thinker, for example, considered the demand for female emancipation to be a direct result of female masculinity, whether acquired or innate.[4] He proclaimed: 'A woman's demand for emancipation and her qualification for it are in direct proportion to the amount of maleness in her' (1906: 64). By emancipation, however, Weininger did not mean economic autonomy, political enfranchisement or gender equality, he meant rather the 'deep seated craving to acquire man's character, to attain his mental and moral freedom, to reach his real interests and creative power' (ibid.: 65).

In other words, women with any kind of social, aesthetic or political aspirations must in some sense not be women at all and, furthermore, he claimed, the heroic women held up by feminists as examples of female genius and aptitude–Sappho, George Sand, Catherine the Great–were not simply 'great' women rather they were virtual men, and their masculinity, according to him, 'presupposes a higher degree of development' (66). Obviously a theory of sex and character like Weininger's is deeply misogynist in that it attributes all female ambition to a male disposition; femininity itself then corresponds to a low and even regressive form of human development and it cannot be the root of either genius or power. In other parts of the book, Weininger links his odious ideas on gender to equally sinister notions of race: Jews, he claimed were a feminized and therefore a doomed race. While Weininger's ideas reflected both the anti-semitism and the masculinism of the first decade of twentieth-century Europe, they do provide insight into the ways in which female masculinity might have been understood simultaneously as a gender or sexual perversion, and as a superior form of female evolution. Weininger believed in fact that the two went together and that even where a successful woman was not known to be homosexual, her homosexuality would be legible on her body. Weininger explicitly connects the 'ugly', masculine woman to homosexuality and he even formulates a woman's homosexuality as an outcome of her masculinity. Weininger's idiosyncratic and controversial response to feminism then concludes with a modest proposal: 'Let there be the freest scope given to and few hindrances put in the way of all women with masculine dispositions who feel a psychical necessity to devote themselves to masculine occupations and are physically fit to undertake them' (1906: 71). But freedom for the masculine woman predictably comes at a price for the feminine woman: 'away with the whole 'women's movement' with its unnaturalness and artificiality and fundamental errors' states Weininger ominously. This split between emancipation for the invert and confinement for the feminine woman sets female masculinity at odds with feminism, indeed sets female masculinity at odds with womanhood, and creates a double bind for the masculine woman and for masculine female modernists. Does the masculine woman cleave to a masculinist politics that sets her at the top of a hierarchy of women or does she recognize her solidarity with feminine women and set her sights on feminist goals? Gertrude Stein, for one, was extremely attracted to Weininger's ideas precisely because he associated female masculinity with female genius, but other writers like Djuna Barnes had to work out how to rescue female masculinity for a feminist aesthetic. For many nineteenth-century writers, however, femininity was a symptom of modern degeneration and the only solution they offered was to recreate a virile culture.

For obvious reasons then, many feminists studying the rise of models of inversion within modernism have associated female masculinity with an anti-feminist and anti-feminine understanding of modern gender. Some feminist critics, like Lilian Faderman (1981) for example, have long claimed that the female invert, the masculine woman, was indeed an invention of the sexologists and a masculinist and heterosexist one at that; but others, particularly queer historians like George Chauncey (1989) and Lisa Duggan (1993) have been far more willing to believe that the category of invert was a collaboration between doctors and sexual communities; and while the term 'invert' may well have covered over other more elaborate and colourful sexual vernaculars, they assert, it was not forced upon unwilling subjects.[5] But it is the split between gender variance and feminist politics that interests us here and that echoes in contemporary debates about the meaning of transgenderism.

Contemporary debates

Nowadays we can look to the debates about 'womyn only' space at the Michigan Womyn's Music Festival, and the founding of Camp Trans as a protestation of these policies, to see that territorial, semantic and membership debates are alive and well in those areas of gender politics which focus upon transgender embodiment.[6] While I am interested in the new loci of contestation over the queering of definitions of 'women' and 'men', femininity and masculinity, that have emerged in recent years, I also think that debates about transgenderism have turned a little stale and we would do well to concentrate on re-imagining the terrain of struggle rather than rehearsing the positions that have emerged. This essay, consequently, is less of an attempt to summarize the impact of transgenderism on feminism and vice versa and more of a search for new ways of articulating some of the mutual projects of a politicized transgenderism and a gender - queer feminism.

Boi's just wanna have fun

> Most bois are in their twenties and have come of age in a time when women's and gay rights seem like more of a given and less of an urgent struggle than they did to lesbians ten or twenty or more years older. So it makes sense that they—like young women in general—have the luxury to prioritize play and pleasure in a different way, and that worrying about things like male privilege seems old-school and uncool. (Levy, 2004: 25–8)

An edition of *New York* magazine featured two articles of interest to anyone contemplating the present, past and future of queer genders, lesbian representation and feminism. In the first article, the cover story, the magazine proclaimed that the Showtime series 'The L Word' offered images of women who are decidedly 'not your mother's lesbians'. (Bolonik, 2004). Another story in the same edition discussed the new phenomenon of 'boi' culture and proposed to tell us why, as the byline put it, 'some young lesbians are going beyond feminist politics, beyond androgyny, to explore a new generation of sex roles' (Levy, 2004: 24). 'The L Word' and 'boi' culture both advertise themselves in terms of a much-needed Oedipal displacement of those older models of queer, and especially lesbian, culture in serious need of upgrades. The sleek lipstick lesbians of 'The L Word', are not 'your mother's' lesbians apparently because they are beautiful, ambitious, monied, reproductive, classy, urban; the fashionable 'bois' at clubs like *Meow Mix* in New York and *The Lex* in San Francisco have similarly gone 'beyond feminism' because they are 'young, hip, sex positive, a little masculine and ready to rock' (Levy, 2004: 25). One boi describes the relationship of bois to butches as generational and, for her, while bois are into fun and sex, butches are '… adult.

If you're a butch, you're grown-up. You're man of the house' (ibid.: 25). What are we to make of these new forms of trans and lesbian culture? Why is feminism posited as both an embarrassing mother who must be pushed aside and a humourless butch aunt who stands in the way of the pursuit of pleasure? Are there other models of generation, temporality and politics available to queer culture and feminism?

Of course, to say that this year's lipstick lezzies are not your mother's lesbians is to posit a rigidly Oedipal frame for generational change. And indeed this Oedipal frame has stifled all kinds of other models for thinking about the evolution of feminist politics. From women's studies professors who think of their students as 'daughters', to next-wave feminists who see earlier activists as seriously 'out of touch', Oedipal dynamics and their familial metaphors snuff out the potential futures of a powerful feminism. Many Women's Studies departments around the United States, indeed, currently struggle with the messy and even ugly legacy of Oedipal models of generationality. In some of these departments the Oedipal dynamics are also racialized and sexualized, and so an older generation of mostly white women might be simultaneously hiring and holding at bay a younger generation of, often queer, women of colour. The whole model of 'passing down' knowledge from mother to daughter is quite clearly invested in both white, gendered and heteronormativity; indeed the system inevitably stalls in the face of these racialized and heterosexualised scenes of difference. And while the 'mothers' become frustrated with the apparent unwillingness of the women they have hired to continue their line of inquiry, the 'daughters' struggle to make the older women see that regulatory systems are embedded in the paradigms they so insistently want to pass on. The pervasive model of women's studies as a mother–daughter dynamic ironically resembles patriarchal systems in that it casts the mother as the place of history, tradition and memory and the daughter as the inheritor of a static system which she must either accept without changing or reject completely.

Eve K. Sedgwick proposes one way in which queer cultures have managed to sidestep the stifling reproductive logics of Oedipal temporality. In an essay on the perils of paranoid knowledge production, Sedgwick calls attention to the temporal frame within which paranoid reasoning takes place; arguing that paranoia is anticipatory, that it is a reading practice which is 'closely tied to a notion of the inevitable'. Sedgwick tells us that paranoid readings and relations are 'characterized by a distinctly Oedipal regularity and repetitiveness: it happened to my father's father, it happened to my father, it is happening to me, and it will happen to my son, and it will happen to my son's son' (Sedgwick,

2003: 147). By contrast, Sedgwick claims, queer life unfolds differently. She writes: 'But isn't it a feature of queer possibility ... that our generational relations don't always proceed in this lockstep?' (2003: 147). While obviously, heterosexual relations are not essentially bound to 'regularity and repetitiveness', the bourgeois family matrix, with its emphasis on lineage, inheritance and generation, does tend to cast temporal flux in terms of either seamless continuity or total rupture. And by casting generations of feminism as somehow at odds, both young and old feminists engage in paranoid models of interaction.

The stability of heteronormative models of time and transformation has effects all over the map of social change; as J.K. Gibson-Graham point out in their feminist critique of political economy, if we represent capitalism, heteropatriarchy and racist economies as totalizing and inevitable, as seamless and impermeable, then we have 'little possibility of escape' from those systems, and few ways of accessing a 'non-capitalist imaginary' (Gibson-Graham, 1996). And as Roderick Ferguson argues in a brilliant book about 'queer of color critique', the normative temporal and spatial frames of historical materialism have ironically forced a congruence between Marxist and bourgeois definitions of 'civilization', both of which cast racialized non-normative sexualities as anterior, and as signs of disorder and social chaos within an otherwise stable social system (Ferguson, 2003). The contingency of queer relation, its uncertainty, irregularity and even perversity, promises new models of generation. Queer relation also prompts us to refuse the normative temporal logics of progress, deterioration, supercession, replacement and hindsight while recognizing other possible non-oedipal logics including a focus on the ephemeral, the momentary, the surprise, simultaneity, contradiction, intergenerational exchange. This might mean rejecting the model of feminism which posits generational relations in terms of mother–daughter bonds and conflicts; it might mean recognizing alternative futures in alternative readings of the past, it could introduce an element of surprise in place of the anticipatory paranoid scheme within which all causes and all outcomes are predicted in advance.

Queer temporalities, I argue emerge from the specifications of lives lived beyond the hetero-reproductive matrix (Halberstam, 2005). This is not to say that all gays and lesbians choose to avoid reproductive logics or that all heterosexuals live within them; nor is it to argue that all families and all those people who reproduce participate in the normativity of parenthood, bourgeois family and heterosexual scheduling practices. 'Queer', in this context might include communities of colour, single mothers, sex workers or transgender people. Queer might also signify as a form of critique that identifies and exposes the contradictions within universalizing discourses of identity and politics.

In my book I identify queer subcultures as one queer site within which normative temporal modes are shaken up and from which different models of adulthood, maturity and feminist practice emerge. When a multi-racial punk band like Tribe 8, for example, perform a song like 'Frat Pig' while performing a ritual castration on a dildo on stage, they make a link back to earlier models of radical feminism from the likes of Valerie Solanas but they also split from pacifist forms of feminism by casting futurity in terms of a kind of menace, a potential for feminist violence.[7] Tribe 8 also break the un-useful binary between 'your mother's and not your mother's lesbians' – with their tattoos and scars, their alternative genders, their blending of femme guitar heroics with butch rock star antics, Tribe 8 remind us that there is more to feminist generationality than assimilation versus separatism. When 42-year old white butch Breedlove takes off her shirt, dons a dildo in the middle of Tribe 8 shows and makes a male fan give her a blowjob before chopping the dildo to bits, and when 40-year old Asian American femme guitarist Leslie Mah performs a long guitar solo in a skirt and combat boots, they resignify the gendered and the sexed body, the aging body, the masculine and the feminine body, the raced body, and they stage feminism as precisely this reordering of time, flesh and femaleness. And while Leslie Mah and Silas Flipper play the guitars and remake punk, Breedlove literally plays the dildo and remakes the symbolic terrain of gender politics. The dildo cannot be read back into flabby narratives of penis envy or castration anxiety, it reads instead as a marker of transgender feminism, a transgenderism in fact which, since the publication of *Gender Trouble*, has been cast as both the stigma of feminism (the man-hating butch and the castrating femme) and as one of its potential outcomes (an escape from the restrictions of normative and hegemonic femininity and masculinity) (Butler, 1990).

In queer subcultures, I am arguing, some performers re-imagine gender by reordering the temporal logics within which normative embodiment unfolds. They do not imagine identity as unfixed, fluid, as flexible (which is the dominant trope for lesbian desire in a show like 'The L Word' for example), no, queer subcultures understand the identities they inhabit and the knowledges they produce as utterly contingent, as fragile, risky, deliberately peripheral, short term, ambivalent rather than ambiguous, as related to what came before and productive of what lies ahead but not bound by fidelity to the past or commitment to the future. The transgender body, as the article on 'bois' that I discussed earlier suggests, captures some of the ambivalence about change and transformation that haunts feminist communities and feminist models of time and transmission. In many queer communities and in many feminist conversations, feminism and transgenderism have been cast as at odds with one another – particularly when we are talking about female to male transitions or queer female masculinities, the transgendered body has sometimes been cast as the betrayal of a particular model of feminism and its investments in certain understandings of womanhood. Or, the transgender body has been cast as a symbol of the splintering of prematurely unified understandings of womanhood and female embodiment. In fact, transgenderism has actually been an interesting site for examining generational struggle in the culture at large and transgender characters often appear in popular film to signify rupture, unanticipated change and odd disruptions to heteronormative order. Both Female-To-Male's (FTM) and Male-To-Females's (MTF) challenge stable conceptions of identity, generation, gender and community.

Forgetful fish and the future of feminism

> Hermaphrodism is a successful way of life for many species; my guess is that hermaphrodism is more common in the world than species who maintain separate sexes in separate bodies (called gonochronism). The separate-sex/separate-body state is often viewed as 'normal', suggesting that something unusual favors hermaphrodism in plants, on coral reefs and in the deep sea. Alternatively, hermaphrodism may be viewed as the original norm, prompting us to ask what there is in mobile organisms in the terrestrial environment that favors separate sexes in separate bodies. (Roughgarden, 2004: 34)

In looking for models of alternative temporalities, other modes of embodiment and the whacky modes of affiliation and relation that they engender, we do not only have to rely solely upon avant-garde productions. Popular culture produces, almost accidentally, plenty of perverse narratives of belonging, relating and evolving and they often associate these narratives with, or at least in proximity to, transgender characters. Significantly, these same narratives locate transgenderism alongside a broader narrative of species diversity and within a historical framework of forgetfulness. Forgetfulness, in the early twenty-first century indeed, has become a major trope of mainstream cinema; and while most forms of forgetting in mainstream cinema operate according to a simple mapping of memory onto identity and memory loss onto the loss of history, location and even politics, a few films, often unintentionally, set forgetting in motion in such a way as to undermine dominant modes of historicizing. While serious films like *Memento* or *The Eternal Sunshine of the Spotless Mind* (or *The Manchurian Candidate* or *Code 46*) all equate memory manipulation with brainwashing, loss of humanity and state intrusions on privacy, a set of comedic films tackle the same topic with different and wildly unpredictable results. Let's look closely at two non-serious films in this developing genre, *Finding Nemo* (2003, Pixar Animation Studioe) and *Fifty First Dates* (2004, directed by Peter Segal), to see how they deploy forgetting for radically different ends. Both films feature surreptitious narratives about transgenderism and both sidestep overt discourses of feminism. Both also represent transgenderism as part of a 'natural' order of species diversity.

Let me say at the outset of my discussion of *Fifty First Dates* (*FFD*), that I am not at all interested in endorsing this film particularly given its racist depictions of native Hawaiians, its colonial depiction of Island culture and its transphobic use of queer characters. However, precisely because the film stages its drama of memory loss against the backdrop of Hawaii, and its narrative of heteronormativity against the seeming perversity of transgenderism, the trope of forgetting becomes interesting and potentially disruptive of the dominant narrative. *Fifty First Dates*, features Drew Barrymore as Lucy, a woman afflicted by short-term memory loss due to an injury to her 'temporal lobe'. Adam Sandler is Henry Roth, a zoo veterinarian by day who romances tourists by night. And, Hawaii operates as the setting for Roth's promiscuity as the island seems to offer an endless supply of single women looking for a few nights of fun. Hawaii is thus cast as the place of pleasure without responsibility, a paradise of course, but one that must be left behind during the white male's quest for adulthood. Henry's dating exploits are watched with voyeuristic glee by his native Hawaiian friend Ula, played by Rod Schneider in brownface who has kids and a wife; and Ula, far from representing an alternative Hawaii or an alternative model of kinship, is just cast as a buffoon whom marriage has reduced to a kind of infantile state. Other native Hawaiians serve as friendly onlookers to the scene of white romance and one immigrant Chinese man is cast as a crazy guy in the local restaurant who watches Henry and Lucy's romance and makes wry and pointedly critical comments about Henry ('stupid idiot' being the most frequent). Since Henry is a zoo veterinarian, a panoply of animals take up minor roles in the comedy.

The basic premise of the film rests upon Lucy's memory loop which forces her to relive the same day, the day of her accident, over and over again and Henry's desire to interrupt that loop by using her desire for him as a way of stalling her memory loss and replacing it with the permanent and long-term scenarios of marriage and family. Amazingly, there are at least three characters in this film who are cast as transgender in some way or another and these transgender characters serve no obvious purpose in terms of advancing the narrative – like the animals Henry works with in the zoo, they are merely supposed to represent the diversity of nature and culture!

Fifty First Dates, it must be said, unlike other recent comedies set in Hawaii like the cartoon *Lilo and Stich* for example, has no particular interest in the geo-political significance of its Island setting. *Lilo and Stich* at least weaves its narrative of family and kinship through complex subplots about native hostility to tourists, the influence of US popular culture on colonized locations and the paternalistic function of the state. *Fifty First Dates*, on the other hand, utilizes Hawaii as a kind of blank slate, a place emptied of political turmoil and a perfect metaphor for the state of mind produced by the erasure of memory. Unwittingly, of course, the film's emphasis on short-term memory loss does raise issues about national memory and histories of colonization; and the film allows the discerning reader to understand the status of Hawaii in relation to state-authorized forms of forgetting. Tensions between Hawaii and the mainland, between native Hawaiians and white Americans, between the history of colonization and the narrative of statehood are all wiped away like damaged memory of the film's romantic heroine. And yet, those tensions linger on and cannot be resolved as easily as the romantic obstacles.

Henry's solution to Lucy's memory loss problem is to create a videotape for her to watch every morning which gives her a quick account of world news and then reminds her of the traumatic accident and its aftermath which has left her in her afflicted state. At certain points, Lucy tries to replace the video record with her own diary in order to 'tell herself' the narrative and to steer clear of the clear 'Stepford wives' implication of the image of the woman being programmed every morning to perform her familial duties. And yet, the narrative cannot pull itself clear of the 'brainwashing' motif and so ultimately it reveals heterosexual romance to be nothing more than the violent enforcement of normative forms of sociality and sexuality. Forgetting, surprisingly, stalls the implantation of heteronormativity and creates a barrier to the conventional progress narrative of heterosexual romance. The film, unconsciously, analogizes US imperialism to heterosexuality and casts memory as the motor of national belonging. By implication then, forgetting, when directed at a dominant narrative rather than at subaltern knowledges, could become a tactic for resisting the imposition of colonial rule.

In an excellent new book about *'Aloha Betrayed: Native Hawaiian Resistance to American Colonialism'*, Noenoe Silva studies the erasure of local histories through the imposition of English language histories and interpretations of indigenous culture (Silva, 2004). Of the struggle between English texts about Hawaii and oral accounts she writes: 'When the stories told at home do not match up with the texts at school, students are taught to doubt the oral versions' (Silvia, 2004: 3). Obviously then forgetting has been a colonial tactic in the past and has produced a hierarchical relationship between foreign and native knowledges; but in order to remember and recognize the anti-colonial struggles, other narratives do have to be forgotten and unlearned. I am suggesting that a 'stupid' film like *FFD* unconsciously reinforces the power of forgetting and it disrupts the seamless production of white settlers as 'native Hawaiians' by demonstrating how national memory constructs those 'locals' as 'natives'. When Lucy 'forgets' Henry, she forgets patriarchy, heterosexuality, gender hierarchies; the film despite itself allows us the occasion to think about forgetting as a tactic of anti-colonial resistance.

The host of transgender characters in the film also reveals how dependent normative heterosexuality is upon the production of non-normative subjects. From Alexa, Henry's androgynous and sexually ambiguous assistant at the zoo, to Doug, Lucy's steroid pumping brother and to John/Jennifer, an FTM transsexual from Lucy's past, the transgender characters represent the dangers of life outside of the nuclear family. In order for Lucy and Henry's bizarre and even disturbing courtship to seem authentic and chosen, these other characters must model a kind of freakish excess which is then associated with too much freedom (the single and predatory Alexa), not enough maternal guidance (Doug) and adolescent angst (Jennifer/John). The native Hawaiian characters are similarly cast as sexually depraved (Ula), fetishistically phallic (Nick) and physically repugnant (Ula's wife). Hence, Henry and Lucy, despite their potentially perverse arrangement, can occupy the place of the ideal family by turning short-term memory loss into less a metaphor for the constant training that women endure in order to become mothers and wives and more the necessary preamble to national and familial stability. That the new family sails off at the end of the film to another utopian colony/state, Alaska, suggests that they go in search of new 'blank' landscapes upon which they hope to write their persistent tales of whiteness, benevolence and the inevitable reproduction of the same.

Forgetting as a practice is already a necessary part of all kinds of political and cultural projects. At the end of Toni Morrison's (2004) novel *Beloved*, for example, the ghost of Sethe's child and of all the 'dis-remembered and unaccounted for' people lost to slavery, disappears and allows Sethe and Denver to enter a space of forgetfulness, a space where the horrors of slavery do not have to haunt them at every turn but where life can fill up the spaces that previously were saturated with loss, violation, dehumanization and memory. Morrison describes the effect of Beloved's departure on those who remained: 'They forgot her like a bad dream. After they made up their tales, shaped and decorated them, those that saw her that day on the porch quickly and deliberately forgot her. ... Remembering seemed unwise' (Morrison, 2004: 274). Morrison's embrace of the act of forgetting has a very specific function and is not intended, obviously, as a wholesale endorsement of forgetting as a strategy for survival. Rather, Morrison situates forgetting as contingent, necessary, impermanent but also as a rupture in the logic of remember-ing (the conventional slave narrative for example) that shapes memories into acceptable and palatable forms of knowing the past. Forgetting is also what allows for a new way of remembering and so while the sur-vivors of slavery forget the ghost that has haunted them in Morrison's novel, they also learn how to live with the traces she leaves behind.

In *Cities of the Dead*, Joseph Roach (1996) writes: 'memory is a process that depends crucially upon forgetting' and he describes how culture reproduces itself as a receptacle for both remembering and forgetting through performance and substitution. Describing performance cultures as a form of 'surrogation', Roach identifies the actor as a substitute or effigy, who, as Roach suggests, covers over the gap between what was and what is and attempts to reproduce the past in the present and the dead in the living; surrogation is capable of making a real connection between the past and the present, but it only ever does so imperfectly. And so, according to Roach, performance represents not only what has been remembered and carried forward but also what has been lost in the act of transmission. He writes provocatively: 'Performance ... stands in for an elusive entity that it is not but that it must vainly aspire both to embody and to replace' (1996: 3). Surrogation, quite obviously, is not reproduction; it is not faithful to the original and it does not aspire to authenticity; while Roach does not say this, we can surmise that surro-gation is queer in its commitment to the copy and its repudiation indeed its wilful forgetting of the original.

Perhaps this notion of 'surrogation' can help to explain the visibility of the transgender body, in *FFD*. The transgender body seems to represent anxiety and ambivalence about change and transformation in general but also it allows Henry and Lucy to understand their wilfully artificial productions of family, gender and affiliation as authentic, if only because there is an abundance of clearly inauthentic bodies surrounding them. If Lucy is stuck in one time loop through memory loss, she is delivered by Henry into another through heterosexuality. The trans characters edging the semi-sinister narrative then suggest that change can mean loss of tradition, family, history. Another memory loss narrative however shows that change and memory loss can produce distinctly queer and alternative futures. An odd little animated feature, *Finding Nemo* positioned queerness, and transgender queerness at that, in ways that may be helpful to us as we look for more nuanced and less Oedipal ways of telling time in queer feminist contexts and in relation to explicit renderings of the transgender body. *Finding Nemo* tells the story of a clown-fish family that, in the film's tragic opening, is decimated by a hungry shark. The mother fish and almost all of her eggs are consumed leaving a very anxious adult male fish, Marlin, with one slightly disabled offspring (he has a small fin on one side), Nemo. Marlin, whose voice is supplied by Albert Brooks, becomes understandably paranoid about the safety of his only son and he nervously and even hysterically tries to guard him from all of the dangers of the deep. Inevitably Nemo grows tired of his father's ministrations and, in a fit of Oedipal rebellion, he tells his father he hates him and swims off recklessly into the open sea only to be netted by a diver and placed in a fish bowl in a dentist's office. Marlin, his paranoid fears now realized, begins a mad search for his missing son and swims his way to Sydney, Australia. When he finally finds him, he and Nemo orchestrate a fish uprising against their human jailors and they work out a different, non-oedipal, non-paranoid mode of relation.

Like *Chicken Run*, then, the Gramscian cartoon about organic chicken intellectuals, *Finding Nemo* weds its story of family to a tale of successful collective opposition to enslavement, forced labour and commodification. And like another 'stupid' narrative (where 'stupid' represents a generic classification) *Dude, Where's My Car*, *Finding Nemo* both thematizes the limits to masculinist forms of knowing and it posits forgetting as a powerful obstacle to capitalist and patriarchal modes of transmission (forgetfulness literally stalls the reproduction of the dominant in these films). *Finding Nemo* also makes queer coalition, here represented by a seemingly helpful bluefish named Dory whose voice is supplied by the queer Ellen Degeneres, into a major component of the quest for freedom and the attempts to reinvent kinship, identity and collectivity.

Dory accompanies Marlin on his quest for Nemo. Dory, however, suffers from 'short term memory loss' and so only remembers intermittently why she and Marlin are swimming to Australia, and her odd sense of time introduces absurdity into an otherwise rather straight narrative and it scrambles all temporal interactions. When explaining her memory problem to Marlin, Dory says she thinks she must have inherited it from her family but then again she comments, she cannot remember her family so she is not sure how she came to be afflicted. In her lack of family memory, her exile in the present tense, her ephemeral sense of knowledge and her continuous sense of a lack of context, Dory offers fascinating models of queer time (short term memory), queer knowledge practices (ephemeral insights) and anti-familial kinship. By aiding Marlin without desiring him, finding Nemo without mothering him, and going on a journey without a telos, Dory offers us a model of cooperation which is not dependent upon payment or remunerative alliance. Dory, literally, swims alongside the broken family without becoming part of it and she helps to repair familial bonds without being invested in knowing specifically what the relations between Marlin and Nemo might be. The fact that they are father and son is of no more interest to her than if they were lovers or brothers, strangers or friends.

I focus here on *Finding Nemo* because I believe that popular culture, particularly non-earnest and non-serious popular culture, can offer narratives and images for the project of thinking through what J. K. Gibson- Graham call 'non-capitalist imaginaries'. Furthermore, *Finding Nemo*, covertly harbours a transgender narrative about transformation. Clownfish, we learn from a new book by transgender theoretical ecologist, Joan Roughgarden, are one of many species of fish who can and often do change sex. Roughgarden's wonderful study of evolutionary diversity explains that most biologists observe 'nature' through a narrow and biased lens of socio-normativity and they therefore misinterpret all kinds of bio-diversity. Transsexual fish, hermaphroditic hyenas, non-monogamous birds, homosexual lizards all play a role in the survival and evolution of the species but mostly their function has been misunderstood and folded into rigid and unimaginative familial schemes of reproductive zeal and the survival of the fittest. Roughgarden explains that human observers misread competition into often cooperative activities, they misunderstand the relations between strength and dominance and they overestimate the primacy of reproductive dynamics. In the case of the clownfish, according to Roughgarden, the mating couple does tend to be monogamous; so much so that if the female partner should perish (as she does in *Finding Nemo*), the male fish will transsex and become female. She will then mate with one of her offspring to recreate a kinship circuit. Roughgarden explains clownfish behaviour, along with all kinds of other such morphing and shifting, less as evidence of the dominance of the reproductive circuit and more as an adaptive process of affiliation that creates stable community rather than familial structures.

Roughgarden's remarkable readings of bio-diversity and 'social' as opposed to 'sexual' selection ask us to reconsider the very process of evolution as well as the nature and function of diversity. Dory, for example, the helpful bluefish in *Finding Nemo*, becomes recognizable in her relation to family if we use Roughgarden's narratives of social cooperation and the sharing of resources within any given animal community to replace hackneyed notions of the dominance of the biological family, the centrality and stability of the parent–child bonds and the deliberate exclusions of non-relatives. *Finding Nemo*, with its subtle critique of Oedipal narratives of pleasure and danger, with its inspiring visions of collective fish rebellions and with its queer models of friendship and affiliation, and with its emphasis on the here and nowness of political relations, speaks directly to a queer feminist imaginary and the possibilities of social change. In this film, as in a number of blockbuster films of the last few years, memory is linked in very material ways to the project of re-imagining kinship.

It is significant that in both *Finding Nemo* and *Fifty First Dates* the drama of short-term memory loss plays out against the backdrop of the missing mother and in relation to a host of transgender characters. The mother, in both films, comes to represent the relation to the past and when she dies, memory dies with her. And the transgender characters in each film represent the disorder that the death of the mother introduces into the system. Forgetting can easily be cast as a tool of dominant culture, a mode of oppression, but it is also a necessary distraction from the weight of the past and the menace of the future. In *The History of Forgetting*, Norman Klein links the uncertainty of memory to the fragility of place in ever-changing urban landscapes. Klein rejects an empiricist project of salvaging memory and instead turns to a method he mines from Borges, namely 'selective forgetting' and he writes: 'selective forgetting is a literary tool for describing a social imaginary: how fictions are turned into facts, while in turn erasing facts into fictions' (Klein, 1997: 16). And Nietzsche reminds us that forgetting can be 'active and that in its "active" mode it serves as a "preserver of psychic order" '. Indeed, for Nietzsche, there can be no 'happiness, no cheerfulness, no hope, no pride, no present, without forgetfulness'

(2003). If we take up forgetting as an act, as a productive force, we can then understand the 'forgetting' films as opportunities to rethink, restage and resist the reproductive imperative and its grim emphases on cyclical time, family space and normative development while producing new queer social imaginaries.

All of these films cast forgetfulness as an affliction associated with immaturity, adolescence even and all recommend hetero marriage as a way of fixing, once and for all, the jarring sensation of waking up every day and not knowing who you are, where you have been and where you are going. I suggest that the link between feminism and transgenderism might be rethought through a resistance to the historical/Oedipal fix which demands that each generation of feminism set itself up in opposition to each new version of gender variance; transgenderism, as we see in the comic films discussed here, often functions as a symbol of transformation itself and feminism, in recent years, has been cast as an obstacle to change and as a conservation project. A transgender feminism is one invested in change, motion, collectivity and queer temporalities; in this sense, we can take our cues from Dory by resting a while in the weird but hopeful temporal space of the lost, the forgotten and the unmoored.

Notes

1. 'Boi' is a term that entered queer vernacular fairly recently and it can refer to a boyish gay man or a female born person with masculine but not mannish features. It has become part of a generational conversation about categories and categorization itself.
2. Janice Raymond basically saw MTF transsexuals as part of a medical conspiracy to infiltrate women's space and replace women with men. She saw MTF's, furthermore, as tools of patriarchy and saw their attempt to become women as imperialist and violent. She had less to say about FTM transsexuals but did cast them as confused lesbians.
3. See Seth Koven (1992: 376).
4. Otto Weininger's book, *Sex and Character*, was immensely popular at the beginning of the twentieth century. He wrote this book originally as a PhD dissertation and showed it to Freud who advised him to do more research to back up some of the book's more outrageous claims. The book made connections between Judaism and femininity and Christianity and masculinity and fed into discourses about degeneration, anti-semitism and politically motivated misogyny. Weininger committed suicide shortly after the book's publication but it went on to influence all kinds of early twentieth-century intellectuals including Gertrude Stein.
5. For her critique of sexology see Faderman (1981); for different readings of sexology and medical discourse see Chauncey (1989); Duggan (1993).

6. In recent years, Michigan Women's Music Festival, an annual event that has traditionally been 'for women only', has become a target of trans groups and trans women in particular who seek to be admitted to the festival under an expanded notion of 'womanhood'. These debates about who counts as a woman have often turned vicious and trans activists have set up a protest camp at the entrance to the festival named 'Camp Trans'.
7. Valerie Solanas was the author of the notorious SCUM Manifesto which called for the abolition of men. SCUM stands for the Society for the Cutting Up of Men. Solanas was considered too extreme for liberal feminism, too violent for cultural feminism and too crazy for lesbian feminism. She shot Andy Warhol after he refused to return the only copy of a play she had written, Up Your Ass. For more on Solanas see Avital Ronell's introduction to the latest reissue of SCUM Manifesto by Verso Press in 2004.

6
The Value of a Second Skin

Rosemary Hennessy

Toward a social ontology: material for feminist–queer intersection

The human person is never merely an individual but lives always in social relation. How we understand those relations affects how we act to change them. My work in the university and in communities outside it has been supported by thinking social relations through feminism, historical materialism, queer studies, and the 'good sense' of working people. Together they offer a powerful explanation of what it means to be human. All begin with the premise that human beings make history, though not necessarily under conditions of our own choosing. The continued survival of humans as a species depends on meeting human needs or what Marx referred to as the requirements of our 'species being'. Expanding upon Marx, some feminist social theorists have recently called this way of seeing human history 'social ontology' (Bakker and Gil, 2003: 17). Ontology in the philosophical sense involves the study of the nature of existence. The notion of social ontology conceptualizes the constituents of existence as social being; it underscores the social relations through which the needs of human 'being' are met. These relations span political economy, juridical and cultural forms: where work mediates the social and natural orders and becomes labour; where legal and disciplinary regimes regulate action, mobility, life and death; where individuals become subjects, and bodies become meaningful through and against normative prescriptions. Social ontology also addresses the dialectical relationship between the actions of human beings upon the social world and its mediation of human agency.

As human beings we work and desire, we have needs and sensations. All at the same time. But modern culture has been shaped by paradigms that separate these activities and capacities. This is itself a historical consequence. Over the course of capitalism's development desire and labour, sensation and need have been isolated from one another in the prevailing ways of making sense of the self and society. This segregation is not accidental nor is it simply philosophical. It is best understood as a historical effect consolidated some time in the nineteenth century and not coincidentally at the dawning of consumer capitalism. It has registered in the irreconcilability of the two great western analytics of desire and need – psychoanalysis and Marxism – and more recently in the tenuous relationship between two major discourses of social movement: feminism and queer theory.

Marx situates the labouring subject at the centre of capitalism's social relations and relegates gender and sexuality to the footnotes of his analysis where its bearing on market exchange is noted but not theorized. With few exceptions (such as the Frankfurt school and in particular the work of Herbert Marcuse (1966)), most of the tradition of Marxist thought throughout the next century will all but ignore sexuality. Socialist and marxist feminism intervened in this situation by making visible the gendered division of labour and its value as a cultural and ideological system. But the voices within these feminist traditions that confronted sexuality as a problem were few and far between.

In the late twentieth century, some intellectuals' discontent with this bracketing of sexuality in social theory, many of them influenced by the gay liberation movement yet critical of the identity politics that overtook it, argued that explanations of human being must also take into account economies of desire and identification in such a way as to speak to the differences suppressed by their heteronormative organization. They embraced the sign 'queer' and recast its value, transforming shame into a standpoint for critique. Queer theory emerged as a critical effort to de-naturalize how we think about sexuality, posing it as an unstable symbolic construction and cultural effect. It offered a critique of the 'straight mind', that is, of heterosexuality as a normative regime and of the arbitrary and neat distinctions it enforces.[1] It also opened the monolithic identities 'lesbian' and 'gay' to the ways they are inflected by heterosexual norms, race and ethnic differences.

Queer theory is far from being a monolithic discourse. Yet, as I argue in my book, *Profit and Pleasure* (2000), underneath the debates there is often a recurring set of assumptions that separates the critical understanding of sexuality from capitalism. For example, Judith Halberstam presents 'queer' along these lines when she asserts that a 'queer way of life' encompasses 'subcultural practices, alternative methods of alliance, forms of transgender embodiment, and those forms of representation dedicated to capturing these willfully eccentric modes of being' (Halberstam, 2005: 1). While Halberstam tells us that the times and places of queer subcultures inhabit the 'logics of labor and reproduction' under capitalism, or may even open spaces outside of capitalism, the force of her insights pertains almost exclusively to the 'non-normative logics and organizations of community, sexual identity, embodiment and activity' (ibid.: 6). In this respect, her work is fairly representative of the main drift of the discourses of queer studies.

It is not insignificant that much work in queer studies also embraces what Halberstam calls 'a developed understanding of the local, non-metropolitan ... and the situated' (ibid.: 12) a way of knowing that pits the local against the global and advocates cultural investigation and political intervention that is particular and specific. Halberstam underscores this point when she argues that work on globalization inevitably skims the surface of local variations and reproduces its homogenizing effects (ibid.: 12). But surely we should think twice before closing off the possibility of understanding the relation of a subculture's particularities to the dominant social relations of which it is a part or against which it manoeuvres? We know that capital accumulation is global in scale and that it proceeds by way of strategies aimed at specific local sites, at infiltrating local communities and subcultures and inviting community members to see only as far as their immediate and particular interests— for jobs, for 'convenient' and 'affordable' commodities, even for the valorisation of a 'subculture'. Coca Cola and Wal-Mart are only two examples among many. No inevitable homogenization necessarily follows if we tackle the impact of these multinationals on specific communities, nor is there any point in pretending their effects are sufficiently understood if we see only the local particulars.[2]

The tradition of historical materialist feminism has long recognized and continued to develop analyses that connect capitalism's transnational reach to its local impacts.[3] Materialist feminism's accounts of gender insist that we take into account that most of the world's poor are women and that the socially necessary domestic labour of reproducing labour power remains primarily women's work; that homeworking, also primarily women's work, has become a requisite ancillary sector for assembly production, while in the service economy women predominate among the casual workers and freelancers who revolve like satellites on part-time contracts around a shrinking core of permanent workers; that the traffic in women's bodies remains a major facet of global trade and is controlled by transnational syndicates that make profits by the billions. Materialist feminists argue that these facts beg for a social ontology that addresses the interface of normative regimes with these relations of labour and their impact on the particular relations through which human life is sustained in the everyday lives of women and men.

Celebrating local communities as self-defined spaces for affirmation, cultural identity or political resistance can play into capitalism's opportunistic use of localizing – not just to open sites for production or new market niches but as a way of knowing. Local ways of knowing can have a powerful appeal because they authorize groups that have been disenfranchised and excluded from public times and spaces. They enable those of us who have been marginalized, dehumanized and excluded to seize a certain degree of public legitimacy, to speak and act on our own behalf. They call attention to oppression. But they also have a limited political scope. The challenge is to articulate the particular histories we most immediately live and experience to the less visible social relations they are shaped by and support.

Recent work in queer studies is re-examining some of the presuppositions in what we might call its main current and advancing this sort of materialist analysis of gender and sexuality, one that articulates their mediation by (and of) capitalist social relations. It is here that the politically urgent discourses of materialist feminism and queer studies converge. This materialist direction in queer studies situates analyses of specific sexual formations in relation to globalization's exploitative relations and imperial histories as they are shaped by race and ethnicity and the changing relations of labour throughout the modern period, including neo-liberal and neo-imperial capitalism's new bargains with the state. Examples include Kevin Floyd's (forthcoming) analysis of the roots of queer politics in the emergence of consumer culture; the late Lionel Cantú's (2002) work on the impact of migration, structural adjustment policies and the Mexican government's development of the tourism industry on the commodification of Mexican 'gay' culture and space; and Roderick Ferguson's (2003) treatment of the consolidation of a racialized heteronormative patriarchy within Marxism, sociology and revolutionary nationalist movements. Materialist work in queer studies affirms its debt to feminism, to lesbian and gay social movement, and like Ferguson and others, probes this history. Engaging a 'new gender politics' that acknowledges the persistence of gender discrimination against women and also calls attention to normative violence against transgender and transsexual identities that do not neatly align with normative prescriptions, materialist queer studies insists that no politics will get us very far without a critical purchase on the ways gender and sexual formations, whether normative, non-normative, new or traditional, feature in capitalism.

As capitalism's modernizing impulses aggressively invade bodies and pleasures and enmesh properly flexible subjects in neo-liberal and neo-imperial structures of feeling and desire, sectors of value in the ontology of humanness are being formed that often elude critical examination. We need analyses that can address those zones where exchange value and cultural value, labour and desire, meet. Here are crucial local-global sites that any effort to assess the damage to individual and collective modes of being human and to forge alternative social relations must take into account. Along with other materialist critics, I am suggesting that we pursue this work by beginning not with a subcultural community of queers or with women, but with human needs. That is, in terms of a 'social ontology' that will allow us to connect local (individual and collective) identity formations to the relations of social reproduction to which they are bound. My reading of gender and sexual identity as what I call a 'second skin' is a contribution to those efforts to situate the value attached to the identities through which everyday experience is being narrated in some particular localities (in this case in northern Mexico) in such a social ontology, placing the lived and contested cultural values of identity in relation to the surplus value capital relies upon. Here the critically urgent insights of feminism and queer studies intersect.

Let me begin to elaborate by first turning to two threads in recent work in queer studies from which this notion of 'second skin' is derived. One is re-examining the social constructionist premise of queer theory, the other is reopening the question of value. The phrase 'second skin' is the title of a book by Jay Prosser (1998) on the body narratives of transsexuals. Prosser's analysis is also a critical reading, or re-reading, of the social constructionist paradigm that overtook theories of gender in the past twenty years or so, a paradigm spurred on by the publication and reception of Judith Butler's *Gender Trouble* in 1990. Prosser reads social constructionism as an important critique of the positivist notion that biology determines gender. But along with other transsexual critics, he emphasizes that the unfortunate effect has been to replace the scientific concept of gender as the expression of a natural core identity with a new understanding of gender as a purely discursive reiterative practice (Brandenburg, 2004: 21).[4] Lost in this account of gender, which has so comprehensively influenced queer studies, is the relation between psyche and body in shaping gender identity. Sven Brandenburg, another theorist of transsexual identity, argues that queer theory was incapable of accounting for the irreconcilable gap between the 'felt' gendered perception (gender identity) of the transsexual and the visual perception of the physical body that stands in contrast to it (Brandenburg, 2004: 24). The salient point of this critique of queer studies is not to revert to the body as the generator of identity, but rather to re-examine the ways the social constructionist argument closed off the complex interfaces between the values encoded in bodies and identities.

Recent work in queer studies by Janet Jakobsen (2005) and Miranda Joseph (2002) on the question of value also calls our attention to embodiment. In separate publications each returns us to Gayatri Spivak's 1985 essay, 'Scattered Speculations on the Question of Value'.[5] Although I am critical of Spivak's argument in many respects, like Jakobsen and Joseph I am interested in her speculation on the relation between domination and exploitation, a relation that Spivak posits as complicitous rather than analogous. One of Spivak's concerns in this essay is what she calls 'the materialist predication of the subject'. She contends that the moment when capital is fully developed arises when the subject as labour power is 'freed' to produce surplus labour, that is when the subject is predicated as 'super adequate to itself', in other words, as a subject who desires to sell its labour power (Spivak, 1987: 162). It is here in the 'use value' of a subject 'super adequate to itself' that cultural value plays a crucial role in that the use value of labour power itself is determined by dominating cultural values. As Jakobsen notes, Spivak reads domination as a tool of exploitation and 'in some sense preceding exploitation' (Jakobsen, 2002: 58). Jakobsen underscores that in 'de-naturalizing' labour and opening it up to domination, Spivak's argument 'leads to the question of embodiment, of how bodies that labor are themselves produced in relation to the differential production of value' (Jakobsen, 2002: 57). Embodiment, Jakobsen reminds us, is always itself a double discourse articulated in domination as abjection, 'as a splitting that abstracts the subject from that which it excludes (the abject) even as it (the abject) is inscribed within the subject' (Jakobsen, 2002: 58). The 'abject' designates what has been expelled from the body, discharged as excrement, literally rendered 'Other.' Through this expulsion the alien is effectively established as a 'not me', a 'not me' that sets up the boundaries of the body which are the first contours of the subject (Butler, 1990: 133). As a mechanism by which the subject's bodily boundaries are established and dominated, abjection is a social and normative process. This concept of abjection has been extended to understand the social repudiation of bodies for their sex and/or colour as an 'expulsion' followed by a 'repulsion'. It is this mechanism of abjection, by which the subject harbours and expels a 'not me', that is inscribed within the social mandate to sell a part of one's human capacities, a mandate I suggest we consider analogous to 'taking on' and 'giving over' a second skin. In this respect, what Spivak calls the 'material predication of the subject' opens the door to the abstraction of value from labour power (Jakobsen, 2002: 58). Through the social processes of abjection, domination becomes complicit with exploitation because it produces embodied subjects that can be exploited (Jakobsen, 2002: 58).

The important point here is the speculation that 'exploitation is never itself 'value free' because it is *both* dependent on *and* structured by values carried by the normatively inscribed, the dominated, body' (Jakobsen, 2002: 58 original emphasis). Capitalism would not make sense, would not work, if the disciplining of the body to enter the market, to sell the second skin of one's labour power, were not underway. As I use it, the phrase 'second skin' pursues these critical re-visions at the intersection of feminism and queer theory. It directs us toward the imaginary construction of abjection as a precarious relationship to one's body, not only within a field of images and representations but within a set of social relations of labour as well. As I turn to the value attached to the embodied identities through which everyday experience is being narrated in some particular localities in northern Mexico, I am reading within such a social ontology, placing the lived and contested cultural values of identity within the fundamental logic of the extraction of surplus value, the source of profit.

In my book *Profit and Pleasure* (2000) I looked at the incorporation of queer subjects into the marketplaces and consumer niches in advanced capitalist sectors over the last decades of the twentieth century and the economies of visibility that process depends upon. The corporate marketing to gays, lesbians, queers, trans and other flexible subjects is part of an international division of labour in which Mexican maquiladora[6] workers participate. The fuller elaboration of this relationship would have to address the operation of the 'second skin' of value across this international division of labour, in the relations that bind the debates over gay legitimacy and the value of gay workers as labour power in the one-third world's advanced sectors to the values embedded in the feminization of the workforce in the maquilas.

Standing with and for maquiladora workers

I encountered the people whose narratives I will share through an international coalition that introduced me to grassroots organizations in four maquiladora communities along Mexico's northern border. Almost all of the people I talked to were or had been involved in groups that were members of this coalition. I began to record their stories from a sense that the sparks flying here are ignited in part by something that rarely appears in training manuals, theories, or formal lessons. Something that eludes the critical frameworks I have just been discussing, something almost impossible to name, that I still only vaguely call passionate politics. In tracking this elusive fabric of organizing I did a version of what ethnographers do. I collected narratives through visits and interviews. I attended meetings, hung out, and lived with a family for a stretch. I took notes. I was involved in the lives of the people whose narratives I heard to different degrees, and I still am. I am a member of one of the cooperatives that formed in the wake of a strike at one maquila, and I continue to work with many of these groups through the international coalition, through email, and occasional visits.

My relationships to those whose narratives I represent here are of course part of the story; they filter nuances and navigate distances, from *gringa profesora*, to *companera, madrina*, friend and partner. I knew that whatever I made of the stories I told through those mediations would not have the same authority as workers' testimonies. And so this project spurred on another, a collaborative collection of workers and farmers' reports, testimonies, analyses in their own words entitled *NAFTA From Below* (2005). Both projects raise the question: can one be of the one-third world and for the two-thirds world? If the answer is 'yes,' as it surely must be, how to exercise that alliance is far from settled. I agree with Chandra Mohanty that in a tightly integrated capitalist system the particular standpoints of poor, indigenous, and two-thirds world women provide the most inclusive view of power. This is a claim, she reminds us, grounded in historical materialism: 'Narratives of historical experience are crucial to political thinking not because they present an unmediated version of the 'truth' but because they can destabilize received truths and locate debate in the complexities and contradictions of historical life' (Mohanty, 2003: 244). They can write subjects into history against the grain of their normative predications. They can create openings, make waves.

The passionate politics of organizing in the maquilas

By the time we crossed the bridge into Mexico Fela had been waiting for hours and she looked tired when we picked her up and continued driving to the beauty shop on the far side of Nuevo Laredo in Colonia Peru. Carmen's *estetica* is huddled in a row of stores along the railroad, on one side a small food stand and on the other a taco place. When we pulled up it looked at first like no one was there. But in a few seconds, sure enough, a short, dark man peeked out and after a moment's hesitation gave us a shy welcome before slipping away to summon Carmen. She arrived in a flourish, a wave of energy swooshing into the room with warm embraces all around. Fela laughed and commented on the new name, but Carmen dismissed it as she summoned her *esposo*[7] – 'Mi Amor, ven!!' – proudly announcing that she is pregnant, and stretching her shirt across her belly to reveal a slightly plump *panza* as the evidence of this miraculous conception. She beckoned me, 'Sit here, *hija*',[8] motioning to the spot next to her, and began to tell about the years she worked at a garment factory in Nuevo Laredo that was a major supplier for Wal-Mart. Her job was sewing waistbands, pockets and zippers on pants and sleeping bags, sometimes made of camouflage material.

'*I was a worker at Fabricas de Calidad*', she begins, '*and I always introduced myself with my real name. I said my name is Andrés Rosales Martínez at your service. I am a homosexual and a homosexual is like any person. I am one person who says we are workers and we have to accomplish something. If we are going to do that – all the people – we'll have to put nerves aside. A person who is homosexual does not have to be humiliated and I was humiliated in all my rights physically and morally.*' Carmen reports that workers in production were paid 350 pesos a week and a 50 peso bonus for meeting the quotas. '*In one night you had to finish 1000 shirts, if not they disciplined you. Do you think a salary of 350 pesos ($US 35) and a bonus of 50 pesos ($US 5) was enough?*' she says, voice rising. '*With fifty miserable pesos I can't clean my ass!*'

'*They gave you pills that were vitamins*', she continues, '*they made us work at 100% capacity with these vitamins. Things worked out to perfection! We were two or three days without sleep. It was pure work and they fucked us until something happened to Ofelia. With the women it was too much because they were giving them a pill supposedly to sleep, and with that pill they didn't get their periods, las pobres, or when they did get their periods they were bleeding so much it was like they were having a miscarriage, and the only thing they were telling them was, "Espera me afuera" [wait for me outside] and they were bleeding with big spots of blood all over their clothes.*'

'*So now my friend, Ofelia, was working two days de puro trabajo y pura pastilla without sleep and she was shaking and shaking and then half of her body was paralyzed. But instead of taking her to the hospital the union delegate took her to the kitchen and he was saying to her, "Don't be a clown!!"*

"Don't be faking!" Ofelia was Pati's partner; she was lesbian. It was something where you were saying "Why did this happen to her? Why was she paralyzed? Why were they making her work more with the pills? Why?" Something that you cannot accept.'

When the workers at Fabricas de Calidad went on strike in 1999 Carmen was one of the leaders.[9] Events came to a head when the owners sold the company and refused to give the workers their legally mandated severance pay. When it seemed they were simply moving the company to another plant and just giving it a new name, the workers united and said *'Enough! Either give us our severance pay or hire us in this new plant!'* They mobilized for 43 days. They drew up a list of grievances and a criminal complaint against the manager for the amphetamines that paralyzed Ofelia and gave her co-worker, Gloria, a miscarriage. Carmen was among them and in the front, one of the women. But then he was Andrés. He and Caretino were the only gays, the only men involved in the movement.

When they went to the bosses with a lawyer, Carmen recounts, the bosses said, *' "Why, Andrés, why do you have so much anger? Why did you stir up all the workers?" The lawyer replied for me: "Remember how you humiliated him when you told him you are a homosexual, a shit?" The humiliation for being openly gay was continuous. They would say that I pooped my pants. They were telling me I was a normal shit or diarrhea. If I was putting up with all that it was because I had to. But then I said no one is going to humiliate me any more, no one is going to step on my rights any more. I am a person, a citizen. My mistake or not mistake was to be gay.'*

In the end the workers got the embargo, and the company had to give everyone 100 per cent severance pay. What is remarkable about the Fabricas de Calidad mobilization is that the rights of gay workers were on the list of demands and that two openly homosexual men were respected leaders. As Carmen says, *'We were in the front and we ... showed them that as homosexuals we are here in Laredo Mexico! And many people supported us and many were saying, "Keep going! Ser adelante, mi hija." '*

If Carmen's story makes visible the fact of gay identified workers in the maquilas it also highlights the ways abjection is folded into the conditions of exploitation. The bosses humiliated Carmen by representing her to herself as that which has been expelled from the (social) body, as the abject, the alien. But this was not a novel representation; indeed it was already in place in the cultural system outside the factory. Mary Douglas suggests that the body is a synecdoche for all social systems and that all social systems are vulnerable at their boundaries. In this cultural logic bodily margins are specifically invested with power and danger (cited in Butler, 1990: 132). Any kind of unregulated permeability can constitute a site of pollution. Moreover, bodily orifices are mapped in terms that constitute heterosexual gender exchange. The boss's abjection of Carmen pursues this cultural logic and it is one that she both acknowledges and rejects. Her exclamation, 'I am a person, a citizen' in relation to the 'mistake or not mistake' of being gay underscores her dis-identification from this abjection, a dis-identification that she enacts when she refuses to 'put up with this' and recasts the 'second skin' that dispossesses her.

Carmen's self-representation also suggests that the notion of a feminized workforce as female needs to be re-examined. Much has been written about the impact of the gendered division of labour on women workers in the maquiladoras.[10] Little or no research has been done on the cultures of same-sex desire in this massive female workforce. Are the maquilas where thousands of women have worked together day after day a breeding ground for lesbians? In this concentrated all-female work environment did women develop new or different affective and sexual relationships with one another? Is 'lesbian' an adequate term for them if they did? How did these relationships feature in the dynamics of organizing? At what point did 'gay' men enter the maquila workforce? And how? Are gay identified men and lesbians 'out' at work in the maquilas, and what are the consequences if they are? How does sexual identity, no matter how unstable a category, feature in the work cultures of the maquilas? And in the extraction of surplus value?

These are very general questions. Answers would need to take into account particular differences across regions, cities and industries. In Mexico assumptions and practices about non- normative sexuality are unevenly shared, sometimes don't travel very far, and are inflected by varied local historical influences. Practices and concepts that may be commonplace in northern border towns do not necessarily hold in Mexico City or the Yucatan, and cultural variations between *mestizo* and indigenous groups are considerable. The reification of sexuality that was one of the conditions for the emergence of homo and heterosexual identities around the turn of the twentieth century in Europe and the United States also took hold in urban centres in Mexico in the early twentieth century as the state defined previously untaxonomized sectors and behaviours to regulate the national body, but they were reified along a different trajectory than the ones many North American and European theorists have charted. The bonds between sexuality and gender remained more integrated through the rules of traditional *machista* patriarchal culture, and sexual identity has not been displaced from family alliances along the paths of scientific and clinical discourse as in the North. [11]

If big business in the United States has realized that 'there is more value in incorporating queers who will work for them since that at least creates the possibility of an alternative market' (Quiroga, 2000: 7), capital's trajectory in Mexico is not quite that, or not yet. Many treatments of neo-liberal capitalism's impact make use of a North–South paradigm to measure the emergence of 'new' families and lifestyles in the service economy of the North against a feminized industrial workforce in the South, freed from the constraints of domestic production yet still bound by traditional heterogender norms at work and by the reproductive labour of daughter, wife and mother at home. However, changes in the gendered division of labour in the maquila workforce invite us to rethink the concept of the 'feminization of labour'.

From the inception of the Border Industrialization Program in 1965 through the next decade, the overwhelming majority of unskilled production workers in the maquiladoras were women. Women were construed as more docile toward authority and as a temporary workforce whose primary interests lay in family and home. At the same time, the 'femininity' that was recruited had to do with a set of meanings that were dislodging femininity from the home and traditional family production and reconstituting it as a set of characteristics that could ostensibly apply to men or women: dexterous, docile, tolerant and cheap (Salzinger, 2003: 37). Men were the preferred labour force in firms making transportation equipment, leather and synthetic goods, wood and metal furniture, photographic, sporting, and paper goods (Pearson, 1995: 140). In those sectors where labour was the major portion of manufacturing costs, women workers predominated.

Now, however, the proportions are changing. The majority of maquiladora workers are still women, but almost half are men. The gradual changeover began to happen in the 1980s when the demand for maquila workers increased but the market of women willing to work in the factories was saturated. Ultimately, the demand for cheap labour made adjustments in the demographics of the workforce inevitable (Salzinger, 2003: 43). By the 1990s women workers had already proven to be less 'docile', as their involvement in strikes and work stoppages indicates, but at the same time the standard profile of the maquiladora worker had been set. Men were being hired, but the profile of 'feminine' expectations continued to define the preferred worker. This 'feminine' ideal was an imaginary phantom by which cheap, disposable labour could be extracted.

When I asked a group of workers from Sara Lee, makers of Hanes garments, in Frontera, Coahuila how many workers there are in their plant they replied, '*40 percent men, 50 percent women and 10 percent gays*'. This unprompted naming of gays surprised me. I asked Horacio how they knew there were 10 per cent gays in the plant and he said it was obvious. '*The gays are men who look and act feminine.*' He said there are lesbians too and you know them '*because they look and act masculine.*' We went on to talk about the possible intricacies of this gendered division, but the nonchalance with which 'gays' (even if understood in these het-eronormative terms) were included in the population of workers seemed notable. He said while gays are accepted at work there is no politics around their presence, either in the organizing in the factory or in the community. Nelly Benitez, an out lesbian, former maquiladora worker and organizer in Nuevo Laredo, agrees. '*There are lots of gays and lesbians in Nuevo Laredo,*' she says; '*it's a really big community, but they have a social not a political presence.*' When she worked in the maquilas, Nelly said, there was a group of lesbians who would hang out on their breaks together. Everyone knew they were gay. Sometimes they were harassed. Some of the lesbian workers would talk about the fact that they don't have the same rights as married workers – health insurance for their partners, for example. But while the politics of sexuality has featured in the workshops Nelly has helped organize, it has focused on sexual harassment and women's reproductive rights, not these concerns.

Another former maquila worker, Mariana, says she saw changes in the maquila workforce over the several generations she worked there. '*By the 1990s,*' she says, '*the culture inside the maquilas was changing. There was the biggest invasion of maquilas to the border cities during this decade and they really needed workers. It was then that the informal filters that kept gay men out started to relax. Of course there was no official policy against hiring gays, but informally this was the practice. They would even write it in the comments on the application. But by the 1990s the maquilas needed all the workers they could get, and gay men started appearing as operators on the line along with the women. By then the lesbians were more open, too.*' Another worker, Iván, from Reynosa, theorizes that gay men in the 1990s became the 'new women' of the maquilas. Homosexual men who are 'open' have typically few options for work. But during these years they entered the maquilas and were welcomed. As he puts it, '*The more dependent you are on the work the more you are going to be here, and gay men cannot risk having work outside. So they inverted the role and exchanged women for gays.*' Two years after Iván offered this observation, as many maquilas on the border are closing or moving, another organizer reported that 30 workers at one factory in Reynosa were fired after having been singled out as 'gay'.

Iván also stated that when he worked in the maquilas in the early 1990s gay men were being recruited into management positions. When I asked him how he understands this he responds that of course it is a matter of class. *'There is a saying,'* he says, *'that goes "how they see you they treat you." This has a lot to do with class. But it also has to do with the question of identity. One thing can't be separated from the other. It would be,'* he sums up, *'like eating cheese without cheese. Without the flavor of cheese it tastes like milk.'* Iván's oblique comment points to some of the complex mediations that organize the relation between domination and exploitation, between perception and being, stressing as he does that the politics of sexual identity is a matter of class position and that class position is relational. The lived being of sexual identity – how they see you and treat you – is filtered by class, a difference that splits cheese into 'not cheese', into cheese that tastes like milk. In other words, for Iván the visibility of 'gay' workers or managers in the factory does not simply turn on the epistemology of the closet, for the substance that matters is the ground this body stands on – whether on the side of labour or management.

The second skin of labour power

While he did not address sexuality *per se*, what Marx has to say about what he called the 'queer commodity' labour power is pertinent, and I want now to turn briefly to that for it brings us back to the concept of the body's value as it is incorporated in the worker's second skin. First and foremost, Marx tells us in *Capital* Volume 1, commodities are things. They cannot go to market themselves, but 'must have recourse to their guardians, who are the possessors of commodities. Because commodities are things, they therefore lack the power to resist man. If they are unwilling, he can use force; in other words, he can take possession of them' (Marx, 1977: 178). At this point Marx adds a footnote: 'In the twelfth century, so renowned for its piety, very delicate things often appear among these commodities. Thus a French poet of the period enumerates among the commodities to be found in the fair of Lendit, alongside clothing, shoes, leather, implements of cultivation, skins, etc. were *'femmes folles de leur corps'* (Marx, 1977: 178).

What are we to make of this 'wonton woman' wedged obliquely into the midst of Marx's explanation of commodities? Her body is in the market fair, but she is outside the body of the text, exiled to the bottom of the page, beside the point, her place in a revolutionary theory of the commodity left to trail off, an afterthought, unthought. We can imagine Marx stumbling upon the text of this anonymous twelfth-century French poet one day in the British Museum, perhaps in a moment when he needed a break from Ricardo and Smith, and finding her there. A distraction, perhaps a curiosity, even a delight. Nonetheless, he gives us her in the Lendit market, one delicate thing among the rough wares at the fair, her delicate-ness inseparable from her body and her labour, her '*corps*,' and perhaps inseparable from her person as well. This attachment between '*femmes*' and '*corps*' seems in any case a rather loose one. Loose, too, is her connection to the commodity as she is like and yet different from the leather, tools and skins that are being traded. Should she one day centuries later go to work in a factory, the imprint of 'delicate thing' and this 'loose' relation to her body will go with her, perhaps even mark her as a preferred worker. Her value will be in the very cell structure of her second skin, the commodity labour power she exchanges for a wage. This 'second skin' will mark her as already not completely her own guardian, but rather only loosely in possession of herself.

Within the marketplaces of capitalism commodities are exchanged. The commodity the worker brings to exchange for a wage is her power to labour. In chapter 6 of *Capital* Volume 1 'The Sale and Purchase of Labor-Power', Marx explains: 'we mean by labour-power, or labour-capacity, the aggregate of those mental and physical capabilities existing in *the physical form, the living personality*, of a human being, capabilities which he sets in motion whenever he produces a use value of any kind' (Marx, 1977: 270, emphasis mine). Marx understands labour power to include both a physical dimension and this other part that he calls 'the living personality'. In order for the worker to sell his labour power, Marx says, he must have it at his disposal, 'he must be the *free proprietor of his own labour-capacity, hence of his person*' (Marx, 1977: 271, emphasis mine). For Marx, when the worker and the capitalist meet in the market, they enter into relations with each other 'on an equal footing as owners of commodities. Both are therefore equal in the eyes of the law' (Marx, 1977: 271). But clearly this is not a relationship between equals. As Spivak's argument on the 'predication of the subject' reminds us, the subject who enters the marketplace ready to sell his or her labour power is already dominated, his or her body disposed and somewhat dispossessed. In order to offer his or her labour power for sale the worker has had already to 'abject' it. Moreover, as Carmen/Andrés recognizes, some citizens are further abjected from the social body, considered a 'mistake' in their very being. The 'real individuality' of our particular living personalities that accompanies labour power is a corporeal, meaningful second skin. It is supplemental in the sense that it is both an extra and requisite. Seemingly irrelevant to one's ability to assemble wiring, sew sleeves, wait tables, flip burgers, or ... this second skin is an aspect of a worker's subjectivity that can be claimed by someone else, managed and disciplined. Sutured to the particularity of our human capacities, it is simultaneously at risk of being out of our hands.

Free market exchange relies on and takes advantage of the political and cultural dispossession of certain subjects, a dispossession that registers in the body. This dispossession is the effect of the process of abjection-domination I referred to earlier. The 'second skin' of femininity is embodied, but not anchored in biology. It pertains to gender but also organizes sexual identity. When a feminized second skin accompanies the exchange of labour power for a wage, it offers a tacit promise to the buyer that the supervision of the physical life and living personality of the bearer of this commodity is out of her hands. To bear a feminized second skin is to doubly forfeit claim to one's capacities. There is a degree to which they are more fully loosened from one's possession than is the case for a worker who is not feminized. This dispossession lowers the cost of labour power and so enhances the value added to whatever commodities the feminized worker produces. Feminized workers are not only the subjects of surplus labour; they are more accurately the hyper-exploited.

The second skin of femininity enshrouds the value of labour outside the marketplace as well – in the non-productive circuits of capital that nourish, reproduce, and care for workers, children, the elderly and sick: in the street, the bedroom and the kitchen. This is the case for Carmen. *'My mother said I prefer to see you dead rather than a homosexual, and my brother said if I see you dressed like a woman I will kill you,'* she says. *'But in the zona roja this is what I wore. I never asked for a taco from them. I was the one who was giving to them. When my twin sister was in the hospital I went and she said, "What you are doing here in the hospital if you are a pinche joto? I am ashamed. You are a piece of shit," and I said, "I was the one who was paying the bills." And then she cried and cried and said, "I didn't know." I told them I was in the red zone working as a prostitute and all of them were able to eat from my fucking in the Papagayo and the Siete Negro.'*

Sex and sexual identity are for Carmen inseparable from her labour, as maquiladora worker, as sex worker, and as son. She is the only one who cares for her father, and he is dying. *'At Christmas time every night he would wake up crying and shaking me like this,'* she says and shakes the arm of the *esposo* who is still sitting there, eyes wide. *'He begs to die. When I ask my brothers or sister to come and care for him they say "No – es bien feo!" I bathe him and wash his ass and clean up the excrement. I am the only son who does this. I am the homosexual and I am the only son who cares for him.'* The *esposo* shakes his head. He, too, it seems has a part in this care for the father who is waiting for death in the long hours of the night. *'It is not right and it is not fair that my father should be alone with no one,'* says Carmen/Andrés. *'I am the homosexual and I am the son who cares for him.'*

As Carmen's story of her time at Fabricas de Calidad reveals, this place where cultural and economic value meet is not just a place of exploitation but also a wedge into the dominant tale of who the worker is, disclosing in what has been offered as the way things are an alternative story of how they can be. Her actions demonstrate the possibility of interrupting what Melissa Wright (2001) has referred to as 'the dialectic of still life', capital's ambivalent positioning of feminized workers between their value (as cheap labour) and as waste (disposable labour). Compañeras who refuse to 'put up with this' pry from that 'still life' image of the feminized cheap and disposable worker the possibility of social movement.

So far as I can tell, the Fabricas de Calidad campaign where gay rights were on the agenda and two homosexuals were in the front was an extraordinary event. Among organizers in maquila communities there are many who are homosexual, gay, lesbian or transgendered, but those who are openly so are rare and they face enormous challenges. Mariana reports that *'the company would tell the workers, "The only reason she is organizing is to have all of you women as her lovers."'* 'Many women who become organizers so disrupt Mexican *machista* culture that they are threatened by their husbands and accused of being lesbians, yet they face few options outside the economic support heteronormative identity offers. Iván says that after some of the other organizers began making comments openly about his gay sexuality, his credibility was so undermined that he had to leave the group he was working with. *'It's like the waves of the sea'*, he says, extending his arms. *'One has to walk like this. If you go against the current you are going to drown. But there is always the chance that a wave is going to break and you might catch it.'*

Some organizers in the maquilas are making waves that others may catch. They bear on their second skins the tattoo of capital's monstrous possibility. A few, like Carmen, Iván and Mariana, put in motion predications of the subject that re-narrate the scripts of abjection. Meeting locally, regionally, and at times with peasants from the south, small groups of Mexican maquiladora workers and former workers are building alliances and imagining alternatives. Out of the immense challenges of massive unmet need, the resources of traditional knowledge, and the legacy of radical intellectual thought, they are developing critical 'social ontologies', forms of political education and action. Often, very often, their organizing founders on homophobia. While some are working to insert its re-narration as an issue in their popular education workshops, this is rare. This second skin of abjection that binds the feminization of labour power to homophobia has yet to be transformed into a life jacket.

Capital pursues workers whose labour power is cheap. That pursuit depends on norms that devalue some human beings and value others, on an abjection-domination embedded in a second skin that carries the promise of continual dispossession. The loose second skins of thousands who are dispossessed of their bodies and of the dignity of a human 'mode of being' are incorporated into their labour: in jobs where this second skin enhances profits as it is literally incorporated into the value of what is produced at the same time it serves as an alibi for diminished wages; in the times and places of caring labour at home. The result is a cycle of dispossession, of needs for food, housing, education, rest, nurturing that cannot ever be fully met under capitalism. Whether marked as queer, *maricón*, *marimacha*, or woman – workers' second skins are sewn into the commodities they produce, the pants and sleeping bags, blenders and TVs that 'new gender' folks and 'new family' consumers buy at their local Wal-Mart. If not all queer workers wear the same second skins, this may tell us much about the relationship of culture to class, or as Iván would have it, about the points at which cheese becomes milk.

Capital depends on the production of value, including the cultural norms embedded in the exchange of labour for a wage. Without this systemic and particular relationship between capitalist and worker capitalism is something else. Maquiladora workers are only one small sector of the millions who make up the majority of the world's working people whose human needs routinely and brutally go unmet. The most incisive politics of feminism and queer studies converge here: in addressing the social relations through which the material and cultural value of human being is filtered. Here both feminism and queer politics aim to transform the deprivation of *what is* into *what can be*. Those times and places where cultural value meets surplus value are crucial to this undertaking. They beg for further critical work – across universities, community centres, workshops and *encuentros*, within and across national borders. And that work we have only just begun.

Acknowledgements

I wish to thank the editors of Rethinking Marxism for permission to reprint portions of this essay that appear in a Special Section on *Queer Theory and Marxism*, 18 (2006), as well as the Rockefeller Foundation's Sexuality, Race and Globalization Project at the University of Arizona for research and writing support. I also owe a special thank you to the Mexican workers who share their lives here.

Notes

1. The phrase 'the straight mind' is Monique Wittig's (1992). Though she did not embrace the formulation 'queer', her critique of heterosexuality is an important materialist intervention. On this point see Hennessy (1993b).
2. The Killer Coke campaign that is taking off on college campuses where Coke monopolizes the soft drink franchise is making visible and opposing Coke's ad campaigns that target local subcultures while decimating local water sources (India) and violently suppressing union organizing by Coke's bottlers (Colombia). This campaign is an example of coordinated efforts that address local impacts and their transnational reach, as are the burgeoning campaigns that take on Wal-Mart's low wages, gender discrimination, union busting and contamination of water sources.
3. See for example, Ramamurthy (2004); Mohanty (2003); Salzinger (2003); Wright (2001).
4. In a reading that is critical of Prosser yet advances his general argument for the important ontological role of the body in sexed subjectivity, Sven Brandenburg emphasizes that psychic investment arises from perception. He contends that the notion of perception underscoring the neo-constructionist version of gender draws upon a rationalist account of perception that confuses being with appearance, idea with image. As a result, it forecloses the processes involved in the mediation of perception, the formation of the unconscious, of a 'gestalt' or visual field, and the role of physical difference here – the bodily differences with which the subject is confronted. He contends that as one gives meaning to these differences and to one's own body, nature and culture are both necessary, though neither serves as guarantor of meaning.
5. For an analysis that carries their elaboration of Spivak's argument on value to the other side of the US–Mexican border see Zimmerman (2005).
6. Factories run by US companies in Mexico that benefit from exploitive labour costs and minimal regulation of health and safety.
7. Husband.
8. Daughter.
9. Carmen is the name Andrés adopted. She did not discuss with me why or when she changed her name. I refer to her for the most part as Carmen, the name she used to introduce herself. The slips between Carmen and Andrés in her story mark both the gender complexity of her life and the places where feminism's attention to gender discrimination and queer politics' attention to transgendered subjects meet.

10. The maquiladora concept of assembly for export was initially developed in the mid 1960s to lure corporations to 'free trade zones' that offered opportunities for a wider profit margin. Companies that moved their production there got tax breaks and low or no tariffs on imports. Materials enter Mexico duty free so long as the finished product is exported. The corporation realizes a wider profit margin because it does not have to provide health and safety equipment, decent working conditions or safe disposal of toxic wastes. Over one million Mexican workers are employed in almost 3000 maquiladoras and live in the *colonias* (shantytowns) that surround them. They earn between $35–$50 for a 48-hour work week. The goods they assemble include everything from electrical harnesses for cars to small appliances. The parent companies of about 90 per cent of these factories are US corporations. On the gendered division of labour here see Fernandez-Kelly (1987); Salzinger (2003); Tiano (1994); Wright (2001).
11. For studies of the history of the lesbian and gay social movement in Mexico see Carrier (1995); Lumsden (1991); Mejia (2000); Mongrovejo (2000); Priuer (1998).

7

Refiguring the Family

Towards a Post-Queer Politics of Gay and Lesbian Marriage

Chet Meeks and Arlene Stein

Strange bedfellows: the institution of marriage and the LGBT community

In November 2003, the Massachusetts Supreme Court ruled that same-sex couples are entitled to equal marriage rights. Later the following year, voter initiatives designed to ban same-sex marriage were passed in 11 state ballots throughout the United States, and pundits declared that a sizeable proportion of George W. Bush's support for the presidency came from 'values voters' who saw gay marriage as a threat. Bush and Republican members of Congress proposed a federal Constitutional Amendment that would ban same-sex marriage. The Massachusetts decision has deeply divided the United States.

In its opposition to gay and lesbian marriage, America is unusual among advanced nations.[1] At a time when same-sex relationships have been legally recognized in Scandinavia, the Netherlands, Belgium, France, Canada, Germany, Hungary, Austria, South Africa, the United Kingdom, and, for immigration purposes, Australia, Americans are virtually alone in their widespread resistance to same-sex marriage, a situation that Adam (2003) terms a 'gay marriage panic'. The combined effect of a well-organized and increasingly powerful religious conservative movement (Hunter, 1991; Stein, 2001) and the absence of a strong welfare state that provides government supports to alternative family structures (Lyall, 2002; Adam, 2003) may account for this lack of progress.

Our focus in this chapter is not on the opposition to lesbian and gay marriage by the American mainstream, but rather on the debates within the lesbian and gay community about this issue. Since the first widely publicized challenges to heterosexual marriage emerged in the early 1990s, lesbian and gay communities in the United States have been divided. Proponents of lesbian and gay marriage have tended to embrace what we call a politics of normalization. We define a politics of normalization as a rhetorical strategy that simultaneously advances the cause of gay civil rights while constructing rigid and regulative definitions of 'normal' gay sexuality. Not every form of civil rights politics is normalizing, but normalizing arguments have been dominant in the struggle for same-sex marriage. Opposing the politics of normalization are those who argue that the lesbian and gay community should reject marriage altogether. These arguments are grounded in a tradition of feminist and queer politics that views marriage as central to patriarchal, heterosexist and class forms of domination (see e.g., Radicalesbians in Blasius and Phelan, 1997). Same-sex marriage would force lesbian, gay and queer people to conform to a script that is essentially heterosexual, and would strengthen a culture that views sexual behaviour as a key indicator of one's moral status as a 'moral' or 'polluted' individual. We should instead create new, more egalitarian intimate arrangements and family forms, they argue.

In the following, we outline a 'post-queer' argument for same-sex marriage, one that understands the battle for same-sex marriage in relation to historical changes in family structure and lesbian/gay lives. Queer and feminist critics often portray marriage as a static institution, one that, if lesbian and gay people were to enter into it, would assimilate all of our differences, creativity and identities. What this critique misses is that the struggle for lesbian and gay marriage comes at a time when the structure of 'traditional' marriage has weakened (Stacey, 1990; Coontz, 1997). In Scandinavia, for example, lesbian and gay marriage has accompanied the weakening, not strengthening, of patriarchy, compulsory heterosexuality and rigid marital norms, much to the dismay of many conservatives (see, e.g. O'Sullivan, 2004). In the United States, too, the emergence of lesbian and gay marriage as a possibility has paralleled increases in divorce rates, growing autonomy for women in heterosexual marriages, and increased rates of cohabitation before marriage and instead of marriage. Static views of marriage must give way to more accurate accounts of the way institutions that intersect with intimate life change, and specifically, how they might change if they accommodate lesbian and gay marriage.

The queer rejection of marriage also fails to take into account the ways lesbian and gay lives have changed. Specifically, many lesbians and gay men are living closer to the 'mainstream' of American society than in the past. George Chauncey (2004) identifies increased visibility in popular culture, the impact of HIV/AIDS on intimate matters such as visitation rights and inheritance, and the 'lesbian baby boom' of the 1990s, as forces that re-oriented the lesbian and gay community away from sexual liberation and toward marriage as a primary political priority. Corroborating Chauncey's observations, a 2004 poll found that a clear majority (83%) of lesbian, gay and bisexual Americans rated obtaining civil marriage 'extremely important', and more than three quarters ranked obtaining a marriage license a top personal priority ('Strategic Insights Survey', www.hrc.org). These figures may not be wholly representative, but many others have documented a re-orientation of lesbian and gay people away from issues of sexual liberation and community building and toward creating and protecting families (Weston, 1991; Lynch, 1992; Weeks, Heaphy and Donovan, 2001; Seidman, 2002; Sullivan, 2004). A community that once branded marriage a 'rotten, oppressive institution' (Wittman in Blasius and Phelan, 1997: 382) seems increasingly to want the protections and status associated with it. Many queer scholars and activists have attributed this to 'false consciousness', but we believe a modified theoretical framework is in order.

Our 'post-queer' framework for analysing the politics of marriage borrows from the work of Anthony Giddens and Cheshire Calhoun to argue that same-sex marriage would contribute to the trend toward increased reflexivity and expanded autonomy in intimate and sexual life. Just as divorce reform and the repeal of miscegenation statutes relaxed some of the rigid customs that regulated marriage, replacing its governance with norms of reflexive choice, so too would same-sex marriage. Additionally, same-sex marriage would be a step toward the accomplishment of one of queer politics' long-stated aims – de-centring heterosexuality. Heterosexual dominance rests on the claim that heterosexuality is foundational to civilization, making marriage a natural right. Same-sex marriage would expose the fallacy of this claim, forcing heterosexuals to view their relationships as deliberately enacted social practices, 'life-styles' that are dependent on recognition of the state, rather than inevitable, 'natural' accomplishments.

Marriage and the politics of normalization

The first legal challenge to the marriage ban was waged in 1970, just months after the Stonewall riots, by Richard Baker and James McConnell. *Baker* v. *Nelson* was followed by six legal challenges between

1970 and 1993. None of these early legal battles for same-sex marriage were broadly embraced by the lesbian and gay community. Nor did they stimulate much debate. Most of the Justices who heard these challenges barely took the claims seriously, and none of the complaints ever made it to the Federal level. Only in 1993, with *Baehr* v. *Lewin* in Hawaii, did marriage become a central feature of lesbian and gay politics. And only then did marriage become a source of intra-community debate, since marriage became coupled with the politics of normalization.

Noble and ennobling love

Andrew Sullivan moved to the forefront of LGBT politics in the 1990s as one of a handful of vocal and visible 'gay conservatives'. For Sullivan, marriage should be the gay community's central concern, because it is the political equivalent of 'coming out'. Because homosexuality is associated with shame in Western societies, Sullivan explains, 'the gay teenager learns ... that that which would most give him meaning is mostly likely to destroy him in the eyes of others' (1995: 12). Shame, in turn, leads to 'distinctions between ... sexual desire and ... emotional longing ... [and to] an ethic more of anonymous and promiscuous sex than of committed relationships' (ibid.: 12–13). This promiscuous sexual ethic is 'infantalizing and liberating at the same time' (ibid.: 192) and deepens the divide between gay and straight worlds. To Sullivan, lesbian and gay subcultures nurture sexual norms that distance gay and lesbian Americans from mainstream society.

Opposing the shame-based sexuality of the lesbian and gay subculture, Sullivan argues, marriage is 'noble' and 'ennobling'. Marriage would be personally and socially beneficial, because it would re-couple sex and intimacy (especially for gay men), and because it would admit gay men and lesbians into civilization's most civilizing institution. Marriage, notes Sullivan, 'is the only political and cultural and spiritual institution that can truly liberate us from the shackles of marginalization and pathology' (1998: 63). Marriage would make family values lesbian and gay values, mend the cultural divide that separates homosexuals and heterosexuals, and attenuate what Sullivan sees as unhealthy sex practices amongst gay men.

Marriage would be beneficial for one last reason. Rather than demanding what Sullivan characterizes as 'special rights' (e.g. a Federal hate crimes bill or any legislation that recognizes the unique circumstances or shared politics of lesbian and gay people), marriage would be politically beneficial because it 'allows homosexuals to define their own future and their own identity and does not place it in the hands of the other [sic].

It makes a clear, public statement of equality while leaving all the inequalities of emotion and passion to the private sphere, where they belong. It does not legislate private tolerance; it declares public equality. It banishes ... victimology and replaces it with ... integrity' (1995: 186). Marriage should be central, then, because a politics focused on marital rights can be framed as an issue of individual rights, essentially uncoupling the struggle for gay and lesbian equality from the collective political identity of the gay and lesbian community.

While few advocates of same-sex marriage fully embrace all of Sullivan's ideas, their arguments are shaped by a politics of normalization that maintains the following:

1. Homosexual oppression is the result of individual acts of bigotry or the organized efforts of irrational (religious) extremists, and not the result of the socially patterned privileging of heterosexuality.
2. The family is pre-political, bound together by love rather than institutionalized forms of privilege.
3. LGBT politics is a struggle for individual civil rights, not an attempt to transform institutions or cultural meanings. The marriage struggle requires no serious consideration of the relationship between the family and a broad range of economic, racial or sexual inequalities.
4. Lesbian and gay intimacy is a positive adaptation of heterosexual virtues, a pluralization of what mainstream society thinks of as sacred. Sub-cultural/political identifications with the lesbian, gay or queer community, and non-conforming sexual practices, are pathological.

The politics of normalization, then, advances gay and lesbian civil rights while installing regulative and disciplinary constructions of normal, gay sexuality within the lesbian and gay community. Marriage has been a central feature of these constructions.

Love makes a family, nothing more, nothing less

At the 1987 March on Washington, lesbian and gay activists held a mass wedding ceremony, presided over by Pastor Dina Batchelor who noted, 'it matters not who we love, only that we love'. The mass wedding's official slogan was posted on a large placard: 'Love makes a family, nothing more, nothing less' (Botkin, 1987: 16). Although this mass wedding occurred six years before the *Baehr* v. *Lewin* Hawaii decision, the idea that 'love makes a family' would become central to a politics of normalization.

Normalizing arguments view homosexual oppression as the result of individual forms of bigotry, *not* as the result of widespread, entrenched institutional and cultural forces, such as the absence of marital protections, of Federal hate crime legislation, or the cultural entrenchment of rigid sex and gender roles. Rather, if gays and lesbians remain unequal, it is due to the bigotry of the unenlightened. The American religious right is perhaps the most obvious culprit. Evan Wolfson, attorney for Lambda Legal Defense and Education Fund and head counsel for Baehr, noted that 'religious extremists are trying to shut down the nation's discussion on how the denial of marriage rights harms real-life couples before most Americans have had a chance to think about it' (in Dunlap, 1996: A13).

In this view, gays and lesbians are oppressed because of the persistence of stereotypes propagated by the religious right. Commenting on the 1996 Defense of Marriage Act, Elizabeth Birch wrote: 'Religious political extremist organizations shoved gay marriage into America's collective face in their quest for a new fundraising tool that they hoped would have the added bonus of torpedoing Bill Clinton's re-election' (Birch, 1997: 6). And Bruce Bawer noted that 'right wingers have used social and theological arguments to rally opposition to the legalization of same-sex unions; such arguments, aside from being invalid, are irrelevant to any discussion of marriage as a legal contract' (Bawer, 1995: 80).

Lesbian and gay inequality, then, is the result of bigoted individuals and the organized efforts of the religious right. The exclusion of lesbians and gay men from marriage 'brands us as inferior, second-class citizens, thus justifying and reinforcing stereotypes and prejudices as well as other discrimination' (Wolfson, 1996: 84). The American religious right undeniably plays an important role in the subordination of lesbian and gay Americans by deploying negative and homophobic stereotypes. What is striking about these arguments is that they ignore marriage's own institutional role in lesbian and gay subordination. They suggest that if we could simply enlighten fundamentalist preachers and their parishioners, if we could 'pierce the aura of marriage, helping people ... to think about it objectively' (Bawer, 1995: 80), then gay and lesbian oppression would disappear.

'Piercing the aura of marriage' entails constructing marriage-bound lesbians and gay men as the guardians of 'the traditional family.' Gabriel Rotello noted that same-sex marriage 'is in many ways a conservative issue. Those who love to portray gays as promiscuous and predatory are bewildered by images of gentle lesbian and gay ... couples living in connubial and monogamous bliss' (Rotello, 1996: 15). Like heterosexual opponents of same-sex marriage, they suggest that marriage is a pre-political institution. Andrew Sullivan defines the family as 'an emotional commitment [shared] by two people to each other for life', that exists 'prior to the liberal state' (Sullivan, 1995: 186–7).

If the family is pre-political and comprises fixed 'traditional' meanings (love, child-rearing, commitment, etc.), then the struggle for same-sex marriage is *not* connected to feminist struggles against patriarchy, nor to struggles against the pathologization of sexual difference. Rather, as Jonathan Rauch recently argued, the struggle for same-sex marriage is a struggle aimed at *strengthening* the family:

> It [same-sex marriage] is ... good for the institution of marriage ... Far from opening the door to *all sorts of scary redefinitions of marriage* ... same-sex marriage is the surest way to shut that door. Far from decoupling marriage from its core mission, same-sex marriage clarifies and strengthens that mission. Far from hastening the social decline of marriage, same-sex marriage shores up the key values and commitments on which couples and families and society depend. (Rauch, 2004: 6 original emphases)

Appealing to these traditional and traditionalizing definitions, Rauch assures sceptical heterosexuals that same-sex marriage 'offers the best hope of stopping the proliferation ... of marriage-like and 'marriage lite' alternatives' (ibid.). In this view, lesbians and gay men are not threatening traditional family values; they are simply pluralizing those values.

Appealing to traditional, pre-political definitions of marriage serves two functions. First, it normalizes the symbolic image of homosexuality. Against the arguments of religious conservatives who portray homosexuality as deviant and polluted, it argues that homosexuality is simply a positive *adaptation* of America's core sexual and family values. 'The decision [of the Hawaii State Supreme Court in *Baehr* v. *Lewin*] lays out ... the truth about our lives: that we are good parents; that our children are happy and well-adjusted; that we form committed, loving relationships' (Wolfson in Gallagher, 1997: 63). Such an argument is simultaneously regulatory: 'If gay men want to create a sustainable culture ... it has to draw explicit connections between sex and intimacy, reward self-restraint and ... end ... the pervasive belief that those who are living on the fringes of gay sexual life are somehow the most liberated and the most gay' (Rotello, 1997: 14). Same-sex marriage 'evokes a picture of people not so different from heterosexuals except for affectional preference' (Gallagher, 1996: 22).

While pre-political definitions of the institution of marriage help these activists to normalize homosexual imagery, they also de-politicize lesbian and gay struggle. The struggle for marriage is not a struggle against heterosexual dominance. As Andrew Sullivan notes, same-sex marriage 'requires no change in heterosexual behavior and no sacrifice from heterosexuals ... it marries the clarity of liberalism with the institution of conservatism' (1995: 183–4). Rather, the struggle for marriage is simply a struggle for individual, human rights. 'Withholding marriage', noted Democratic Assembly woman Sheila James Kuehl, 'denies the humanity of minority groups' (in Dunlap, 1996: A13). Just as these arguments regulate sexual imagery, they also regulate political imagery. As one critic suggests, 'The gay sub-culture unfortunately provides an ample supply of shocking counter-cultural images to wet the appetite of any conservative defender of family and douse the flame of the most ardent liberal' (Levado, 1994: 57; see also Birch, 1997).

In the end, we should be suspicious of these arguments, not because they are *for* marriage, but because of *how* the arguments are constructed. A political rhetoric that argues that gays and lesbians share 'traditional' family values and are 'normal' only deepens the divide between conforming and non-conforming sexualities. Being 'normal' means an 'individual' who is not attached to subculture or political community. Being 'normal' means behaving in sexually appropriate ways. And being 'normal' means asking for equal rights and demanding inclusion in society's cherished institutions, but never altering these institutions or their most basic, taken-for-granted meanings.

Queer politics and the rejection of marriage

During the same years the lesbian and gay community began fighting the Baehr case in Hawaii and the 1996 Defense of Marriage Act in Congress, social movement organizations like ACT-UP and Queer Nation created a revival of 1960s and 1970s liberationist and radical feminist politics, which stood in stark contrast to the normalizing politics of the same-sex marriage movement.

Central to queer politics is a conception of lesbian and gay oppression that intersects with other (class, gender and racial) forms of subjugation. In this vision, lesbians and gay men are not merely discriminated against by bigoted individuals and religious extremists. Rather, the dominant culture systematically enforces rigid rules of gender intelligibility, installs marital heterosexuality as a sacred norm, and carefully monitors a whole range of hierarchies: between men and women, whites and people of colour, upper and lower economic classes, and of course, heterosexuals and homosexuals. Central to lesbian, gay and queer oppression is the bourgeois nuclear family and the institution of marriage.

The ennobling and the demeaning go together

Michael Warner's *The Trouble with Normal* was written as a critique of the normalizing politics of activists like Andrew Sullivan. 'To a couple that gets married', Warner notes, 'marriage just looks ennobling ... Stand outside of it ... and you see [that] you and your relations are less worthy. Without this corollary effect, marriage would not be able to endow anybody's life with significance. *The ennobling and the demeaning go together'* (1999: 82 original emphasis). Warner's critique is not aimed at the way that lesbians and gay men have been excluded from marriage, but rather at what he calls an 'ethic of social shame'. This ethic operates by privileging a narrow range of desires, sexual practices and identities as normal. This privilege accrues as a result of the pathologization of sexual differences which do not conform to 'the normal'. Marriage is central to the ethic of sexual shame; it 'brings the machinery of administration to bear on the realm of pleasures and intimate relations ...' (1999: 112).

In opposition to Sullivan's claims about (gay male) sexuality, Warner rejects the idea that queer personal lives dissociate sex and intimacy. 'People who think that queer life consists of sex without intimacy are usually seeing only a tiny part of the picture. ... The most fleeting sexual encounter *is*, in its way, intimate' (Warner, 1999: 115). The idea that sex and intimacy are severed amounts to misrecognition of the richness of queer life, a dismissal of the creativity that has resulted from living outside the spaces of mainstream society. Lesbians and gay men often combine sex, intimacy and friendship in ways that heterosexuals do not. Marriage would limit the variety of intimacies that have been cultivated by queer people, and in doing so, deny a wide variety of needs. 'If there is such a thing as a gay way of life, it consists in ... a welter of intimacies outside of ... institutions and ordinary social obligations' (1999: 116). Same-sex marriage would only further subject queer life to the ethic of sexual shame.

Warner sees the struggle for same-sex marriage as a violation of the queer movement's historical purpose. Gay liberation, he notes, 'resisted any attempt to make the norms of straight culture into the standards by which queer life should be measured. ... [i]t insisted that any vision of sexual justice begin by considering the unrecognized dignity of these outcasts ... and the hierarchies of abjection that make them secondary ... or deviant' (Warner, 1999: 88–9). Furthermore, same-sex marriage would only strengthen the state's capacity to regulate intimate life; in effect, the lesbian and gay community would become the new enforcers of sexual normality: 'Gay couples don't just want households, benefits, and recognition. ... This trend comes at a time when ... non-standard households ... [are] increasingly targeted by a neo-conservative program of restricting divorce, punishing adultery, stigmatizing illegiti-macy, and raising tax incentives for marriage' (1999: 125). Same-sex marriage, in other words, would re-draw moral boundaries – granting legitimacy to same-sex relationships that can pass as normal, but exacerbating the dilemmas faced by non-standard households and non-normative forms of intimacy.

Warner's and other queer critiques of marriage are underpinned by a common set of assumptions and a political world view:

1. Queer oppression is the result of more than the actions and beliefs of bigoted individuals. Oppression results from the systematic privileging of a narrow range of sexual practices and identities.
2. Marriage is a political institution that has been used to disqualify queer people from full citizenship. Marriage is central to the maintenance of homosexual oppression and a broad range of social hierarchies. The cultural images associated with 'family values' are used to pathologize sexual and intimate differences.
3. Queer politics is transformational. Queer politics should not simply secure rights for lesbians and gay men, but transform social institu-tions and dismantle socially patterned inequalities. Queer sexuality is thus inescapably political.
4. The queer community fashions new forms of intimacy. The prolifera-tion of sexual difference is the only way to challenge heterosexuality and the normalizing politics of the mainstream gay community.

Let us examine the queer critique of same-sex marriage more closely.

The centrifuge's crush and the untold cost of the awful lie

In *Choosing*, feminist attorney and poet Mary Dunlap defines marriage as 'this myth, this centrifuge of sexist conformity, built on a vicious cycle of female inferiority, tossed, cajoled, and ultimately smashed these beings into a sameness: increasingly fearful deference to the male. ... Can we these most unwelcome outsiders, we these gay and lesbians lovers, be let in? ... Without destruction of all we have learned outside, feminist, heterodox lessons about the centrifuge's crush and the untold cost of the awful lie' (Dunlap, 1997: 125, 127–8).

This image is quite different than the 'Love Makes a Marriage' ideal seen at the 1987 March on Washington mass wedding ceremony. Dunlap's poem suggests a queer politics that revolves around a different conception of marriage, a different view of sexual citizenship, and a different conception of the relationship between intimate choices and sexual justice, all underpinned by a different understanding of queer oppression.

Recall that in pro-marriage arguments, lesbian and gay oppression is the result of individual bigotry and the influence of the religious right. Queer critics of marriage, on the other hand, insist that queer oppression is more complicated than the acts of bigoted individuals and religious extremists. Rather, queer oppression is *institutional*. Underlying these criticisms of the LGBT community's adoption of marital politics is an idea inherited from radical feminism and gay liberationism – heterosexuality is compulsory (see Rich, 1983). Compulsory heterosexuality enforces a rigid gender and sex role system in which men and women must behave in gender-intelligible ways, including making the appropriate erotic-object choices. Gender intelligibility requires the enforcement of strict rules concerning sex and pleasure, narrowly construing some sexual practices and relations as legitimate and sacred, and policing the boundaries of this 'charmed circle' (Rubin, 1993) in search of potential deviances that can be branded as polluted threats to 'family values'.

Compulsory heterosexuality is supported by all social institutions – the media, the state, expert knowledges, criminal and civil law and capitalism. Linking all of these institutions to compulsory heterosexuality is marriage itself. Indeed, marriage plays a foundational role not only in sustaining compulsory heterosexuality, but in the maintenance of a whole range of social inequalities. As Chrys Ingraham (1999) argues, the bridal industry turns the white, female, underweight and airbrushed body into an unattainable yet erotically charged and desirable object – heterosexuality's fantasy of itself, a fantasy which excludes most women but which nonetheless exerts a powerful normative, libidinal and regulatory force. Heterosexuality creates and enforces inequalities not only between heterosexuals and homosexuals, but between men and women, and as Ingraham shows, amongst heterosexual women. Moreover, as Patricia Hill Collins (2004) has argued, marriage is central to regulating the social intercourse between the races. Strict legal and normative marriage rules have always consisted not only of *de jure* prohibitions against same-sex unions, but of *de facto* proscriptions against different-race unions (see also Henwood, 2004). And economically, marriage bestows middle-class benefits on those who conform to its norms and imagery, reinforcing class inequalities by binding material benefits to marital status (Polikoff, 1993; Duggan, 1996).

If institutionalized dynamics ensure conformity and maintain hierarchy, queer critics reason that same-sex marriage would not change marriage as much as it would merely shift (and deepen) normative boundaries. As one activist noted, 'Extending state-sanctioned marriage to lesbian and gay couples wouldn't end discrimination ... it would merely shift the lines. ... Lesbians and gay men who are not or choose not to be involved in any relationship will still be paying the price for not conforming to the norm' (McBride, 1990: 9). Lesbian and gay relations that do not conform to heterosexual, middle-class norms would not only still face discrimination, but might be even more vilified. Cathy Cohen (1996: 37) noted that 'the ability of gays and lesbians to marry will further split and divide our communities ... [instilling] yet another hoop of normality' – dividing same-sex couples who can pass as conventional from those who remain unconventional. The least powerful among us (also the least likely to be married) would be 'propped up as targets for right wing, and increasingly, liberal attacks on the welfare system ... teen and single mothers, whose most horrible sin has been their inability or unwillingness to conform to a normative family structure'.

Marriage is not a pre-political institution; its history is imprinted with economic, racial, gender and sexual inequality. At stake in the queer opposition to marriage are not only marital rights themselves, but a broader vision of social justice. Sexuality, in the queer critique, is not just a private feature of the liberal citizen, but the central feature of an oppositional political ethos. 'Queer relationships are, by their very nature ... political statements because they don't fit the mold. ... When we try to fit our queer lives into the mold of heterosexual marriage, we damage ourselves as queers [by accepting] the idea that our queer relationships are real only when given a heterosexual shading through a wedding ritual' (Burnworth, 1993: 80).

For pro-marriage advocates, marriage would mean formal equality, finally allowing gay and lesbian Americans to *simply be individuals* and Americans. The arguments against marriage draw on a different notion of citizenship:

Being gay or lesbian in this society has always meant challenging ourselves and those around us to develop new, creative and changing ways of love. That process has included the active participation of our lovers, our friends, our families, and our communities. I, for one, do not trust that we can integrate a capitalist, patriarchal, homophobic state into such a process without seriously compromising the role that lesbians and gay men can play as a force of social change. (McBride, 1990: 9)

Opponents of marriage seek to foster political consciousness, to shape a collective political identity. Queer citizens should resist the allure of the mainstream, its institutions and its way of granting rights. Queer politics consists not so much of demanding changes to existing institutions, but rather to creating an alternative personal and community sexual ethic.

As stated at the beginning of this chapter, though, a majority of lesbian and gay Americans seem not to be persuaded by this critique. While queer and liberationist perspectives are important tools for understanding the institutional nature of heterosexual domination, a politics of liberation has been largely replaced in America in favour of a reformist approach to gay and lesbian civil rights, including struggling for marriage. Many queer and feminist critics tend to view this desire to marry as false consciousness. As Warner says: 'It is undeniable that many gays and lesbians want to marry. ... From age to age, serfs have revered their masters. ... Why should gay people be immune to similar mistakes about their interests?' (Warner, 1999: 105). Similarly, Judith Butler views the battle for marriage as 'amnesia about what the alliances of the lesbian and gay movement used to be' (Butler, 2004: 20–1). Lesbian and gay people who believe that the marriage battle is worthwhile and even crucial have bought into the myth and the lie that Dunlap wrote about in her poem. Writing about the lesbians he knows who have gotten married since the Massachusetts decision, Michael Bronski describes 'the women who were raised on Barbie – that rubberized icon of femininity, whose most sublime apotheosis was a beautiful Bride'. He asks, 'Is there any doubt, in anyone's mind, that we live in a society that is completely dominated by a Marriage Culture that tells us from the age of consciousness that the only way to be happy is to be married?' (Bronski, 2004: 22).

While the queer critiques of marriage are grounded in valuable insights about institutions, inequality and the dangers of gay and lesbian normalization, they are sorely out of touch with post-queer realities. We need a better way of conceptualizing marriage.

Marriage as a post-queer struggle

A critique of marriage does not require a rejection of same-sex marriage. The ethical work of queer theory and politics – the focus on building new relations, new forms of sexuality and intimate values, and different familial relations – is important; but this ethical work needs to be translated into a politics that *directly* intervenes in the standard operation of actually existing institutions. We believe this, not only because marriage might be the most efficient means of securing long-denied rights; rather, as we argue in this section, lesbian and gay marriage could actually serve the ends of a progressive, perhaps even radical, sexual politics. This requires a reassessment of the relationship between the institution of marriage and sexual politics.

First, while marriage critics rightly highlight its political nature and its role in sustaining heterosexual dominance, marriage needs to be re-conceptualized as a dynamic and changing, rather than static, institution. Marriage is often construed to operate today in precisely the same way it did 50, 100, or 150 years ago. Such a static view neglects the real changes that have occurred in the institution of marriage and the role feminist and queer politics have played in creating these changes. This view ultimately neglects the active and reflexive role that individuals play in re-shaping (within limits) social institutions to meet their own interests and needs. We offer Anthony Giddens's conception of the 'pure relationship' as a way of re-conceptualizing the actual dynamics of marriage as a social institution and the role of the reflexive sexual citizen in (re)shaping it.

Second, while lesbian and gay inequality intersects with other forms of inequality that are sustained by marriage, the denial of sexual citizenship to same-sex couples is a *relatively* independent feature of compulsory heterosexuality. The privileges that marriage accords to heterosexuals operate in very specific ways that cannot be collapsed into marriage's role in sustaining class, gender or racial inequality. We find persuasive Cheshire Calhoun's argument about the role same-sex marriage could play in de-centring heterosexuality.

Toward 'pure' relationships

Anthony Giddens (1991: ch. 7; 1992. ch. 1, 8) argues that while the family has its roots in patriarchy, it has undergone a radical restructuring. Out of pre-established, rigid, 'traditional' forms, the family has been opened up to new forms of self-reflexivity in which individuals can actively re-shape the family into an entity that meets their own emotional, and sexual needs (see also Stacey, 1990; Weston, 1991; Beck-Gernsheim, 1999; Weeks, Heaphy and Donovan, 2001). The introduction of romantic love into what had previously been a political and economic arrangement, as well as the influence of feminist and lesbian and gay politics, have transformed intimacy and family. For the last 150 years marriage has moved towards what Giddens (1992: 58) calls a *pure relationship*: 'where a social relation is entered into for its own sake, for what can be derived by each person ... and which is continued only in so far as it is thought by both parties to deliver enough satisfactions for each individual to stay in it'.

The 'pure relationship' is a powerful concept because it incorporates a conception of marriage's institutional dynamics, and its relationship to multiple forms of domination. Such relationships are not pre-political; their very possibility is the result of a long struggle against patriarchy and other restrictions on sexuality and intimate diversity. While 'marriage involves hierarchies that have systematically subordinated certain people's personal, economic, and social interests' (Eskridge, 1996: 75), same-sex marriage is not the same as 'buying into a rotten institution; it is only buying into an institution that is *changing*' (ibid.: 76). Marriage, in other words, is an imperfect, but flexible institution.

What would a politics of same-sex marriage centred on the notion of the pure relationship look like? To begin with, it would aim its critique at those features of marriage that bind it in rigidity and inflexibility. If notions of bloodline once made marriage a rigid institution, then the way it binds sex, emotion, and *property* remain, today, a source of rigidity that limit choice and autonomy. Lisa Duggan forcefully criticized this feature of contemporary marriage, noting that '[i]t assumes that sexual/emotional ties are properly joined to economic interdependencies' (Duggan, 1996: 5). To the extent that marriage in its contemporary form binds our economic well-being to our needs for sexual and emotional fulfilment, it remains a deeply problematic institution. A politics of marriage must confront the twenty-first century realities of American economic life, where more than 40 million Americans lived without health insurance in 2003, and where the stewards of what is left of the welfare state offer marriage up as the solution to economic despair. What is the potential for reflexive agency in the realm of sexual and familial relations given the current dynamics of American re-feudalization?

Given these realities, socialist feminists have rightly been sceptical about prioritizing lesbian and gay marriage. As Duggan asks, 'Why can't we find ways of recognizing next of kin relationships that don't assume biological or sexual relations, or enduring sexual relationships that don't lead to economic interdependency ...' (ibid.). A politics that pushes marriage in the direction of the 'pure relationship' must begin with a critique of relations of power (economic, social and cultural) that sustain marriage's rigidity and the material limits placed on intimate choice and autonomy. Duggan and others suggest that we separate the struggle for social recognition from economic considerations, arguing that primary legal support should be given to relations involving child-rearing and economic dependency, regardless of the sexual and emotional nature of those relationships. Relationships that involve sex, emotion and intimacy would receive secondary forms of legal protection (e.g. visitation rights). State and legal institutions, in other words, would take a mostly neutral position with respect to intimacy and sexuality, and would instead subsidize and protect relations of economic dependence.

Economic dynamics impose a continued rigidity on marriage, but the solutions posed by Duggan and other socialist feminists are not viable if the 'pure relationship' is our goal. As Jean Cohen has argued persuasively, autonomy and choice in the intimate and sexual realms are not mere matters of being left-to-be by a state actor that only regulates *negatively* (Cohen, 1997). Reproductive rights, for example, have not been achieved because women have demanded that they be 'left alone' by the state. Rather, these rights have been achieved because women have demanded that the state act *positively* to provide them with legally protected autonomy. Separating intimate and sexual life from economic 'households' might be preferable, but Duggan and other socialist feminists underestimate the necessity of forcing the state to positively recognize same-sex intimacies as legitimate, and to protect them accordingly. Such recognition would further expand and protect agency in the intimate realm, and would highlight the moral worth of policies that protect intimate choice and diversity.

In addition to critiquing the forces that limit choice and autonomy, then, it is also necessary to work toward pluralizing the forms of sex, intimacy and emotional commitment the state will recognize and endow with positive legal protections. Pure relationships are those in which emotional work, commitment, shared intimacies and love have become relatively independent, freely chosen and deliberately enacted. These features cannot flourish if the state takes a neutral role with respect to sex and intimacy while focusing its efforts on providing rights for economic 'households'. This means that the struggle for same-sex marriage must be re-framed from a struggle for acceptance, integration and normalization, to a struggle to pluralize the forms of intimate agency the state will protect. As E. J. Graff notes, 'same-sex marriage seems fair only if you accept a philosophy of marriage that, although it's gained ground in the past several centuries, still strikes many as radical: the idea that marriage (and therefore sex) is justified not by reproduction but by love. ... Marriage is – marriage always has been – variations on a theme' (Graff, 1996: 12).

Finally, centring same-sex marriage struggles on the 'pure relationship' would frame it as a struggle for expanded reflexivity in the intimate realm. The lesbian and gay struggle for same-sex marriage is important not only because it would change the institution of marriage, much as feminist struggles to reform divorce and rape laws did. Same-sex marriage would open marriage to expanded reflexivity; it would subject the roles, rituals and performances of marriage to expanded self-consciousness, where married partners, ideally, would be aware of the scripts they are following, the roles they are performing and where those scripts and roles could be shaped deliberately by both parties to suit particular interests and needs.

De-Centering heterosexuality through marriage reform

In addition to pushing the institution of marriage toward 'the pure relationship', same-sex marriage could contribute to the de-centering of heterosexuality. This does not mean, of course, that same-sex marriage would completely solve the injustices associated with compulsory heterosexuality, but same-sex marriage would seriously challenge the notion that fitness for family life (heterosexuality) *automatically* qualifies one for full citizenship in civil society.

In her book, *Feminism, the Family, and the Politics of the Closet,* Cheshire Calhoun argues that contemporary feminist theory too often collapses heterosexism into sexism. The privileges that accrue to heterosexuals often appear to be 'part of a broader array of interlocking practices built on the distinction between ...'man' and 'woman'. The social penalties visited upon lesbians and gay men for their gender and sexual deviance appear to be simply a special case of the systematic penalization of *anyone* who departs from the gender and sexual norms that support male dominance and female oppression' (Calhoun, 2001: 6). But in order to understand the contemporary dynamics responsible for lesbian and gay inequality, we must recognize heterosexism as a conceptually distinct system of oppression, related to male and other forms of dominance, but having its own independent features. Calhoun challenges us to engage in a thought experiment:

> Imagine a society that is not structured around male dominance. It might be a society that draws no gender distinctions but still emphasizes male–female sexual differences ... Could that society have a stringent taboo on homosexuality and lesbianism? Could social practices and social relations be systematically structured around heterosexuality ... It would seem to me that the answer ... is yes. (ibid.)

If heterosexism has its own relatively independent features, making lesbian and gay inequality distinct from gender-based and other forms of inequality, then, Calhoun reasons, surely 'a central point of lesbian and gay subordination is to preserve the heterosexual marital couple's foundational place within the social structure' (ibid.: 7). Heterosexism installs heterosexuality as the foundation of civilization, while 'displac[ing] gays and lesbians ... by refusing to recognize that [they] belong in either the public or the private sphere' (ibid.: 123).

Calhoun examines the US 1996 Defense of Marriage Act (DOMA) as an example of a politics that aims to displace lesbians and gay men. This Act rested on several assumptions about marriage and sexuality. First, marriage is argued to be, as one proponent of DOMA put it, 'the foundation of our society; families are built on it and values are passed through it' (DOMA cited in Calhoun, 2001: 123). Second, if marriage is the foundation of civilization, it is also pre-political. State and legal institutions thus do not *choose* to recognize heterosexual marriage; they *must* recognize it given its foundational status. Finally, in claiming that their unions are the foundation of civilization, heterosexuals claim to be society's most essential citizens. Their citizenship is inevitable and automatic – a Lockean natural right.

The fear that motivates supporters of DOMA and US President George Bush's call for a Constitutional Amendment stipulating marriage's heterosexuality is not based simply on the idea that homosexuality is immoral or unnatural. Rather, the fear is that same-sex marriage would reduce heterosexuality to one option among others. If the state were forced to recognize plural forms of intimacy, then the political dimensions of marriage would become transparent. Heterosexuals would lose their claim to possessing a *natural* right to participate in society's 'foundational' institution. This explains why, Calhoun argues, a growing number of Americans seem willing to extend legal rights (including domestic partnerships and civil union protections) to gays and lesbians, while remaining unwilling to extend full marriage. As Calhoun puts it, '[f]ree, self-defining, sociable citizens may choose to enter a variety of voluntary relationships with each other ... [but] marriage falls in a different category. Marriage is not one among many voluntary associations that citizens might choose to enter. ... Heterosexuals are not *just* free, rational, self-defining persons. They are also naturally fit to participate in the one institution that all societies, liberal or otherwise, must presuppose' (ibid.: 126–7). Thus the fear behind DOMA and like policies is that same-sex marriage would de-center heterosexuality by making heterosexual marriage one option amongst a variety of morally equivalent options. Heterosexuality would become a 'life-style'.

Doesn't the word 'natural' (as in, heterosexuality is *natural*) connote practices that do not have to be made self-conscious, a set of scripts and rituals that make one's social practices appear as the inevitable outcomes of some transcendental force? Doesn't the ban on same-sex marriage afford heterosexuals with this privilege – a *natural right* consisting of the privilege to live without reflection, the privilege to see one's roles as developing in accordance with principles of inevitability and not according to deliberated choices and self-conscious performances? 'Life-style' 'choices' appear as relations that are not, by contrast, inevitable or 'natural'. Wouldn't same-sex marriage de-center this dynamic, or at least move in that direction, forcing heterosexuals to see their sexuality, their intimate practices, their daily emotional lives as in fact not inevitable or natural, but chosen, scripted, performed? Wouldn't same-sex marriage jeopardize the *natural right* status of heterosexuality? Perhaps this is the source of the anxiety that underlies the conservative rallying cry to 'rescue ... traditional marriage from descent into a cold Scandinavian hell' (O'Sullivan, 2004: 95), and the dogged heterosexual insistence that 'marriage is not ... merely the creation of the state. ... Marriage is ingrained on the human conscience as existing solely between a man and a woman' (Crews, 2004: 99–100).

Conclusion

While queer and feminist critiques of the institution of marriage are indispensable, these critiques must also confront the 'post-queer' reality of contemporary lesbian and gay life. Today, many lesbian and gay identified individuals believe that same-sex marriage should be a political priority because their lives have come to be organized in ways that make marital rights more symbolically and materially significant for them than it was for their liberationist predecessors. This does not negate the power of the queer critique; it simply suggests this critique must engage with existing institutions, rather than reject them in favour of an inward-looking focus on sexual ethics.

As the rest of the industrialized world moves towards more fully integrating its lesbians and gay citizens and granting them legal recognition, the United States has lagged behind, a fact that is ironic considering that the lesbian/gay liberation movement began here three decades ago. The reasons for this are many, including the rise of the religious right, and a weak welfare state. We have focused on the ways that the peculiar nature of American identity politics have also contributed to this lag: American gays and lesbians have themselves been divided between those who seek integration in the family system, and all the rights, privileges and obligations it entails, and those who want to stand outside of it.

As the politics of marriage moves to the centre of lesbian and gay political organizing and action, it is clear that how we intervene in the ongoing cultural conversation about marriage will shape what it comes to mean in the future. If we reject marital institutions, we cede the cultural conversation about gay marriage to those who embrace a politics of normalization. But queer and feminist theorists have a role to play in moving the discussion beyond the liberation-versus-assimilation deadlock, framing the debate in ways that speak to the changed realities of lesbian and gay lives today.

Notes

1. Since this chapter was first published in our collection in 2006, the situation in the US has changed somewhat with the legalisation of gay marriage in several – mostly liberal – states. However, strong resistance towards these legal moves continues amongst state legislators, national politicians and the media. The overall arguments of the chapter are as relevant now as they were in 2006.

8
Practically Between Post-Menopause and Post-Modern

Angelia Wilson

Hanging above my desk are a few postcards which undoubtedly formed the wallpaper of many feminist lesbian graduate students over the years: 'we are everywhere'; 'be a bloody train driver'; and Rosie the riveter with defiant strong fist. As a collection they occasionally fan flames of motivation, but one in particular has begun to irritate me: 'I'll be a post-feminist in post-patriarchy'. I must have purchased it before my encounters with 'post' modern theory, because initially I thought it had a certain utopian appeal. Now, the simplistic binary opposition is seductive in its political directness but the underpinning defiance of all things post-modern is disappointing in its dismissive tone. The postcard may also irritate me because, after years of exposure to the sunlight coming through my office window, it is beginning to fade. Symbolically, this becomes my irritation with feminism – that 'it' seems to forever belong to a baby-boomer few who fought at its vanguard and, having earned the right to pass on wisdom, have become its only spokeswomen; that while students, and those on the 'Queer omnibus', may support equal pay, women's right to divorce and child-care initiatives, they would wince at being labelled with the 'F-word'. While feminism seems to belong to one generation, queer seems to belong to another: one respected but dated, the other cutting-edge and cool. As a lesbian feminist with a soft-spot for deconstruction and pragmatism, my own research nestles, uncomfortably, amongst this clan like a middle sister. It is from this position that I offer a few observations about my siblings' recent conversations.

Before I begin, however, it is worth noting that my commentary is limited to writers who themselves tend to focus on the United Kingdom.

This selection is primarily for reasons of brevity but also enables an element of socio-political shared experience. Second, perhaps because of the first, they each published pieces around the dawn of the Millennium which were underpinned by angst about the past and future of either feminism or lesbian, gay, bisexual, transgender, queer (lgbtq) politics. I do not presume that they offer a collective 'state of play' for either feminism or lgbtq politics. Some are explicitly attempting to do that; others implicitly refer to this as they construct more particular research agendas. Considered together, the level of anxiety about the past, present and future is almost tangible and therefore in itself indicative of the reflective moment inspired by the Millennium and, more importantly, of the agendas and opportunities for future conversations.

The feminist texts selected, *The Whole Woman* (1999), *Why Feminism?* (1999) and *Sacred Cows: Is Feminism Relevant to the New Millennium?* (1999), come from those familiar strong voices that have informed British feminism, from broadly different perspectives, for over 30 years: Germaine Greer, Lynne Segal and Ros Coward. Similar themes lurk in material by lesbian and queer academics although none of these voices explicitly address 'the state' of lgbtq politics/activism. Their words are found in academic journals such as *Sexualities* (1999 and 2000) and *Feminist Review* (2000) and consider particular topics rather than a full-blown analysis of any social movement. Nevertheless, they each share a similar unease and urgency about the state of lgbtq politics. All of this may simply be coincidental. It may be that a methodology that focuses on a particular slice of time blinkers one's view as to the historical political context and preceding debates. Furthermore, this particular selection may not be sufficiently inclusive of the content of the rich political and conceptual debates taking place in broadly defined 'feminist' or 'lgbtq' academic/political exchanges. However, I do think the writers here are fairly representative of current British debates and, as academics and journalists, will continue to shape its parameters in the near future. So, it is at least interesting to listen to this conversation at the turn of the century as expression is given to angst concerning the past and future of individual and collective understanding of 'their' politics.

Each writer voices this unease differently, but the murmurs, or shouts, of disillusionment, or panic, are detectable. Imagine a scene at a crossroads: a debate about which road to take; a hunt for a map, any map; a worry about the length of the journey; where the kids might run off to; the arguments over which street address is the correct, original, one. If nothing else, the turn of the century caused more than a few people to stop the car, get out, look around, and have a family meeting to think about where to head next. Obviously there are different bits of conversations and discourses at play here; different agendas, and different political histories. Nevertheless, I argue that the similarities are striking and offer signs about directions of the coming journey.

Feminism 2000

Three texts, to which I refer loosely as 'Feminism 2000', appeared in bookstores across the United Kingdom just before the dawn of the new Millennium, each offering a version of the last 30 years of the women's movement and contemplating feminism in the twenty-first century. My initial reaction was somewhat cynical. Is it only at historical moments that we take time to consider the 'state of feminism?' Why it is that each of these 'Feminism 2000' texts was written by a particular generation of feminists? Do those born in the 1960s or 1970s or even 1980s worry about the 'state of feminism?' If not, what does that fact alone tell us about the 'state of feminism?' Setting cynicism aside, I found that these elder stateswomen seemed to share a twofold concern about the future of British feminism: 'What the hell were we doing then? /'What the hell are we doing now?'

Unsurprisingly each text provides answers from strikingly different perspectives. In *The Whole Woman*, Germaine Greer writes 'it's time to get angry again' and bids women to take up the mantle of radical, or at least vocal feminism in the face of continued global discrimination and exploitation. From a very different space, Ros Coward asks 'Is feminism relevant to the new millennium?' and her answer is reflected in the book's title, only if feminists sacrifice a few *Sacred Cows*. For Coward, feminism was a specific by-product of 1960s and 1970s socio-economic and political culture. The following 20 years saw the feminization of the economy and the breakdown of traditional family norms. The result of which was not a 'gender trouble' to be celebrated but bemoaned. Lamentably, she argues, feminism will not be relevant to the millennium unless it addresses seriously or sufficiently the crisis of masculinity. Somewhere betwixt the two, Lynne Segal asks and answers the question *Why Feminism?* Her account offers a clear and interesting guide to the varied terrain explored by feminism, and gender theory more broadly. Segal proudly holds onto her socialist feminist agenda.

> Why feminism? Because its most radical goal, both personal and collective, has yet to be realized: a world which is a better place not just for some women, but for all women. In what I still call a socialist

feminist vision, that would be a far better world for boys and men, as well. (1999: 232)

Below I consider their deliberations about the state of feminism, but first I want to note a tone of writing that resonates across these texts. Taken in turn, each author's process of reflection reveals the comfort of wisdom that comes with age and the accompanying discomfort of memory that fades.

For example, in the beginning chapters each author readily admits that political interests are generational, are defined by a particular socio-historical moment. Each refers in passing to the distance between their experience of 1970s (university-based) UK feminism and the social, sexual and political experience of 'girls' in the late 1990s. Germaine Greer acknowledges the rise of 'girl power' thus: 'the longest revolution has many phases, false starts and blind alleys, all of which must be explored before a way through can be found' (1999: 310). Nevertheless, she predicts, second-wave feminism will gather momentum in the coming generations. Taking up where *The Female Eunuch* (1971) left off, she hopes her words in *The Whole Woman* will be a renewed call to arms.

Ros Coward recognizes a similar generation gap but believes the battles of feminism should be left in the past. With that particular territory now charted, young women may feel rather daunted by the feats of the amazons who marked the way.

Few, surely, can fail to recognize that the opportunities and expectations facing young women in the new millennium make thirty years ago seem like another planet. When I left university, the sex discrimination act and equal opportunities legislation had only just become law; battles about combining careers and motherhood still lay ahead. Now, rather than feeling there are uncharted waters in front of them, young women are more likely to feel daunted by the potency of the female icons before them. (1999:7)

Continuing she describes the ubiquitous state of feminism for young girls:

Individual feminists still meet with resistance and problems, but feminism as a movement has been extraordinarily successful; it has sunk into our unconscious. Our contemporary social world – and the way the sexes interact in it – is radically different from the one in which modern feminism emerged. Many of feminism's original objectives have been met, including the principle of equal pay for equal work and the possibility of financial independence. Girls now are growing up in a world radically different form the one described by the early feminists. Feminism no longer has to be reiterated but simply breathed. (Ibid.)

Segal is not quite so sure. In fact, she laments the distorted picture of feminism drawn by the likes of Coward. For Segal, the resulting polarization in the 1980s of 'totalizing and sanctimonious feminism' and those who 'caricature feminism as prudish and puritanical' is a deplorable 'twist in this tale of two generations of feminism' (1999: 7). One analogy drawn by Segal goes to the heart of the generational differences and the resulting difference in 'politics':

Around 1980 it would have been hard to find a single self-respecting feminist in Britain who had not trekked out to Grunwick's factory in west London, in support of the predominantly Asian women on strike, or at least considered such action. Two decades later, it would be hard to find a self-respecting feminist who had even heard of the predominantly Asian women on strike at Burnsall in Birmingham [over almost identical issues] (1999: 25)

A second note that resonates across the three texts is a slight aggravation with the fluidity of memories. Individual recollections fade; new commentators describe the past through contemporary lenses; intensity, passion is redirected, reinterpreted and reinvented. It is helpful to locate their distinctly different interpretations of 'feminisms remembered' alongside Sheila Rowbotham's comments on her first attempts to articulate feminism:

perceptions can be there one minute and gone the next ... as the years go by, what was once a contemporary account comes to reveal a particular historical movement, not simply because of what is said but in the very way it is written. (Rowbotham,1999: 2, also noted by Segal, 1999: 17)

Simplistic readings, Segal points out, overwrite the complexity of earlier formulations. She bemoans the affects of time on political ideals and energy: 'What often leaves erstwhile political crusaders with little more than mournful and confusing feelings of loss and regret – whatever our capacities for irony – is the way in which new narratives emerge as collective memories fade, writing-over those which once incited our most passionate actions' (1999: 9).

Coward, alternatively, welcomes the space to lay to rest the ghost of feminism and move on. Her relationship with feminism, her fading belief in the 'idea of being a feminist', and, in her view, feminism's continued obstinacy over socio-economic gender divisions draws attention to the distance time can place between oneself, politics and knowledge.

> When I first encountered feminism in the 1970s, it had the force and attraction of a profound explanatory system. ... Is feminism relevant at all now? It took me a long time before I allowed myself to ask this question. My intellectual and political formation were in feminism and it feels a bit like casting myself adrift and betraying friendships which have formed me, but for the past few years I have had a growing sense that, at some point ... I would have to look at feminism afresh. ... I needed to understand why feminism had once been so important and why I now felt it had become a strait-jacket. (1999: 3–4)

Such a position enrages Greer who reflects upon her own relationship to developments in feminism and her dismay at fading memories that lead to betrayal:

> For thirty years I have done my best to champion all the styles of feminism that came to public attention ... though I disagreed with some of the strategies and was as troubled as I should have been by some of the more fundamental conflicts, it was not until feminists of my own generation began to assert ... that feminism had gone too far that fire flared up in my belly ... it would have been inexcusable to remain silent. (1999: 1)

The distance travelled since the heady university days of the 1970s compels each of these icons to provide us with their personal, and (of course/therefore) political interpretation of feminism past and future. Collectively, this millennial can't may be simply a tale of the disharmony in 'the feminist movement' but there is more here than the familiar assertion of different feminisms or a sinister marketing ploy for publishers. One can detect a hint of urgency, a need to revive, to redirect, or perhaps to let go of that to which one gave birth.

Taking each in turn then, I want to briefly consider the assessment of the current state of feminism and subsequent roadmaps for the future by

'Feminism 2000'. The process of contextualizing their own beginnings in feminist politics feeds the direction for the future, but all agree on one point: for future success, feminism must change. As we have seen, Coward insists that feminism can only survive if a few 'sacred cows' are slaughtered, among them essentialist notions of power and oppression associated with a gender/sex binary. She believes there has been an overwhelming shift in gender politics:

> Feminism had come into being to attack a world of male privilege, a world where the economy was driven by male work and where individual homes mirrored this economic reality. In the 1980s this ceased to be true in any simple sense; the sexual composition of the workforce changed out of all recognition ... men were appearing in the opposite light. The huge increase in male unemployment, both in heavy industrial and small businesses accompanied by visible signs of recession suddenly revealed men as disproportionately affected ... feminism had give women the confidence to move into masculine areas. ... Men by contrast, were experiencing their work changes, this so-called feminization of labour, more like a smack in the eye. (1999: 44, 51)

According to Coward, men are experiencing a crisis in masculinity alongside, if not as a result of, the questioning of gender norms by feminists. While most would agree that the changing role of women since the 1960s has resulted in an increased awareness of the social construction of masculinity, I am not sure that as she maintains 'suggestions of a real crisis have been dismissed by many feminists with a reassertion of female rights and male inadequacies' (1999: 146). Nor do I think that 'men' are in crisis. Some white, heterosexual men privileged by patriarchy may be worried about any slight change in the balance of power but arguably others have welcomed attempts to deconstruct such rigid conceptions of masculinity (see, for example, Kimmel and Messner, 1992). Coward constructs a particular picture of feminism that has its social analysis and politics stuck somewhere in the late 1970s. Her journalistic style fails to engage with a more contemporary multi-faceted analysis of masculinity offered by 'old' feminists such as Segal and Campbell (1993). Her chapters on 'Whipping Boys' and 'Redundant Fathers' imply that some authors wish to undermine all men rather than acknowledging that contemporary feminist theory comfortably targets a range of oppressions based on 'genders'.

Greer movingly inspires followers in the opposite direction:

> The personal is still political. The millennial feminist has to be aware
> that oppression exerts itself in and through her most intimate
> relationships, beginning with the most intimate, her relationship
> with her body. More and more of her waking hours are to be spent in
> disciplining the recalcitrant body, fending off the diseases that it is
> heir to and making up for its inadequacies in shape, size, weight,
> colouring, hair distribution, muscle tone and orgiastic efficiency, and
> its incorrigible propensity for ageing. More of her life is wasted cleaning
> things that are already clean, trying to feed people who aren't hungry
> and labouring to, in, from and for chain-stores. Too much of her
> energy is sapped by being made to be afraid of everything but her real
> enemy, fear itself. (1999: 329–30)

While I agree generally with the values underpinning Greer's position,
I must admit that having survived the individualism of the 1980s, I do
not think it offers political priorities that inspire social change. Yes, the
listed daily female grind is burdensome. Yes, the deconstruction of this
intimate oppression would indicate success of feminist politics.
Nevertheless, in focusing on the personal, one can lose sight of the
social and the global. Fighting my own battles with intimate oppression is important. But it is not enough. Feminism may have begun by
politicizing the (white, middle-class) personal, but feminists over the
last 30 years did not stop there. Feminism has learned to hear and
respond to the diversities of individual oppressions and to evaluate
social structures that provide support for some women at the expense
of others.

Arguably, Segal offers a more balanced version of the journey
feminism has taken, including its relationship to gender theory and to
queer theory. She maintains a steady course toward transformative gender
equality. 'After feminism', she writes, 'after gender theory, after queer
theory after all the flaunting of the inherent instabilities or fluidities of
gender and sexuality, the problem remains: we still live in a world haunted
by cultural and personal fixations on sexual opposition' (1999: 65). The
women's movement may not need to let go of the fact that men generally
and individually oppress women in order to accommodate the thought
that some men may be uncomfortably struggling to renegotiate
masculinity. The 'emancipatory point is, surely, the hope that', in Segal's
words, 'we might feel better able to acknowledge and indulge real gender

ambiguities, rather than feel driven to reify or eliminate them, whether in oneself or in others' (1999: 70).

What might we glean from our encounter with these feminist texts? The overwhelming diversity of these three confirms what we already know: feminist politics may be nostalgically linked to 'feminism' but while it may have felt homogeneous and revolutionary for some it was never 'an ideology' embraced by every woman. At its core sits a familiarity with oppression. Those choosing to fight against it do so on different fronts, in different modes of battle and often for very different reasons. Their narratives speak in familiar tones of battles over identity politics. The inflection of voice commands a respect for 'herstories' individually recalled and insinuates worries about the distance from those writing the next chapter of feminism.

Generation Q

On the eve of the Millennium a similar but distinct conversation emerged in the 'gay and lesbian movement' who found itself having a rather queer turn. The 1990s advent of 'queer' politics, supported by a 'crack team' of post-modern (largely American) queer theorists, challenged the identity politics of the traditional 'gay and lesbian' movement. This challenge to traditional gay and lesbian politics can be seen as both political and generational. For example, a recent piece by Jill Humphrey, 'To Queer or not to Queer a Lesbian and Gay Group? Sexual and Gendered Politics at the Turn of the Century' (1999) describes the coalface of the battle over identity politics. This qualitative study of the lesbian and gay group of UNISON captures the difficult practicalities of integrating a traditional political group holding a clear 'credible' civil rights agenda with bisexual and transgendered UNISON members whose agenda and credibility were presumed to be suspect. She observes that for the anti-queer lobby:

> bisexuals and transgendered people represent a threat not only to the identity categories which have sustained lesbian and gay solidarities, but also to the civil rights agendas which have earned them credibility within the union and elsewhere. Or rather the prospect of queering the groups is viewed as tantamount to the extinction of the group. (1999: 224)

Humphrey admits that at the outset her sympathies lay with the anti-queer lobby who might threaten potential political gains. However, these sentiments are altered as she notes at the end of the article:

> Quite simply, it is difficult to justify any vision of justice for lesbian women and gay men if the pursuit of this vision, and its end-product, entails injustices against other sexual and gendered minorities. Or else, equality and emancipation for lesbians and gays constitutes a legitimate first step towards recognizing and remedying sexual and gendered oppressions, but it cannot be legitimate as the final goal, insofar as it is inherently incapable of bringing about emancipation from sexual and gendered oppression for all citizens. (1999: 240)

Her reflection on this process acknowledges histories and in doing so accepts that the challenges of a new generation may mean that change is inevitable and, possibly, necessary.

From a more 'disillusioned from within' perspective Chris Woods (1995: 25), a founder of OutRage! and now a television journalist, rails against the forgetfulness of the queer generation. As Humphrey stretches to acknowledge the political point made by queers in UNISON, Woods is outraged by one generation's need to create an identity in order to distance itself from another. Additionally, Woods worries about liberationist politics being completely lost in a queer, often drugged, culture of consumerism and performance. He argues that as queers strive to be different, a new generation of transgression has led away from a politics of social transformation. A new queer generation may overemphasize performance as transformation and, in doing so, is unable to articulate a clear political agenda.

Relatedly, an almost fundamentalist worship of post-modern theory, particularly in the form of Foucault, can be blind to previous contributions that similarly located the construction of a homosexual script within the complexity of historical and political networks. For example, McIntosh locates 'homosexuality in a comparative historical framework' suggesting that the 'homosexual should be seen as playing a social role rather than as having a condition' (McIntosh, 1981: 33, see also Weeks,1998: 135). In his intensely argued article, "The Homosexual Role" After 30 Years: An Appreciation of the work of Mary McIntosh', Jeffrey Weeks voices a similar dissatisfaction with the way in which some contemporary writers privilege the work of Michel Foucault:

> It is frustrating for those of us who have been toiling in this particular vineyard since the turn of the 1960s and 1970s to have our early efforts in understanding sexuality in general and homosexuality in particular, refracted back to us through post-Foucauldian abstractions and then

taken up as if the ideas are freshly minted. I am struck, for example, by the reception of queer theorists such as Eve Sedgwick (1985, 1990) and Judith Butler (1990, 1993) in recent writing about the body and sexuality (especially in literacy studies) in the Anglo-Saxon world, when, to this perhaps jaundiced eye, they are not saying anything fundamentally different from what some of us have been trying to say for 25 years or so, inspired in large part by a reading of Mary McIntosh's 'The Homosexual Role', which was first published in 1968. (1998: 132)

Here Weeks echoes the discomfort of fading memories found in the 'Feminism 2000' literature. It suggests that reflection necessitates an honest look in the mirror: seeing the lines of history, the retold stories, the fading memories, and the uncomfortableness of identity changing over time. The mirror doesn't lie. Self-reflection reveals both altruism and selfishness; benevolence and competitiveness. To this end, Segal recalls that women's liberation was 'in its heyday a theory and practice of social transformation: full of all the embroiled and messy actions, hostilities and compromises of collective political engagement' (Segal, 1999: 15). Those previously active in the 'gay and lesbian movement' will remember heated arguments over s/m, men-who-love-boys, violence, political lesbianism, AIDS, activism and bisexuality. The late amazing Tejan, Gloria Anzaldúa commented that 'identity is not a bunch of little cubby holes stuffed respectively with intellect, race, sex, class, vocation, gender. ... identity is a river – a process' (1991: 252–3). That may be an accurate description of the identity politics discourse within 'feminism' and the 'gay and lesbian' movement. Moreover, fluidity seems an essential part of that process of political identities and agendas. However, from the above discussions emerges a clear consensus that if identity is a river flowing through time it must carry with it a sense of self, direction and movement. Alternatively, identity is a collection of stagnant water or individual drops disappearing upon contact with arid land. To that end, I want to consider a few works that capture the millennial debate over the future flow of the 'lgbtq' movement.

Material realities

Two special issues of the journal *Sexualities* published at the dawn of the new Millennium addressed, either explicitly or implicitly, the future of 'the movement' from distinctly different perspectives. First, in the November 1999 issue: *Stretching Queer Boundaries: Queer Method and Practice for the 21stCentury*, Clare Hemmings and Felicity Grace bring together papers originally given at the University of North London *Queer Too ... ?* seminar series. The editors claim to be motivated by a concern that queer theory had become 'jaded and lacklustre' 'possibly in danger of ceasing to be relevant to the lives of queer subjects' (Hemmings and Grace, 1999: 390). Moreover, they add:

> we began to wonder if we had simply been imagining queer's theoretical and political importance in the late 1990s. One thinks immediately of similar arguments made about queer theory's strange – given its history in early 1990s AIDS activism – yet enduring inability to inform theory through *material concerns* such as poverty, racism, violence or even sexism. (1999: 390–1 my emphasis)

'We wanted to address', they continue, 'queer theory's "fear of being ordinary" ' (ibid.: 392). The issue includes such under-explored 'material concerns' as representations of gay male sex, the femme narrative and the boredom of butch/femme role play. One article that tackles a topic more traditionally associated with the 'material' considers sexism found in bank lending practices. While the information in this particular article is located broadly within queer theory, the data and analysis would appear less distorted in a more traditional feminist journal. In the final article of the collection, Ruth Holliday discusses 'The Comfort of Identity'. Her comments, employing Sennett's *Flesh and Stone* (1994), on queer, and gay and lesbian, identity, are, to say the least, anxiety-provoking:

> The comfort of identity is thus far from an individual or individualizing state within queer culture. Rather it is always social, though it may sometimes be produced through the rhetoric of individualism. ... [Sennett] implies that comfort provides a kind of social detachment, a kind of separation from real connections with others. Being comfortable – as in comfortably off – implies a lack of necessity to worry about the world or one's position in it. Comfort is an easy, unthinking state. Perhaps, then, comfort means social and personal atrophy. The comfort gained through many uncomfortable years of political struggle, the comfort of a revamped scene, the comfort of a more liberal state and some protection from discrimination in the workplace have all produced a more comfortable (lesbian and gay) identity and politics. (1999: 489)

Holliday posits that such 'comfort is to be feared since it is discomfort, displacement, disruption which moves (queer) politics forward to a more complex and less exclusive or complacent place' (ibid.). I am left unsure how this perpetual discomfort is significantly different form the 'transgression for its own sake' that irritated the issue editors initially. The fetishization of discomfort sits rather uneasily with the initial desire to deal with material realities. Quite simply, 'comfort' is a political and personal goal for many caught in situations of poverty, abuse and oppression. Some of us may need to be less comfortable so that everyone can share in a modicum of comfort, but surely discomfort is not a utopian ideal.

The second special edition *Speaking from a Lesbian Position: Opening up Sexuality Studies*, appeared in May 2000. Clare Farquhar and Tamsin Wilton bring together a collection of work from the British Sociological Association Lesbian Studies Group because

> although sexuality studies is now a rapidly expanding area, lesbian issues continue to be marginalized within it, even within the pages of this journal. ... at the time that this special issue was conceived, the first seven issues had not thrown up a single substantive article about lesbian sexualities. (Farquhar and Wilton, 2000: 131)

Continuing, they observe that lesbians have historically found 'allegiance somewhat torn between gay studies and women's studies' and that queer communities and the academy 'have left such problems behind' (Ibid.). While not highlighted by the editors, the difference between topics in this journal and the *Queer* edition is striking. Lesbians, presumably informed by 'feminism', tackle material concerns such as gender inequalities at work, citizenship, self-insemination and fatherhood. Lesbians thus motivated in their research rarely have been privileged enough to worry about 'ceasing to be relevant', not 'challenging', or 'ordinary'.

As acknowledged by the 'Queer' issue editors, critiques of queer theory often focus on its apparent inability to address material concerns. This familiar topic is poignantly described in a predominantly US focused collection *Queerly Classed: Gay men and Lesbians Write About Class* edited by Susan Raffo, which brings 'working-class made good' writers together to engage with tensions between 'class' and 'queer' (Raffo, 1997). Within this setting, Elizabeth Clare offers an insightful criticism of 'queer elites' celebrating another momentous event:

> The twenty-fifth anniversary of the Stonewall Riots (Stonewall 25) ... was a defining event of queer identity in the '90s. I didn't go. ... I've gone to Lesbian and Gay Pride marches for the last

decade, but Stonewall 25 was a commercial extravaganza of huge proportions. ... Who could afford the benefit dance at $150, the concert at $50, the T-shirt at $25? ... And sliding scales? They're evidently a thing of the past. Stonewall 25 strikes me not so much as a celebration of a powerful and life-changing uprising of drag queens and bull dykes fed up with the cops, but as a middle-and up-class urban party that opened its doors only to those who could afford it. (Clare, 1997: 23–4)

In the late 1990s I attended a (UK) Stonewall fund-raising ball in London. As I recall: it was a 'Tea-Dance', tickets were not cheap and there were no sliding scales, and the London 'lgbtq' elites sat at tables perched above the masses with large men guarding the stairway ensuring those that rose above it all were deserving. This was a fund-raising event and, perhaps, economic reality dictates the 'most people at the highest price' approach. Maybe those that pay more should get better seats. While the elites circulated amongst the crowd, no one in attendance could spot socialist or liberationist principles which had for so long provided a political rudder for 'the movement'. I suspect this could be interpreted as foreshadowing a 'New Labour' approach rather than strictly 'post-modern'. Nevertheless, at the time, it was very queer. It was a great party, but thoughts of 'material realities' were conspicuously absent.

Heated debate

To turn up the heat on this point slightly, I want to highlight one US intervention into this queer conversation. As the designated driver of queer, Judith Butler's voice can be distinctly heard directing deliberations at the intersection of feminist and queer theory. Those that believe her analysis of the journey thus far is inspired and, her performative positionings appealing, dismiss calls for a more direct political narrative. At the beginning of the Millennium this debate reached a particular crescendo in a rather thorough attack on Butler's work by Martha Nussbaum, professor of law and global leader in issues facing women. Nussbaum's commentary on the 'Professor of Parody' characterizes Butler's positioning within queer theory thus:

One is given the impression of a mind so profoundly cogitative that it will not pronounce on anything lightly: so one waits, in awe of its depth, for it finally to do so. In this way obscurity creates an aura of importance. ... It bullies the reader into granting that, since one cannot figure out what is going on, there must be something significant going on. ... Thus obscurity fills the void left by an absence of a real complexity of thought and argument. (1999b: 39)

While I am not going to rehearse Butler's pronouncements here, I do want to pause for a moment over a couple of points which seem to shore up the queer conversation. In paraphrasing, I will undoubtedly loose crucial nuances as this seems to characterize her critics. Firstly, the only avenue for disrupting the gender binarism that defines normative politics, and indeed individual selves, is parodic performance. As Nussbaum notes,

Her best known idea, her conception of politics as a parodic performance, is born out of the sense of a (strictly limited) freedom that comes from the recognition that one's ideas of gender have been shaped by forces that are social rather than biological. We are doomed to repetition of the power structures into which we are born, but we can at least make fun of them; and some ways of making fun are subversive assaults on the original norms. (1999b: 40)

I have some sympathy for this approach to politics – after all, feminism challenged women to believe the 'personal was the political' and therefore every act of resistance to oppression, no matter how minor, was a political act. However, for Butler it seems that individual or collective agency cannot significantly alter the cultural and/or political signifiers that define/oppress. In Butler's own words, there is only limited agency in the parodic performance:

Called by an injurious name, I come into social being, and because I have a certain inevitable attachment to my existence, because a certain narcissism takes hold of any term that confers existence, I am led to embrace the terms that injure me because they constitute me socially. (1997b: 104)

Moreover, the combination of this individualized approach and the absence of a clear narrative for socio-economic change deconstruct the political into intangibility (see Wilson, 1997). Nussbaum warns:

There is a void, then at the heart of Butler's notion of politics. But let there be no mistake: for Butler, as for Foucault, subversion is subversion and it can in principle go in any direction. ... In Butler, resistance is always imagined as personal more or less private, involving no unironic, organized public action for legal or institutional change. ... It instructs people that they can, right now, without compromising their security, do something bold. But the boldness is entirely gestural ... it offers only a false hope. Hungry women are not fed by this, battered women are not sheltered by it, raped women do not find justice in it, gay and lesbians do not achieve legal protections through it ... hope for a world of real justice ... equality ... dignity ... has been banished, even perhaps mocked as sexually tedious. ... it collaborates with evil. (1999b: 43)

Butler collaborating with evil: perhaps in the realms of professional courteous exchange, that goes slightly too far. Nussbaum's words, however, do vociferously express a shared fear of queer: that in failing to engage with material realities it fails to provide an effective challenge to the oppressive structures of modernity. Nussbaum simply cannot give an inch to someone who despite economic and academic privilege immorally refuses to mobilize resources against oppression. I am not sure Butler would recognize herself in this depiction. Nevertheless, this isolates a particular bit of conversation that polarized the debate about the future political agenda for lgbtq citizens. As an American, and a Texan, I can have sympathy for the intensity of Nussbaum's argument. With political power in the hands of the Christian right, parody is not political enough. Privileged Americans often fail to see material realities of any 'other', particularly those that are already doomed to hell. Any US conversation about change must find a common language about material realities and the lived experiences of criminalized, economically, socially and politically excluded US citizens – about equality, and justice.

Relatedly, I would argue that over the last eight years lgbtq citizens in the United Kingdom have witnessed an amazing shift in political, economic and social constructs of our lives. Many heteronormative policies that embodied oppression based on sexual orientation have been removed or replaced by those providing a degree of protection: the repeal of Section 28, equalizing the age of consent, EU anti-discrimination legislation. In 'family policy' lgbtq citizens can register civil partnerships, adopt, foster and have increased access to fertility treatments in order to create families. Any UK university course addressing issues relating to 'the family' whether in politics, sociology, religion, medicine, law or visual arts would be incomplete without addressing this 'new'/now socially sanctioned phenomena of the gay and lesbian or queer family. While it may be an enviable position, a list of policy changes does not give a full political, or material, context. As the US political context sets a particular agenda for opposition, the UK political and material realities have led to an opening up of space for the advancement of lgbtq-friendly policies.

For example, clearly policy recognition of gay and lesbian couples with/without children as 'families' necessitates the reconstruction of the modernist conception of 'family', beyond that recognized historically, socially or, for some, naturally. Such a move deconstructs the heterosexual monopoly of the family. However, it has been argued that this possibility has arisen only because the global capitalist project no longer needs/values the nuclear family model. Lee Badgett's study 'Variations on an Equitable Theme: Explaining International Same-Sex Partner Recognition Laws' (SSPR) suggest that 'tolerant attitudes toward homosexuality, low religiosity, and high levels of cohabitation are the primary predictors of a country's legal recognition of same-sex partners' (2004: 1). She argues that a political conflict model helps 'explain why legislators and voters in countries where marriage is seen as less valuable might be more willing to change the law to allow same-sex couples access to some or all rights and responsibilities of marriage' (2004: 14). Countries with SSPR laws have 'fewer highly religious people, more union members, more gay and lesbian organizations and more left governments suggesting a stronger liberal presence and a smaller conservative religious base for opponents of same-sex partner recognition' (ibid.). She concludes that the presence of civil rights laws do not act as predictors of acceptance of SSPR, but that the potential for change must be seen in context of a whole host of cultural, religious, economic and political factors. When a thing becomes less valuable, the economically privileged are less concerned with exclusive rights to it. Similarly, the extension of UK welfare rights, human rights and anti-discrimination legislation can be seen as necessary to the continued progress of capitalism, for example to enable consistency in the European market (Waaldijk and Bonini-Baraldi, 2004). The emphasis on the economy in the European Union has opened up political space in the United Kingdom to challenge discrimination and establish legal protections for many lgbtq citizens. We may have an easier conversation this side of the Atlantic, a completely different political atmosphere, but the outcome is still intrinsically tied to the modern economic/material realities.

Conclusion

The 'Feminism 2000' authors express fears about the future of feminism, but each worry is significantly different. A 'Greerist' fear is of a loss of message resulting in the unconscious collusion with the oppressors. This does not seem to be reflected in the lgbtq literature considered above. A 'Cowardly' fear is of feminism's inability to take responsibility for the redefinition of gender structures that have had a wide-ranging effect on both women and men and to redefine itself in light of that restructuring. The only fear comparable to her worry about the effects of feminism on masculinity would be a worry about the potential for lgbtq politics to cause a crisis of heterosexuality – something one might welcome. The fear found in Segal is of losing sight of transformative socialist goals while taking seriously the responsibility for changing social structures. While some of the lgbtq writers considered here give this only lip-service, others are anxious that material realities stay at the fore of any political agenda.

In the final pages, Segal posits the need to have an understanding of the complexity of subjectivity, the multiplicity of needs and the creativity required to foster effective change. I doubt she will ever be post-feminist, partially due to the unlikelihood of post-patriarchy, but primarily due to the continued oppressive structures of modern capitalism. On this point, I have sympathy. I think the rumours of the end of modernity are exaggerated, but I have heard a few whispers that we may be post-queer (see Meeks and Stein or this volume). As a political theorist with my 'soft-spot for deconstruction', I welcomed queer theory's deconstruction of modernity's definitions of justice, equality, freedom, identity and sexuality, and its radical politics inspiring individuals beyond monetary contributions to political action groups. However, my 'lesbian feminist pragmatism' cannot set aside the need to concentrate on the material realities in which we construct our daily lives. If this review of 'Feminism 2000' highlighted a tone of angst, that of the lgbtq literature hints at somewhat renewed energy for interventions about poverty, employment, family structure, child-care, etc. Lively conversation of academics/ activists is invigorating and creative, but inevitably the topic returns to oppressive social structures. Lavender or rainbow – surely the point is that the privileged of modern capitalism find us menacing.

References

Adam, B. D. (2003) 'The Defense of Marriage Act and American Exceptionalism: The "Gay Marriage" Panic in the United States', *The Journal of the History of Sexuality*, 12 (2): 259–76.

Adkins, L. (1995) *Gendered Work: Sexuality, Family and the Labour Market*. Buckingham: Open University Press.

Adkins, L. (2002) *Revisions: Gender and Sexuality in Late Modernity*. Buckingham: Open University Press.

Ahmed, S., Kilby, J., Lury, C., McNeil, M. and Skeggs, B. (2000) 'Introduction: Thinking Through Feminism', in S. Ahmed, J. Kilby, C. Lury, M. McNeil, and B. Skeggs (eds), *Transformations: Thinking Through Feminism*. London: Routledge.

Alsop, R., Fitzsimons, A. and Lennon, K. (2002) *Theorizing Gender*. Cambridge: Polity Press.

Anzaldúa, G. (1991) 'To(o) Queer the Writer – Loca, escritora, y chicana', in B. Warland (ed.), *InVersions: Writing by Dykes, Queers and Lesbians*. Vancouver: Press Gang.

Anzaldúa, G. (1992) 'To(o) Queer the Writer – Loca, escritora y chicana', in B. Warland (ed.), *InVersions: Writing by Dykes, Queers and Lesbians*. London: Open Letters.

Anzaldúa, G. (1999) *Borderlands/La Frontera: The New Mestiza*, 2nd edn. San Francisco: Aunt Lute Press.

Arruda, T. (1992) Personal Interview, 27 October.

Badgett, L. (2004) 'Variations on an Equitable Theme: Explaining Same Sex Partner Recognition Laws', Paper presented to American Political Science Association.

Bakker, I. and Gill, S. (eds) (2003) *Power, Production and Social Reproduction*. New York: Palgrave.

Bannerji, H. (1995) *Thinking Through: Essays on Feminism, Marxism and Anti-racism*. Toronto: Women's Press.

Barrett, M. (1992) 'Words and Things: Materialism and Method in Contemporary Feminist Analysis', in M. Barrett, and A. Phillips (eds), *Destabilizing Theory: Contemporary Feminist Debates*. Cambridge: Polity Press.

Bawer, B. (1995) 'The Marrying Kind', *The Advocate*, 9 (19): 80.

Beck-Gernsheim, E. (1999) 'On the way to a Post-Familial Family', *Theory, Culture and Society*, 15 (3–4): 53–70.

Bederman, G. (1995) *Manliness and Civilization: A Cultural History of Gender and Race in the United States 1880–1917*. Chicago: University of Chicago Press.

Bell, D. and Binnie, J. (2000) *The Sexual Citizen: Queer Politics and Beyond*. Cambridge: Polity Press.

Berlant, L. (1997) *The Queen of America Goes to Washington City*. Durham, NC and London: Duke University Press.

Birch, E. (1997) 'Two Victories Down, Two Big Struggles to Go', *Harvard Gay and Lesbian Review*, 4 (2): 6.

Blackwood, E. (2005) 'Transnational Sexualities in One Place – Indonesian Readings', *Gender & Society*, 19: 221–42.

Blasius, M. and Phelan, S. (eds) (1997) *We Are Everywhere*. New York: Routledge.

Bolonik, K. (2004). 'Not Your Mother's Lesbians', *New York Magazine*, 12 January. http://www.newyorkmetro.com/nymetro/news/features/n_9708/index.html, Accessed 14th August 2005.

Bordo, S. (1993) 'Feminism, Foucault and the Politics of the Body', in C. Ramazanoğlu (ed.), *Up against Foucault*. London: Routledge.

Bordo, S. (1998) 'Bringing Body to Theory', in D. Welton (ed.), *Body and Flesh: A Philosophical Reader*. Oxford: Blackwell.

Botkin, M. (1987) 'A Gay Affair', *Gay Community News*, 10 (18): 16.

Braidotti, R. (1994) *Nomadic Subjects*. New York: Columbia University Press.

Brandenburg, S. (2004) 'The Perfection of Vision and Knowledge: The Concept of Perception and of Sexed Subjectivity in Contemporary Gender Theories and Their Political Consequences'. Unpublished Paper.

Bright, S. (1984) 'The Year of the Lustful Lesbian', *New York Native*, 30 July– 12 August.

Brodribb, S. (1992) *Nothing Mat(t)ers: A Feminist Critique of Postmodernism*. Melbourne: Spinifex Press.

Bronski, M. (2004) 'Can Marriage Be Saved: A Forum', *The Nation*, 7 (5): 22.

Bunch, C. (1975a) 'Not for Lesbians Only', *Quest, A Feminist Quarterly*, 2 (2): 50–6.

Bunch, C. (1975b) 'Lesbians in Revolt', in N. Myron and C. Bunch (eds), *Lesbianism and the Women's Movement*. Baltimore, MD: Diana Press.

Burnworth, V. (1993) 'The Matrimonial Noose', *The Advocate*, 10 (19): 80.

Butler, J. (1990) *Gender Trouble: Feminism and the Subversion of Identity*. London and New York: Routledge.

Butler, J. (1992) 'Contingent Foundations: Feminism and the Question of "Postmodernism" ' in J. Butler, and J. W. Scott (eds), *Feminists Theorize the Political*. London: Routledge.

Butler, J. (1993) *Bodies That Matter: On the Discursive Limits of 'Sex'*. London and New York: Routledge.

Butler, J. (1994) 'Against Proper Objects', *differences: A Journal of Feminist Cultural Studies*, 6 (2/3): 1–26.

Butler, J. (1997a) 'Critically Queer', in S. Seidman (ed.), *Queer/Sociology*. Oxford: Blackwell.

Butler, J. (1997b) *The Psychic Life of Power*. Stanford: Stanford University Press.

Butler, J. (2004) 'Can Marriage Be Saved: A Forum', *The Nation*, 7 (5): 20–1.

Calhoun, C. (1995) 'The Gender Closet: Lesbian Disappearance under the Sign "Women" ' *Feminist Studies*, 21 (1): 7–34.

Calhoun, C. (2001) *Feminism, the Family, and the Politics of the Closet*. New York: Oxford University Press.

Califia, P. (1981) 'What Is Gay Liberation?' *Heresies*, 3 (12) 30–4.

Cameron, D. (1997/98) 'Back to Nature', *Trouble & Strife*, 36: 6–15.

Campbell, B. (1993) *Goliath: Britain's Dangerous Places*. London: Metheun.

Cantú, L. (2002) '*De Ambiente*: Queer Tourism and the Shifting Boundaries of Mexican Male Sexualities', *GLQ: A Journal of Lesbian and Gay Studies*, 8 (1–2): 139–66.

Carabine, J. (1996) 'Heterosexuality and Social Policy', in D. Richardson (ed.), *Theorizing Heterosexuality: Telling it Straight*. Buckingham: Open University Press.

Carlston, E. G. (1993) '*Zami* and the Politics of Plural Identity', in W. J. Wolfe and J. Penelope (eds), *Sexual Practice, Textual Theory: Lesbian Cultural Criticism*. Cambridge, MA and Oxford, UK: Blackwell.

Carrier, J. (1995) *De Los Otros: Intimacy and Homosexuality among Mexican Men*. New York: Columbia University Press.

Chancer, L. S. (1998) *Reconcilable Differences*. Berkeley: University of California Press.

Chauncey, G. (1989) 'Christian Brotherhood or Sexual Perversion? Homosexual Identities and the Construction of Sexual Boundaries in the World War 1 Era', in M. Duberman, M. Vicinus and G. Chauncey (eds), *Hidden from History: Reclaiming Gay and Lesbian Past*. New York: Meridian.

Chauncey, G. (2004) *Why Marriage?* New York: Basic Books.

Chou, W. (2000) *Tongzhi: Politics of Same-Sex Eroticism in Chinese Societies*. New York: Haworth Press.

Christina, G. (1990) 'Drawing the Line', *On Our Backs*, 6: 14–15.

Clare, E. (1997) 'Losing Home', in S. Raffo (ed.), *Queerly Classed: Gay men and Lesbians Write about Class*. Boston, MA: South End Press.

Clark, D. (1991) 'Commodity Lesbianism', *Camera Obscura*, 25/26: 181–201.

Clarke, C. (1984) 'The Failure to Transform: Homophobia in the Black Community', quoted in b. hooks (ed.), *Feminist Theory from Margin to Center*. Boston, MA: South End Press.

Cockburn, C. (1993) *In the Way of Women*. London: Macmillan.

Cohen, C. (1996) 'The Price of Inclusion in the Marriage Club', *Gay Community News*, 24 (3–4): 27, 37–8.

Cohen, C. (1997) 'Punks, Bulldaggers, and Welfare Queens', *GLQ: A Journal of Lesbian and Gay Studies*, 4 (3): 437–65.

Cohen, E. (1993) *Talk on the Wilde Side*. New York: Routledge.

Cohen, J. (1997) 'Rethinking Privacy: Autonomy, Identity, and the Abortion Controversy', in J. Weintraub and K. Kumar (eds), *Public and Private in Thought and Practice*. Chicago: University of Chicago Press.

Collins, P. H. (2004) *Black Sexual Politics*. New York: Routledge.

Combahee River Collective (1983) 'Combahee River Collective Statement', originally published 1977, in B. Smith (ed.), *Home Girls: A Black Feminist Anthology*. New York: Kitchen Table Women of Color Press.

Connell, R. W. (1995) *Masculinities*. Cambridge: Polity Press.

Connell, R. W. (2000) *The Men and the Boys*. Cambridge: Polity Press.

Coole, D. (1994) 'Wither Feminisms?' *Political Studies*, 42: 128–34.

Coontz, S. (1997) *The Way We Really Are: Coming to Terms with America's Changing Families*. New York: Basic Books.

Cooper, D. (2004) *Challenging Diversity. Rethinking Equality and the Value of Difference*. Cambridge: Cambridge University Press.

Coward, R. (1999) *Sacred Cows: Is Feminism Relevant to the New Millennium?* London: Harper Collins.

Crews, R. (2004) 'No Court Ruling Can Change the Fact that Marriage is About One Man and One Woman', in R. Baird and S. Rosenbaum (eds), *Same-Sex Marriage: The Moral and Legal Debate*, 2nd edn. Amherst: Prometheus Books.

Cruz-Malavé, A. and Manalansan IV, M. F. (eds) (2002) *Queer Globalizations*. New York: New York University Press.

de Lauretis, T. (1994) 'Habit Changes', *differences: A Journal of Feminist Cultural Studies*, 6 (Summer–Fall): 296–313.

Delphy, C. (1984) *Close to Home: A Materialist Analysis of Women's Oppression.* London: Hutchinson.

Delphy, C. (1993) 'Rethinking Sex and Gender', *Women's Studies International Forum*, 16 (1): 1–19.

D'Emilio, J. (2000) 'Cycles of Change, Questions of Strategy, the Gay and Lesbian Movement after Fifty Years', in C. A. Rimmerman, K. D. Wald and C. Wilcox (eds), *The Politics of Gay Rights*. London: University of Chicago Press.

Dollimore, J. (1991) *Sexual Dissidence*. Basingstoke: Open University Press.

Duggan, L. (1993) 'The Trials of Alice Mitchell', *Signs*, 18 (4): 791–814.

Duggan, L. (1996) 'The Marriage Juggernaut', *Gay Community News*, 24 (3–4): 5, 26, 34.

Duggan, L. and Hunter, N. (1995) *Sex Wars: Sexual Dissent and Political Culture.* New York: Routledge.

Dunlap, D. (1996) 'Fearing a Toehold for Gay Marriage, Conservatives Rush to Bar the Door', *New York Times*, 3 (6): A13.

Dunlap, M. (1997) 'Choosing', in A. Sullivan (ed.), *Same-Sex Marriage: Pro & Con.* New York: Vintage.

Ebert, T. L. (1993) 'Ludic Feminism, the Body, Performance and Labor: Bringing Materialism Back into Feminist Cultural Studies', *Cultural Critique*, 23: 5–50.

Equal Opportunities Commission (2005) *Key Facts about Women and Men in Great Britain*. Manchester: Equal Opportunities Commission.

Escoffier, J. (1990) 'Inside the Ivory Closet: The Challenge Facing Lesbian and Gay Studies', *Out/Look*, 10: 40–8

Eskridge, W. (1996) *The Case for Same-Sex Marriage*. New York: Free Press.

Evans, D. (1993) *Sexual Citizenship: the Material Construction of Sexualities.* London: Routledge.

Faderman, L. (1981) *Surpassing the Love of Men: Romantic Friendship and Love between Women from the Renaissance to the Present.* New York: William Morrow.

Faderman, L. (1991) *Odd Girls and Twilight Lovers: A History of Lesbian Life in Twentieth-Century America*. New York: Columbia University Press.

Farquhar, C. and Wilton, T. (eds) (2000) 'Speaking from a Lesbian Position: Opening up Sexuality Studies', *Sexualities*, Special Issue, 3(2, May): 131–272.

Farwell, M. (1996) *Heterosexual Plots and Lesbian Narratives*. New Year: New York University Press.

Fausto-Sterling, A. (2000) *Sexing the Body*, 2nd edn. New York: Basic Books.

Ferguson, R. A. (2003). *Aberrations in Black: Towards a Queer of Color Critique.* Minneapolis: University of Minnesota Press.

Fernandez-Kelly, P. (1987) *For We Are Sold, I and My People: Women and Industry in Mexico's Frontier*. Albany: SUNY Press.

Flax, J. (1992) 'The End of Innocence', in J. Butler and J. W. Scott (eds), *Feminists Theorize the Political*. London: Routledge.

Flax, J. (1993) *Disputed Subjects: Essays on Psychoanalysis, Politics and Philosophy.* London: Routledge.

Floyd, K. (forthcoming) *Reifying Desire: Male Sexuality and Modern U.S. Culture.* Minneapolis: University of Minnesota Press.

Foster, T. (1990) ' "The Very House of Difference": Gender as "Embattled" Standpoint', *Genders*, 8(Summer): 17–37.

Foucault, M. (1978) *The History of Sexuality, Vol 1*. Originally published 1976, Trans. R. Hurley. New York: Pantheon.

Foucault, M. (1979) *The History of Sexuality, Vol I*. London: Allen Lane.

Foucault, M. (1980) *The History of Sexuality, Vol 1*. Trans. R. Hurley. New York: Vintage Books.

Fraser, N. (1995) 'Pragmatism, Feminism, and the Linguistic Turn', in L. J. Nicholson (ed.), *Feminist Contentions: A Philosophical Exchange*. London: Routledge.

Fraser, N. (1997) *Justice Interruptus: Critical Reflections on the 'Postsocialist' Condition*. London: Routledge.

Fuss, D. (1989) *Essentially Speaking: Feminism, Nature & Difference*. New York and London: Routledge.

Fuss, D. (ed.) (1991a) *Inside/Out: Lesbian Theories, Gay Theories*. New York: Routledge.

Fuss, D. (1991b) 'Introduction', in D. Fuss (ed.), *Inside/Out: Lesbian Theories, Gay Theories*. New York: Routledge.

Gagnon, J. (2004) 'Sexual Conduct Revisited', in J. Gagnon (ed.), *An Interpretation of Desire*. Chicago: University of Chicago Press.

Gagnon, J. and Simon, W. (1974) *Sexual Conduct*. London: Hutchinson.

Gallagher, J. (1996) 'State of the Unions: Love & War', *The Advocate*, 7 (23): 22–7.

Gallagher, J. (1997) 'The Marriage Go-Around', *The Advocate*, 1 (21): 63.

Gamson, J. (1998) 'Must Identity Movements Self-Destruct? A Queer Dilemma', in P. M. Nardi and B. E. Schneider (eds), *Social Perspectives in Lesbian and Gay Studies*. London: Routledge.

Garber, L. (2001) *Identity Poetics: Race, Class, and the Lesbian-Feminist Roots of Queer Theory*. New York: Columbia University Press.

Garber, M. (1992) *Vested Interests: Cross-Dressing and Cultural Anxiety*. New York and London: Routledge.

Garfinkel, H. (1967) *Studies in Ethnomethodology*. Englewood Cliffs, NJ: Prentice Hall.

Gibson-Graham, J. K. (1996) *The End of Capitalism (as we knew it): A Feminist Critique of Political Economy*. London: Blackwell.

Giddens, A. (1991) *Modernity and Self-Identity*. Stanford: Stanford University Press.

Giddens, A. (1992) *The Transformation of Intimacy*. Stanford: Stanford University Press.

Glick, E. (2000) 'Sex Positive: Feminism, Queer Theory and the Politics of Transgression', *Feminist Review*, 64: 19–45.

Goffman, E. (1963) *Stigma: Notes on the Management of Spoiled Identity*. New York: Simon & Schuster.

Goffman. E. (1969) *The Presentation of Self*. London: Allen Lane.

Goffman, E. (1976) 'Gender Display', *Studies in the Anthropology of Visual Communication*, 3: 69–77.

Goffman, E. (1977) 'The Arrangement Between the Sexes', *Theory and Society*, 4: 301–31.

Graff, E. J. (1996) 'Retying the Knot', *The Nation*, 6 (24): 12.

Grahn, J. (1985) *The Highest Apple: Sappho and the Lesbian Poetic Tradition*. San Francisco: Spinsters Ink.

Gray, J. (1996) *Mars and Venus in the Bedroom*. London: Vermillion.

Greer, G. (1971) *The Female Eunuch*. London Paladin.

Greer, G. (1999) *The Whole Woman*. London: Doubleday.

Grewal, I. and Kaplan, C. (eds) (1994) *Scattered Hegemonies: Postmodernity and Transnational Feminist Practices*. University of Minnesota: Minneapolis and London.

Grosz, E. (1994) 'Experimental Desire: Rethinking Queer Subjectivity', in J. Copjec (ed.), *Supposing the Subject*. London: Verso.

Grosz, E. (1995) *Space, Time and Perversion: The Politics of Bodies*. Sydney: Allen and Unwin.

Guillaumin, C. (1995) *Racism, Sexism, Power and Ideology*. London: Routledge.

Halberstam, J. (2005) *In a Queer Time and Place: Transgender Bodies, Subcultural Lives*. New York: New York University Press.

Halperin, D. (1995) *Saint Foucault: Towards a Gay Hagiography*. New York: Oxford University Press.

Hammond, K. (1980) 'An Interview with Audre Lorde', *American Poetry Review*, 9 (2, March/April): 18–21.

Hammond, K. (1981) 'Audre Lorde: Interview', *Denver Quarterly*, 16(1, Spring): 10–27.

Haraway, D. (1990) 'A Manifesto for Cyborgs: Science, Technology, and Socialist Feminism in the 1980s', originally published 1985, in L. J. Nicholson (ed.), *Feminism/Postmodernism*. New York: Routledge.

Hartmann, H. (1978) 'The Unhappy Marriage of Marxism and Feminism: Towards a More Progressive Union', *Capital and Class*, 8: 1–33.

Hausman, B. (1995) *Changing Sex: Transsexualism, Technology and the Idea of Gender*. Durham, NC: Duke University Press.

Hawley, J. (ed.) (2001) *Postcolonial, Queer*. New York: State University of New York Press.

Heller, D. (ed.) (1997) *Cross Purposes: Lesbians, Feminists, and the Limits of Alliance*. Bloomington, IN: Indiana University Press.

Hemmings, C. and Grance, F. (eds) (1999) 'Stretching Queer Boundaries: Queer Method and Practice for the 21st Century', *Sexualities*, Special Issue, 2 (4): Nov.

Hennessy, R. (1993a) *Materialist Feminism and the Politics of Discourse*. New York, Routledge.

Hennessy, R. (1993b) 'Queer Theory: A Review of the *differences* Special Issue and Wittig's *The Straight Mind*', *Signs*, 18(Summer): 964–73.

Hennessy, R. (1994) 'Queer Theory, Left Politics', *Rethinking Marxism*, 7 (3): 85–111.

Hennessy, R. (1995) 'Queer Visibility in Commodity Culture', in L. J. Nicholson and S. Seidman (eds), *Social Postmodernism: Beyond Identity Politics*. Cambridge: Cambridge University Press.

Hennessy, R. (2000) *Profit and Pleasure: Sexual Identities in Late Capitalism*. New York: Routledge.

Hennessy, R. and Ojeda, M. (eds) (2005) *NAFTA From Below: Maquiladora Workers, Campesinos, and Indigenous Farmers Speak Back*. San Antonio, TX: Coalition for Justice in the Maquiladoras.

Henwood, D. (2004) 'Hooking Up, Shacking Up, Splitting Up', *The Nation*, 7 (5): 27.

Hinsch, B. (1990) *Passions of the Cut Sleeve: The Male Homosexual Tradition in China*. Berkeley: University of California Press.

Holland, J., Ramazanoğlu, C., Sharpe, S. and Thomson, R. (1996) 'In the Same Boat? The Gendered (In)Experience of First Heterosex', in D. Richardson (ed.), *Theorising Heterosexuality: Telling it Straight*. Buckingham: Open University Press.

Holland, J., Ramazanoğlu, C., Sharpe, S. and Thomson, R. (1998) *The Male in the Head*. London: The Tufnell Press.

Holliday, R. (1999) 'The Comfort of Identity', *Sexualities*, 2 (4): 475–91.

Hughes, A. and Witz, A. (1997) 'Feminism and the Matter of Bodies: From de Beauvoir to Butler', *Body and Society*, 3: 47–60.

Humphrey, J. (1999) 'To Queer or Not to Queer a Lesbian and Gay Group? Sexual and Gendered Politics at the Turn of the Century', *Sexualities*, 2 (2): 223–46.

Hunter, J.D. (1991) *Culture Wars: The Struggle to Define America*. New York: Basic Books.

Ingraham, C. (1996) 'The Heterosexual Imaginary: Feminist Sociology and Theories of Gender', in S. Seidman (ed.), *Queer Theory/Sociology*. Oxford: Blackwell.

Ingraham, C. (1999) *White Weddings: Romancing Heterosexuality in Popular Culture*. New York: Routledge.

Ingraham, C. (ed.) (2005) *Thinking Straight. The Power, the Promise, and the Paradox of Heterosexuality*. London/New York: Routledge.

Jackson, S. (1995) 'Gender and Heterosexuality: A Materialist Feminist Analysis', in M. Maynard and J. Purvis (eds), *(Hetero)sexual Politics*. London: Taylor and Francis.

Jackson, S. (1996a) 'Heterosexuality and Feminist Theory', in D. Richardson (ed.), *Theorising Heterosexuality: Telling it Straight*. Buckingham: Open University Press.

Jackson, S. (1996b) 'Heterosexuality, Power and Pleasure', in S. Jackson and S. Scott (eds), *Feminism and Sexuality: A Reader*. Edinburgh: Edinburgh University Press.

Jackson, S. (1999a) 'Feminist Sociology and Sociological Feminism: Recovering the Social in Feminist Thought', *Sociological Research Online*, 4 (3): U337–U356. http://www.socresonline.org.uk/socresonline/4/3/jackson.html

Jackson, S. (1999b) *Heterosexuality in Question*. London: Sage.

Jackson, S. (2000) 'For a Sociological Feminism', in J. Eldridge, J. MacInnes, S. Scott, C. Warhurst and A. Witz (eds), *For Sociology*. Durham, NC: Sociologypress.

Jackson, S. (2001) 'Why a Materialist Feminism is Still Possible (and Necessary)', *Women's Studies International Forum*, 24 (2–3): 283–93.

Jackson, S. (2005) 'Sexuality, Heterosexuality, and Gender Hierarchy', in C. Ingraham (ed.), *Thinking Straight. The Power, the Promise, and the Paradox of Heterosexuality*. London and New York: Routledge.

Jackson, S. and Scott, S. (1996) 'Sexual Skirmishes and Feminist Factions: Twenty-Five Years of Debate on Women and Sexuality', in S. Jackson and S. Scott (eds), *Feminism and Sexuality: A Reader*. Edinburgh: Edinburgh University Press.

Jackson, S. and Scott, S. (1997) 'Gut Reactions to Matters of the Heart: Reflections on Rationality, Irrationality and Sexuality', *Sociological Review*, 45 (4): 551–75.

Jackson, S. and Scott, S. (2000) 'Risk Anxiety and the Social Construction of Childhood', in D. Lupton (ed.), *Risk and Sociocultural Theory*. Cambridge: Cambridge University Press.

Jackson, S. and Scott, S. (2004) 'Sexual Antinomies in Late Modernity', *Sexualities*, 7 (2): 241–56.

Jagose, A. (1996) *Queer Theory. An Introduction*. New York: New York University Press.

Jakobsen, J. R. (2002) 'Can Homosexuals End Western Civilization As We Know It? Family Values in a Global Economy', in A. Cruz-Malavé and M. F. Manalansan IV (eds), *Queer Globalizations: Citizenship and the Afterlife of Colonialism*, New York: New York University Press.

Jeffreys, S. (1990) *Anticlimax: A Feminist Perspective on the Sexual Revolution*. London: The Women's Press.

Jeffreys, S. (1993) *The Lesbian Heresy*. Melbourne: Spinifex Press.

Jeffreys, S. (1994) 'The Queer Disappearance of Lesbians: Sexuality in the Academy', *Women's Studies International Forum*, 17 (5): 459–72.

Jeffreys, S. (2003) *Unpacking Queer Politics: A Lesbian Feminist Perspective*. Cambridge: Polity Press.

Joseph, M. (2002) *Against the Romance of Community*. Minnesota: University of Minnesota Press.

Keating, A. (1993) 'Writing, Politics, and las Lesberadas: *Platicando con* Gloria Anzaldúa', *Frontiers*, 14 (1, Fall): 105–30.

Kessler, S. J. (1998) *Lessons from the Intersexed*. New Brunswick, NJ: Rutgers University Press.

Kessler, S. J. and McKenna, W. (1978) *Gender: An Ethnomethodological Approach*. New York: Wiley.

Kessler, S. J. and McKenna, W. (2000) 'Gender Construction in Everyday Life: Transsexualism (Abridged)', *Feminism and Psychology*, 10: 11–29.

Kimmel, M. and Messner, M. (eds) (1992) *Men's Lives*, 2nd edn. New York: Macmillan.

Kirsch, M. H. (2000) *Queer Theory and Social Change*. London: Routledge.

Kitzinger, C. and Wilkinson, S. (1994) 'Virgins and Queers: Rehabilitating Heterosexuality?' *Gender and Society*, 8 (3): 444–63.

Klein, N. (1997) *The History of Forgetting: Los Angeles and the Erasure of Memory*. New York and London: Verso.

Koven, S. (1992) 'From Rough Lads to Hooligans: Boy Life, National Culture and Social Reform', in A. Parker, M. Russo, D. Summer and P. Yeage (eds), *Nationalisms and Sexualities*. New York: Routledge.

Kranich, K. A. (1989) 'Catalysts for Transforming Ourselves and the World: U.S. Women of Color Periodicals 1968–1988', National Women's Studies Association Conference, Towson State University, June. New York: Lesbian Herstory Archives.

Kregloe, K. and Caputi, J. (1997) 'Supermodels of Lesbian Chic: Camille Paglia Revamps Lesbian/Feminism (while Susie Bright Retools)', in D. Heller (ed.), *Cross Purposes: Lesbians, Feminists, and the Limits of Alliance*. Bloomington, IN: Indiana University Press.

Lawler, S. (2000) *Mothering the Self: Mothers, Daughters, Subjects*. London: Routledge.

Leeds Revolutionary Feminist Group (1981) 'Political Lesbianism: The Case Against Heterosexuality', in Onlywomen Press (eds), *Love Your Enemy? The Debate Between Heterosexual Feminism and Political Lesbianism*. London: Onlywomen Press.

Leonard, D. and Adkins, L. (eds) (1996) *Sex in Question: French Materialist Feminism*. London: Taylor and Francis.

'Letters' section (2003) *Lesbian Connection*, 26(2 September/October): 13.

Levado, Y. (1994) 'Family Values', *Tikkun*, September: 57–60.

Le Vay, S. (1993) *The Sexual Brain*. Cambridge, MA: MIT Press.

Levy, A. (2004) 'Where the Bois Are', *New York Magazine*, 12 January: 25–8.

Lloyd, M. (1999) 'Performativity, Parody, Politics', *Theory, Culture and Society*, 16 (2): 195–213.

Lorde, A. (1978) *The Black Unicorn*. New York: Norton.

Lorde, A. (1984) *Sister Outsider: Essays and Speeches*. Freedom, CA: Crossing Press.

Lumsden, I. (1991) *Homosexuality and the State in Mexico*. Mexico City: Colectivo Sol.

Lurie, S., Cvetkovich, A., Gallop, J., Modleski, T. and Spillers, H. (2001) 'Restoring Feminist Politics to Poststructuralist Critique', *Feminist Studies*, 27: 679–707.

Lyall, S. (2002) 'For Europeans, Love, Yes; Marriage, Maybe', *The New York Times*, 24 March: 1.

Lynch, F. (1992) 'Nonghetto Gays', in G. Herdt (ed.), *Gay Culture in America*. Boston, MA: Beacon Press.

MacKinnon, C. (1982) 'Feminism, Marxism, Method and the State: An Agenda for Theory', *Signs*, 7 (3): 315–44.

Mann, S. A. (2000) 'The Scholarship of Difference: A Scholarship of Liberation?' *Sociological Inquiry*, 70 (4): 475–98.

Marcuse, H. (1966) *Eros and Civilization: A Philosophical Inquiry into Freud*. Boston, MA: Beacon Press.

Martin, B. (1992) 'Sexual Practice and Changing Lesbian Identities', in M. Barrett and A. Phillips (eds), *Destabilising Contemporary Feminist Debates*. Cambridge: Polity Press.

Martin, B. (1998) 'Sexualities without Genders and Other Queer Utopias', in M. Merck, N. Segal and E. Wright (eds), *Coming out of Feminism*. Oxford: Blackwell.

Marx, K. (1977) *Capital. Volume 1*. New York: Vintage.

Matisons, M. R. (1998) 'The New Feminist Philosophy of the Body', *The European Journal of Women's Studies*, 5: 9–34.

McBride, J. (1990) 'The Vision of a Different Place', *Rites*, February: 9.

McIntosh, M. (1968) 'The Homosexual Role', *Social Problems*, 16 (2): 189–92.

McIntosh, M. (1981) 'The Homosexual Role', in K. Plummer (ed.), *The Making of the Modern Homosexual*. London: Hutchinson.

McIntosh, M. (1993) 'Queer Theory and the War of the Sexes', in J. Bristow, and A.R. Wilson (eds), *Activating Theory. Lesbian, Gay, Bisexual Politics*. London: Lawrence & Wishart.

McKee, A. (1999) ' "Resistance is Hopeless": Assimilating Queer Theory', *Social Semiotics*, 9 (2): 235–50.

McKenna, W. and Kessler, S.J. (2000) 'Retrospective Response', *Feminism and Psychology*, 10: 66–72.

McLaughlin, J. (2003) *Feminist Social and Political Theory*. Basingstoke: Palgrave.

McLelland, M. (2000) *Male Homosexuality in Modern Japan: Cultural Myths and Social Realities*. Richmond, Surrey: Curzon Press.

McRobbie, A. (2004) 'Feminism and the Socialist Tradition … Undone? A Response to Recent Work by Judith Butler', *Cultural Studies*, 18: 503–22.

Mead, G. H. (1934) *Mind Self and Society*. Chicago: University of Chicago Press.

Mejia, M. (2000) 'Mexican Pink', in P. Drucker (ed.), *Different Rainbows*. New York: Gay Men's Press.

Merchant, H. (ed.) (1999) *Yaraana: Gay Writing from India*. New Delhi: Penguin Books India.

Merck, M., Segal, N. and Wright, E. (eds) (1998) *Coming Out of Feminism?* Oxford: Blackwell.

Mitchell, J. (1982) 'Introduction I', in J. Mitchell and J. Rose (eds), *Feminine Sexuality: Jacques Lacan and the École Freudienne*. London: Macmillan.

Mohanty, C. (2003) *Feminism Without Borders: Decolonizing Theory, Practicing Solidarity*. Durham, NC: Duke University Press.

Mongrovejo, N. (2000) *Un Amor Que se Atrevió a Decir Su Nombre: La Lucha de las Lesbianas y su Relación con los Movimientos Homosexual y Feminista en América Latina*. México, DF: CDAHL.

Morrison, T. (2004). *Beloved* (reprint). New York: Vintage.

Moynihan, R. (2003) 'The Making of a Disease: Female Sexual Dysfunction', *British Medical Journal*, 326 (January): 45–7.

Nestle, J. (1987) *A Restricted Country*. Ithaca, NY: Firebrand Press.

Ng, V. (1997) 'Looking for Lesbians in Chinese History', in M. Duberman (ed.) *A Queer World*. New York: New York University Press.

Nicholson, L. J. (1994) 'Interpreting Gender', *Signs: Journal of Women in Culture and Society*, 7 (3): 515–44.

Nietzsche, F. (2003) *The Genealogy of Morals*, Second Essay, Section One. New York and London: Dover Publications.

Nussbaum, M. C. (1999a) *Sex and Justice*. New York: Oxford University Press.

Nussbaum, M. C. (1999b) 'The Professor of Parody', *The New Republic*, 22 February: 37–45.

Oakley, A. (1972) *Sex, Gender and Society*. London: Maurice Temple Smith.

Okin, S. M. (1994) 'Gender Inequality and Cultural Differences', *Political Theory*, 22 (1): 5–24.

Ollenberger, J. C. and Moore, H. A. (1998) *A Sociology of Women: The Intersection of Patriarchy, Capitalism and Colonialisation*. Upper Saddle River, NJ: Prentice Hall.

O'Sullivan, J. (2004) 'The Bells Are Ringing ... Marriage, Marriage Everywhere', in B.M. Robert and S.E. Rosenbaum (eds), *Same-Sex Marriage: The Moral and Legal Debate*. Amherst, NY: Prometheus Books.

Patton, C. and Sanchez-Eppler, B. (eds) (2000) *Queer Diasporas*. Durham, NC: Duke University Press.

Pearson, R. (1995) 'Male Bias and Women's Work in Mexico's Border Industries', in D. Elson (ed.), *Male Bias in Development*. Manchester: Manchester University Press.

Perry, D. (1993) 'Interview with Gloria Anzaldúa', in *Backtalk: Women Writers Speak Out*. New Brunswick, NJ: Rutgers University Press.

Petievich, C. (2002) '*Doganas and Zanakhis*: The Invention and Subsequent Erasure of Urdu Poetry's "Lesbian" Voice', in R. Vanita (ed.), *Queering India: Same-Sex Love and Eroticism in Indian Culture and Society*. New York: Routledge.

Pflugfelder, G. M. (1999) *Cartographies of Desire: Male-Male Sexuality in Japanese Discourse, 1600–1950*. Berkeley: University of California Press.

Phelan, S. (1994) *Getting Specific: Postmodern Lesbian Politics*. Minneapolis: University of Minnesota Press.

Phelan, S. (2001) *Sexual Strangers. Gays, Lesbians and Dilemmas of Citizenship*. Philadelphia, PA: Temple University Press.

Plummer, K. (1995) *Telling Sexual Stories: Power, Change and Social Worlds*. London: Routledge.

Plummer, K. (ed.) (1985) *Modern Homosexualities*. London: Routledge.

Polikoff, N. (1993) 'We Will Get What We Ask For', *Virginia Law Review*, 79: 1535–50.

Priuer, A. (1998) *Mema's House, Mexico City: On Transvestites, Queers and Machos*. Chicago: University of Chicago Press.

Probyn, E. (1996) *Outside Belongings*. London: Routledge.

Prosser, J. (1998) *Second Skins: The Body Narratives of Transsexuality*. New York: Columbia University Press.

Questions féministes Collective (1981) 'Variations on a common theme' in E. Marks and I. de Courtivron (eds), *New French Feminisms*. Brighton: Harvester.

Quiroga, J. (2000) *Tropics of Desire: Interventions from Queer Latin America*. New York: New York University Press.

Radicalesbians (1973) 'The Woman-Identified Woman', originally published 1970, in A. Koedt, E. Levine and A. Rapone (eds), *Radical Feminism*. New York: Quadrangle.

Raffo, S. (1997) *Queerly Classed: Gay Men and Lesbians Write about Class*. Boston, MA: South End Press.

Rahman, M. and Jackson, S. (1997) 'Liberty, Equality and Sexuality: Essentialism and the Discourse of Rights', *Journal of Gender Studies*, 6 (2): 117–29.

Rahman, M. and Witz, A. (2003) 'What Really Matters? The Elusive Quality of the Material in Feminist Thought', *Feminist Theory*, 4: 243–61.

Ramamurthy, P. (2004) 'Why is Buying a "Madras" Cotton Shirt a Political Act? A Feminist Commodity Chain Analysis', *Feminist Studies*, 30 (Fall): 734–69.

Rauch, J. (2004) *Gay Marriage*. New York: Times Books.

Raymond, J. (1994) *The Transsexual Empire: The Making of the She-Male* (reissue). New York: Teacher's College Press.

Reagon, B. J. (1983) 'Coalition Politics: Turning the Century', in B. Smith (ed.), *Home Girls: A Black Feminist Anthology*. New York: Kitchen Table Women of Color Press.

Rees, A. (2000) 'Higamous, Hogamous, Woman Monogamous', *Feminist Theory*, 1 (3): 365–70.

Rich, A. (1979) 'When We Dead Awaken: Writing as Re-Vision,' originally published 1971, in *On Lies, Secrets, and Silence: Selected Prose 1966–1978*. New York: Norton.

Rich, A. (1980) 'Compulsory Heterosexuality and Lesbian Existence', *Signs*, 5 (4): 631–60.

Rich, A. (1983) 'Compulsory Heterosexuality and Lesbian Existence', in A. Snitow, C. Stansell and S. Thompson (eds) *Powers of Desire*. New York: Monthly Review Press.

Rich, A. (1986) 'Compulsory Heterosexuality and Lesbian Existence', in *Blood, Bread, and Poetry: Selected Prose, 1979–1985*. New York: Norton.

Richardson, D. (1997) 'Sexuality and Feminism', in V. Robinson and D. Richardson (eds), *Introducing Women's Studies: Feminist Theory and Practice*. Basingstoke: Palgrave.

Richardson, D. (2000) *Rethinking Sexuality*. London: Sage.

Richardson, D. (2005) 'Desiring Sameness? The Rise of a Neoliberal Politics of Normalisation', *Antipode*, 37 (3): 514–34.

Richardson, D. (ed.) (1996) *Theorising Heterosexuality: Telling it Straight*. Buckingham: Open University Press.

Riley, D. (1988) *Am I That Name?: Feminism and the Category of 'Women' in History*. Basingstoke: Macmillan.

Roach, J. (1996) *Cities of the Dead: Circum-Atlantic Performance*. New York, NC: Columbia University Press.

Robertson, J. (1998) *Takarazuka: Sexual Politics and Popular Culture in Modern Japan*. Berkeley: University of California Press.

Rose, H. and Rose, S. (2000) *Alas Poor Darwin: Arguments Against Evolutionary Psychology*. London: Vintage.

Rotello, G. (1996) 'To Have and To Hold', *The Nation*, 6 (24): 11–17.

Rotello, G. (1997) 'Creating a New Gay Culture', *The Nation*, 4 (21): 11–16.

Roughgarden, J. (2004) *Evolution's Rainbow: Diversity, Gender and Sexuality in Nature and People*. Berkeley and Los Angeles: University of California Press.

Rowbotham, S. (1999) *Threads Through Time: Writings on History and Autobiography*. London: Penguin.

Rowland, R. and Klein, R. (1996) 'Radical Feminism: History, Politics, Action', in D. Bell and R. Klein (eds), *Radically Speaking: Feminism Reclaimed*. London: Zed Books.

Rubin, G. (1975) 'The Traffic in Women: Notes on the "Political Economy" of Sex', in R. Reiter (ed.), *Toward an Anthropology of Women*. New York: Monthly Review Press.

Rubin, G. (1984) 'Thinking Sex: Notes for a Radical Theory of the Politics of Sexuality', in C. S. Vance (ed.), *Pleasure and Danger: Exploring Female Sexuality*. New York and London: Routledge & Kegan Paul.

Rubin, G. (1993) 'Thinking Sex: Notes for a Radical Theory of the Politics of Sexuality', in H. Abelove, M.A. Barale, and D. M. Halperin (eds), *The Lesbian and Gay Studies Reader*. London: Routledge.

Rubin, G. with Butler, J. (1998) 'Sexual Traffic', in M. Merck, N. Segal, and E. Wright (eds), *Coming Out of Feminism?* Oxford: Blackwell.

Salzinger, L. (2003) *Genders in Production. Making Workers in Mexico's Global Factories*. Berkeley: University of California Press.

Sandoval, C. (1991) 'U.S. Third World Feminism: The Theory and Method of Oppositional Consciousness in the Postmodern World', *Genders*, 10(Spring): 1–24.

Schlichter, A. (2004) 'Queer at Last? Straight Intellectuals and the Desire for Transgression', *GLQ: A Journal of Lesbian and Gay Studies*, 10: 543–64.

Seabrook, J. (1999) *Love in a Different Climate: Men Who Have Sex with Men in India*. London: Verso.

Seajay, C. (1990) 'The Women-In-Print Movement, Some Beginnings: An Interview with Judy Grahn', Part I, *Feminist Bookstore News*, 13 (1, May/June): 19–25.

Sedgwick E. K. (1990) *Epistemology of the Closet*. Berkeley: University of California Press.

Sedgwick, E. K. (1991) *The Epistemology of the Closet*. Hemel Hempstead: Harvester Wheatsheaf.

Sedgwick, E.K. (2003) *Touching, Feeling: Affect, Pedagogy, Performativity*. Durham, NC: Duke University Press.

Segal, L. (1994) *Straight Sex: The Politics of Pleasure*. London: Virago.

Segal, L. (1999) *Why Feminism?* Cambridge: Polity Press.

Seidman, S. (1996) 'Introduction', in S. Seidman (ed.), *Queer Theory/ Sociology*. Oxford: Blackwell.

Seidman, S. (1997) *Difference Troubles. Queering Social Theory and Sexual Politics*. Cambridge: Cambridge University Press.

Seidman, S. (2002) *Beyond the Closet: The Transformation of Gay and Lesbian Life*. New York and London: Routledge.

Sennett, R. (1994) *Flesh and Stone*. London: Faber.

Silva, N. (2004) *Aloha Betrayed: Native Hawaiian Resistance to American Colonialism*. Durham, NC: Duke University Press.

Skeggs, B. (2001) 'The Toilet Paper: Femininity, Class and Mis-Recognition', *Women's Studies International Forum*, 24 (3/4): 295–307.

Skeggs, B. (2003) 'Becoming Repellent: The Limits of Propriety'. Plenary Address to the British Sociological Association Annual Conference, University of York, 20th April.

Skeggs, B. (2004) *Class, Self, Culture*. London: Routledge.

Smart, C. (1996) 'Collusion, Collaboration and Confession: On Moving Beyond the Heterosexuality Debate', in D. Richardson (ed.), *Theorising Heterosexuality: Telling it Straight*. Buckingham: Open University Press.

Smith, B. (1982) 'Toward a Black Feminist Criticism', originally published 1977, in G. Hull, P.B. Scott and B. Smith (eds), *All the Women Are White, All the Blacks Are Men, But Some of Us Are Brave: Black Women's Studies*. New York: Feminist Press.

Spivak, G. (1987) *In Other Worlds: Essays in Cultural Politics*. New York: Methuen.

Spurlin, W. J. (1998) 'Sissies and Sisters: Gender, Sexuality and the Possibilities of Coalition', in M. Merck, N. Segal and E. Wright (eds), *Coming out of Feminism?* Oxford: Blackwell.

Squires, J. (1993) 'Introduction', in J. Squires (ed.), *Principled Positions*, London: Lawrence and Wishart.

Stacey, J. (1990) *Brave New Families*. New York: Basic Books.

Stacey, J. (1993) 'Untangling Feminist Theory', in D. Richardson and V. Robinson (eds), *Introducing Women's Studies: Feminist Theory and Practice*. Basingstoke: Macmillan.

Stacey, J. (1997) 'Feminist Theory: Capital F, Capital T', in V. Robinson and D. Richardson (eds), *Introducing Women's Studies: Feminist Theory and Practice*, 2nd edn. Basingstoke: Macmillan.

Stanley, L. and Wise, S. (2000) 'But the Empress has no Clothes!' *Feminist Theory*, 1 (3): 261–88.

Stein, A. (1992) 'Sisters and Queers: The Decentering of Lesbian Feminism', *Socialist Review*, 22 (1, January–March): 33–55.

Stein, A. (ed.) (1993) *Sisters, Sexperts, Queers: Beyond the Lesbian Nation*. New York: Plume.

Stein, A. (1997) *Sex and Sensibility: Stories of a Lesbian Generation*. Berkeley: University of California Press.

Stein, A. (2001) *The Stranger Next Door: The Story of a Small Community's Battle Over Sex, Faith, and Civil Rights*. Boston, MA: Beacon.

Stein, A. and Plummer, K. (1996) ' "I Can't Even Think Straight": "Queer" Theory and the Missing Sexual Revolution in Sociology', in S. Seidman (ed.), *Queer Theory/Sociology*. Oxford: Blackwell.

Stone, S. (1993) 'The "Empire" Strikes back: A Posttranssexual Manifesto', in J. Epstein and K. Straub (eds), *Body Guards: The Cultural Politics of Gender Ambiguity*, New York: Routledge.

Sullivan, A. (1995) *Virtually Normal*. New York: Knopf.

Sullivan, A. (1998) 'The Marriage Moment', *The Advocate*, 1 (20): 59–67.

Sullivan, M. (2004) *The Family of Woman*. Berkeley: University of California Press.

Sullivan, N. (2003) *A Critical Introduction to Queer Theory*. Edinburgh: Edinburgh University Press and Melbourne: Circa Books.

Thadani, G. (1996) *Sakhiyani: Lesbian Desire in Ancient and Modern India*. London: Cassell.

Tolman, D. (2002) *Dilemmas of Desire*. Cambridge, MA: Harvard University Press.

Turner, W. B. (2000) *A Genealogy of Queer Studies*. Philadelphia, PA: Temple University Press.

Urry, J. (2000) *Sociology Beyond Societies*. London: Routledge.

Vance, C.S. (1992) 'Pleasure and Danger: Toward a Politics of Sexuality', in C.S. Vance (ed.), *Pleasure and Danger: Exploring Female Sexuality*, 2nd edn. London: Pandora.

VanEvery, J. (1996) 'Heterosexuality and Domestic Life', in D. Richardson (ed.), *Theorizing Heterosexuality: Telling it Straight*. Buckingham: Open University Press.

Vanita, R. (ed.) (2002) *Queering India: Same-Sex Love and Eroticism in India Culture and Society*. New York: Routledge.

Vanita, R. and Kidwai, S. (2000) *Same-Sex Love in India: Readings from Literature and History*. New York: St. Martin's Press.

Waaldijk, K. and Bonini-Boaraldi, M. (2004) 'Combating Sexual Orientation Discrimination in Employment: Legislation in Fifteen EU Member States' (Report prepared by the independent European Group of Experts on Combating Sexual Orientation Discrimination).

Walby, S. (1990) *Theorizing Patriarchy*. Oxford: Blackwell.

Walby, S. (1997) *Gender Transformations*. London: Routledge.

Walters, S. D. (2005) 'From Here to Queer: Radical Feminism, Postmodernism, and the Lesbian Menace', in I. Morland and A. Willox (eds), *Queer Theory*. Basingstoke: Palgrave.

Warner, M. (1993) 'Introduction', in M. Warner (ed.), *Fear of a Queer Planet: Queer Politics and Social Theory*. Minneapolis: University of Minnesota Press.

Warner, M. (1999) *The Trouble with Normal: Sex, Politics and the Ethics of Queer Life*. New York: Free Press.

Warner, M. (2000) *The Trouble with Normal: Sex, Politics and the Ethics of Queer Life*. Cambridge, MA: Harvard University Press.

Warner, M. (ed.) (1993) *Fear of a Queer Planet: Queer Politics and Social Theory*. Minneapolis: University of Minnesota Press.

Weed, E. and Schor, N. (ed.) (1997) *Feminism meets Queer Theory*. Bloomington, IN: Indiana University Press.

Weeks, J. (1998) 'The "Homosexual Role" After 30 years: an Appreciation of the Work of Mary Macintosh', *Sexualities*, 1(2): 131–52.

Weeks, J., Heaphy, B. and Donovan, C. (2001) *Same-Sex Intimacies*. New York: Routledge.

Weininger, O. (1906) *Sex and Character*. London: William Heinemann.

West, C. and Zimmerman, D. (1987) 'Doing Gender', *Gender and Society*, 1 (2): 125–51.

Weston, K. (1991) *Families We Choose*. New York: Columbia University Press.

Whisman, V. (1996) *Queer by Choice*. New York: Routledge.

Wilkinson, S. and Kitzinger, C. (eds) (1993) *Heterosexuality: A Feminism & Psychology Reader*. London: Sage.

Wilkinson, S. and Kitzinger C. (1996) 'The Queer Backlash', in D. Bell and R. Klein, (eds), *Radically Speaking: Feminism Reclaimed*. Melbourne: Spinifex Press.

Wilson, A. (1997) 'Somewhere over the Rainbow/: The Future of Queer Politics', in S. Phelan (ed.), *Playing with Fire: Queer Politics/ Queer Theories*. New York. Routledge.

Wilson, E. (1993) 'Is Transgression Transgressive?' in J. Bristow and A. R. Wilson (eds), *Activating Theory. Lesbian, Gay, Bisexual Politics*. London: Lawrence & Wishart.

Winter, B. (1997) '(Mis)representations: What French Feminism Isn't', *Women's Studies International Forum*, 20 (2): 211–24.

Wittig, M. (1980) 'The Straight Mind', *Feminist Issues*, 1 (1): 103–11.

Wittig, M. (1992) *The Straight Mind and Other Essays*. Boston, MA: Beacon Press and Hemel Hemstead: Harvester Wheatsheaf.

Wittig, M. (1981) 'One is Not Born a Woman', *Feminist Issues*, 1 (2): 47–54. Reprinted in M. Wittig (1992) *The Straight Mind and Other Essays*. Boston, MA: Beacon Press and Hemel Hemstead: Harvester Wheatsheaf.

Wittig, M. (1992) *The Straight Mind and Other Essays*. Boston, MA: Beacon Press and Hemel Hempstead: Harvester.

Wolfe, S. J. and Penelope, J. (eds) (1993) *Sexual Practice, Textual Theory: Lesbian Cultural Criticism*. Cambridge, MA: Blackwell.

Wolfson, E. (1996) 'Why We Should Fight for the Freedom to Marry', *Journal of Gay, Lesbian, and Bisexual Identity*, 1 (1): 79–89.

Woods, C. (1995) *State of the Queer Nation: A Critique of Gay and Lesbian Politics in Britain*. London: Cassell.

Wright, M. (2001) 'The Dialectics of Still Life: Murder, Women, and Maquiladoras', in J. Comeroff and J. L. Comeroff (eds), *Millennial Capitalism and the Culture of Neolilberalism*. Durham, NC: Duke University Press.

Zimmerman, B. (1997). ' "Confessions" of a Lesbian Feminist', in D. Heller (ed.), *Cross Purposes: Lesbians, Feminists, and the Limits of Alliance*. Bloomington, IN: Indiana University Press.

Zimmerman, B. and. McNaron, T. A. H (eds) (1996) *The New Lesbian Studies: Into the Twenty-First Century*. New York: The Feminist Press.

Zimmerman, C. (2005) 'Learning To Stand on Shifting Sands: Sonoran Desert Capitalism and Working Alliances For Social Change'. Unpublished dissertation, University of Arizona.

Index